William H. Goodyear

A History of Art

For classes, art-students, and tourists in Europe

William H. Goodyear

A History of Art
For classes, art-students, and tourists in Europe

ISBN/EAN: 9783337193195

Printed in Europe, USA, Canada, Australia, Japan

Cover: Foto ©Thomas Meinert / pixelio.de

More available books at **www.hansebooks.com**

A

HISTORY OF ART

FOR CLASSES, ART-STUDENTS AND TOURISTS IN EUROPE

BY

WILLIAM HENRY GOODYEAR, M.A.

CURATOR OF FINE ARTS IN THE MUSEUM OF THE BROOKLYN INSTITUTE OF ARTS AND SCIENCES
FORMERLY CURATOR OF PAINTING IN THE METROPOLITAN MUSEUM OF ART, NEW YORK
HONORARY MEMBER, ROYAL ACADEMIES OF VENICE AND MILAN; OF THE
SOCIETY OF ARCHITECTS OF ROME; OF THE ARCHITECTURAL
ASSOCIATION OF EDINBURGH; AND CORRESPONDING MEMBER
OF THE AMERICAN INSTITUTE OF ARCHITECTS

TWENTIETH EDITION
REVISED AND ENLARGED, WITH NEW ILLUSTRATIONS

THE A. S. BARNES COMPANY
NEW YORK

Preface

THE study of historical art may appear to be unpractical, or, at least, of very limited use, in a country where, relatively, few remains of the older European art are preserved, and where the interests of the nation are attached to the future rather than the past. Hence a few remarks as to the practical uses and bearings of this study are in place here.

The training of the taste is not purely a matter of ornamental education; nor does it imply, even indirectly, an affectation of luxury, or of the expenditure of wealth. In most branches of trade, and in many branches of manufacture, an artistic taste is a matter of practical importance in the gaining of one's livelihood. There are few kinds of handiwork in which the element of design does not enter, and wherever the arts of design are in question, taste has to be exercised. The general tendency to introduce the practice of drawing into elementary school instruction, results from a public recognition of these practical uses of art instruction.

If, on the other hand, we take the stand-point of the consumer, the question of "household art" is one of comprehensive importance, and the education of taste with regard to it has great value, even as a matter of economy. The tendency to rate things by their expense, or money value, is a very common and very mistaken one. The first condition of good taste is to know how much may be done with little money, and to understand that the manifestation of utility in forms is an elementary principle of art. Moreover, the most practical and hard-working lives ought not to be deprived of mental and spiritual stimulus; and this is to be found in colors and in forms, no less than in music and in books. If we consider the training of taste in art from the stand-point of polite education, there can be no question that, in this sense, it is becoming an undisputed essential.

IF it be admitted that the direction and instruction of artistic taste are matters of practical and economical importance, as well as of polite education, the study of the history of art needs no further apology. Although the most widely spread and most necessary exercise of taste relates to ornamental design and to objects of "household art" rather than to architecture, sculpture, and painting, the training of taste must be largely attained through these latter arts. Modern ornamental art depends on that which went before it, and has been even too dependent on the past. The use of historic ornamental forms, both in good and bad directions, is so absolutely universal that the history of ornament is unavoidably essential to the comprehension of our own. This history is again connected with the great periods of architecture, sculpture, and painting, in such a way that neither the phraseology nor the facts of the subject can be understood without reference to these other arts.

The study of historic art is also made advisable by the consideration that contact with the best examples is the one important thing in the training of the taste. The greatness of the past in all departments of art is as generally admitted as our own preeminence in purely mechanical and material civilization. The study of art history is simply, then, the study of good examples of art, considered in their most natural arrangement and sequence—that of time. Finally, however much our own immediate interest may turn to the present and to its own art productions, we must remember that even in the strength of our sympathy as moderns for modern things lies an important reason for seeking standards and principles of taste in other works. In literary training, for instance, it is generally admitted that modern authors, however excellent, are not the best standards of instruction. General principles of taste in literature are best founded on works which have been tested by time and the criticisms of more than one generation. Personal tastes, one's own chance acquaintances and surroundings, or the fashion of the hour, are apt to be disturbing elements when we use modern work as the standard of appeal for educational purposes. In dealing with the past, we stand on firmer ground. The weight of authoritative criticism is such, and its verdicts are so well known, that the individual instructor becomes the exponent of these, and must be judged by his own rendering and appreciation of them.

The learner then stands in face, not of an individual teacher, but of the criticism of art as determined by its standard authorities. To develop and form an original and independent taste is the object of the learner. To offer a firm basis for this development by the suppression of individual views and by attention to the most general principles must be the object of the teacher. On the whole, the matter of fact is the main thing. The eye can be trained only through the objects which it sees, not through theories or intellectual process. To present the most important works of art in the most natural arrangement and let them work their own results, is the purpose of art history. To this end there is only one thing more important than abundant illustration in the hand-book itself, viz., faithful study of all the originals, casts, photographs, and copies which can be made accessible outside of it.

The specific aim of the present book has been to present such an amount and choice of illustration as have never been previously attempted in similar works, and as a class-book to present the subject in such a way that the use of still further illustration for the combined class will be easy and desirable. The Soule Photograph Company of Boston have made it their mission to supply, at very cheap cost, complete sets of photographic illustrations in all departments of art history, and a choice from their catalogue, suggested by the unillustrated notices of this book, will greatly add to its usefulness.

For the definitions of technical terms and for the pronunciation of foreign words, attention is called to the Index. Pronunciation and definition have generally been entered in the text once, but without subsequent repetition. The Index gives the page on which the pronunciation or definition may be found, as well as the usual matter for reference.

CONTENTS

ARCHITECTURE.

SCULPTURE.

PAINTING.

HISTORY OF MUSIC.

LIST OF ILLUSTRATIONS.

MODERN ARCHITECTURE.

EGYPTIAN ARCHITECTURE.

GREEK ARCHITECTURE.

ROMAN ARCHITECTURE.

BYZANTINE ARCHITECTURE.

ROMANESQUE ARCHITECTURE.

GOTHIC ARCHITECTURE.

RENAISSANCE ARCHITECTURE.

CHALDEAN SCULPTURE.

ASSYRIAN SCULPTURE.

PERSIAN SCULPTURE.

EGYPTIAN SCULPTURE.

GREEK SCULPTURE.

ROMAN SCULPTURE.

MEDIEVAL SCULPTURE.

RENAISSANCE SCULPTURE.

MODERN SCULPTURE.

EGYPTIAN PAINTING.

GRECO-ROMAN PAINTING.

BYZANTINE MOSAICS. EARLY CHRISTIAN ART.

ITALIAN PAINTING. 14TH CENTURY.

ITALIAN PAINTING. 15TH CENTURY.

ITALIAN PAINTING. 16TH CENTURY.

ITALIAN PAINTING. 17TH CENTURY.

FLEMISH AND GERMAN PAINTING. 15TH CENTURY.

FLEMISH AND GERMAN PAINTING. 16TH CENTURY.

DUTCH PAINTING. 17TH CENTURY.

FLEMISH PAINTING. 17TH CENTURY.

LIST OF TEXT ILLUSTRATIONS.

Relief from the Column of Trajan.

LIST OF TEXT ILLUSTRATIONS.

Relief from the Column of Trajan.

ARCHITECTURE.

I.

RELATIONS OF ARCHITECTURE, SCULPTURE, AND PAINTING IN HISTORIC STUDIES OF ART.

IT has just been noted that a systematic knowledge of ornamental art is dependent on a knowledge of the history of art as a whole—of its epochs, and styles, and of the terms which are used to explain and designate them. It is the aim of this work to present such a sketch of the history of art as a whole. In the matter of ornamental design considered as a specialty (as distinct from that general education of taste which is necessary to good perceptions about it), special works of illustration devoted to it must be consulted;* but these can only be used to advantage by possessing the preliminary knowledge here in question.

With regard to the history of art (conceived in the sense of design, as distinct from music, poetry, etc.), the three subjects of Architecture, Sculpture, and Painting are those to be first considered, but whether together or separately is a matter to be determined by circumstances. In the study of historic art, the facts and connections of history itself are of supreme importance. There is indeed no more agreeable and instructive approach to history than that offered by its actual relics and monuments. From the historic point of view, the method which considers all the arts in question in combination, and which unites the description of all for each epoch, is the most natural and satisfactory. The treatment of these topics has, however, been separated in the present book on account of its necessary brevity, and because that kind of knowledge which is most directly applicable to modern art can be most directly presented in this way.

* Owen Jones, "Grammar of Ornament"; Racinet, "Polychromatic Ornament," etc. These and similar works are too large and expensive for private ownership in general, but may be found in most public libraries.

ARCHITECTURE.

I.

RELATIONS OF ARCHITECTURE, SCULPTURE, AND PAINTING IN HISTORIC STUDIES OF ART.

IT has just been noted that a systematic knowledge of ornamental art is dependent on a knowledge of the history of art as a whole—of its epochs, and styles, and of the terms which are used to explain and designate them. It is the aim of this work to present such a sketch of the history of art as a whole. In the matter of ornamental design considered as a specialty (as distinct from that general education of taste which is necessary to good perceptions about it), special works of illustration devoted to it must be consulted;* but these can only be used to advantage by possessing the preliminary knowledge here in question.

With regard to the history of art (conceived in the sense of design, as distinct from music, poetry, etc.), the three subjects of Architecture, Sculpture, and Painting are those to be first considered, but whether together or separately is a matter to be determined by circumstances. In the study of historic art, the facts and connections of history itself are of supreme importance. There is indeed no more agreeable and instructive approach to history than that offered by its actual relics and monuments. From the historic point of view, the method which considers all the arts in question in combination, and which unites the description of all for each epoch, is the most natural and satisfactory. The treatment of these topics has, however, been separated in the present book on account of its necessary brevity, and because that kind of knowledge which is most directly applicable to modern art can be most directly presented in this way.

* Owen Jones, " Grammar of Ornament "; Racinet, " Polychromatic Ornament," etc. These and similar works are too large and expensive for private ownership in general, but may be found in most public libraries.

If the subjects of Architecture, Sculpture, and Painting are to be separately treated in the historical sketch proposed, the question rises which shall be treated first. The following reasons for giving the first attention to architecture are important.

It is the subject through which all the epochs of art history, taken as a whole, may be most readily specified and distinguished and treated in their proper sequence. As far as the history of painting is concerned, attention must be given especially to the Italians, and to certain particular centuries of their history, especially the 14th, 15th, 16th, and 17th centuries. As far as the history of sculpture is concerned, preponderant attention must be paid to the ancient Greeks. But in the history of architecture, all the great historic nations have been, in their individual ways, almost equally great. Every epoch claims a nearly equal amount of interest and attention. Thus the sequence, distinction, and designations of the epochs of art history in general are most easily and clearly studied in architecture.

Architecture is the art in connection with which sculpture and painting took their rise, and with which they have always been, in the greatest times, very closely related. The most famous works of sculpture in existence are the Elgin Marbles in the British Museum in London, which were the architectural decorations of a Greek temple. The most famous pictures in existence are the wall paintings by Michael Angelo and by Raphael in Rome—the architectural decorations of the Sistine Chapel and of the Palace of the Vatican. The most famous sculptures of Greek antiquity were the colossal gold and ivory statues, to hold which the ancient temples were erected. The most important ancient paintings now in existence are the wall paintings of the houses in Pompeii. It is evident, then, that architecture should, if studied separately, be studied first.

Architecture is the most practical and necessary of the three arts, and the one which may be most readily studied by examples, since these surround us on all sides. Some slight knowledge as to the so-called "styles" of modern buildings is, moreover, a matter of almost necessary education.

Finally, since historical forms have had an overwhelming influence on the "styles" of modern buildings, the necessity for a historical treatment of the subject of art in general is here the most obviously apparent; and the general history of art may be most easily approached in this way.

1. ST. PATRICK'S CATHEDRAL, N. Y.

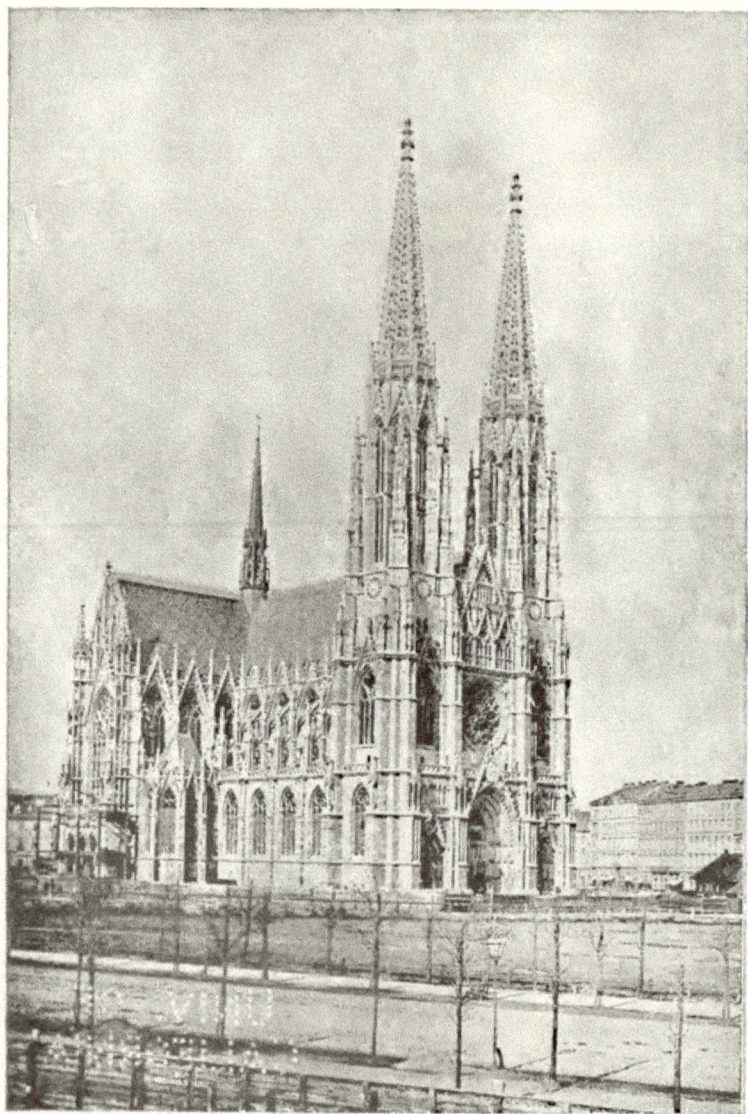

2. VOTIVE CHURCH, VIENNA.

HISTORIC "STYLES" IN MODERN ARCHITECTURE.

It is a very general presumption, or at least a prejudice constantly apparent, that our modern buildings, if pretentious of artistic character, must exhibit or belong to some "style." The prejudice is a manifest mistake to every artistically educated person, and is only a result of the fact that, for several centuries, imitations of historic buildings have been the rage. As a matter of fact, many or most of the best modern buildings do not belong to any "style" at all, unless it be one of which we, as moderns, are unconscious, but which may be seen, at some future time, to represent the peculiar needs and conditions of the century, by general resemblances which are not now apparent.

To devote attention first to the modern buildings which are imitations of historic styles, is not to imply that such imitations are especially to be commended. It is, however, a matter of general knowledge, essential to the comprehension of the latest tendencies of modern art, to understand what these modern historic styles have been, and especially because these latest tendencies are more or less antagonistic to them.

Three of these "styles" are especially pronounced in character, and have been especially affected—each to an extent that in some cities, fifteen or twenty years ago, scarcely a building could be found which did not show the influence of some one of them. These three styles may be designated as the Greek, the Renaissance, and the buttressed Gothic. There are many instances where a spectator, standing in one place, may point to examples of all three.

The Buttressed Gothic Style.*—The Catholic Cathedral of New York and the famous Votive Church in Vienna have been chosen as examples of the modern buttressed Gothic (Illustrations 1 and 2). The traits of the style, as found in the exterior appearance, are the pointed arch (frequently surmounted by an acutely angled gable ornament); the tracery of masonry divisions in the windows in manifold geometrical patterns; the use of similar tracery (originally imitated from that of the windows) on the masonry surface; the use of ornamental carvings based on forms of natural foliage, and

---

* The word "Gothic" is commonly used alone, but the words "buttressed Gothic" are used in order to distinguish it from the "Italian Gothic" style subsequently mentioned.

the use of the buttress—*i. e.*, a perpendicular masonry abutment placed at the corners of the towers, and at equidistant intervals along the walls—in the latter case frequently surmounted by a pinnacle with its top decoration or "finial."

The Greek and Renaissance Styles may be, for the moment considered together as regards their characteristic forms. In both styles the so-called "classical orders of architecture" are used.* We may notice what the elements of the classical orders are, by comparing the view of Girard College in Philadelphia with the Church of the Madeleine in Paris (Illustrations 3 and 4). In these buildings,

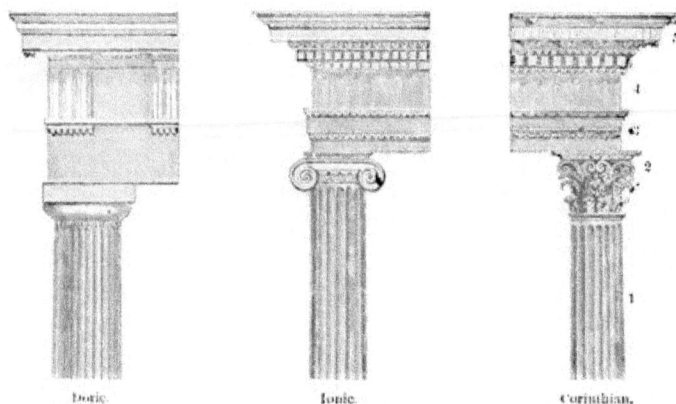

Doric.   Ionic.   Corinthian.

Three Orders of Grecian Architecture.

(1. *shaft* ; 2. *capital* ; 3. *architrave* ; 4. *frieze* ; 5. *cornice*. The entire part above the capital is the entablature. At the bottom of the shaft is the base.)

a portico or colonnade may be observed, which has become so familiar in modern architecture that its frequent appearance seems a matter of course. The columns belong to one of three classes, "Doric," "Ionic," or "Corinthian" (see text-cut), which are most easily distinguished by their capitals, *i. e.*, by the upper terminal ornament of the column. Two lines of beams with certain typical and unvarying decorations (see the ornaments on the Doric "architrave" and the horizontal lines on the Ionic and Corinthian "frieze") are

* The word "Order" is applied in Classical and Renaissance architecture either to a single column and immediate superstructure, to a series of columns and immediate superstructure, or to the general decorative system therewith connected.

A. GIRARD COLLEGE, PHILADELPHIA.

4. CHURCH OF THE MADELEINE, PARIS.

surmounted by a "cornice."* At the ends of the buildings the lines of the roof form a gable, or "pediment." The traits of the classic orders need not be more closely described at present, because they will be considered under the chapter for the Greek Temple Architecture, but they will be immediately recognized as familiar appearances in modern buildings from the diagrams and illustrations.

Distinction between the Greek and the Renaissance Styles.—This lies in the use made of the forms and "orders" in question. If the forms and "orders" are portions of the necessary construction of the building, the style is Greek. For instance, in the Girard College, and the Madeleine (3 and 4), the gable results from the construction of the roof: but in the Boston City Hall (5) the same form is an ornament above the upper central window, which could be removed without destroying the essential parts of the building. In the Renaissance style there are also modifications, or rather variations, of the gable ornament, which may be observed in many examples in every city, as well as in many pieces of furniture. The triangular gable is frequently broken at the center. Its lines rise toward the upper angle, but do not meet it. This variation would be impossible or very unnatural in the gables of 3 and 4, because the angle is there formed, as in other similar roofs, by beams which lean against and support one another; whereas in the smaller and purely ornamental use of the same form, this construction is only imitative, and the modification of the original form is not physically difficult. The same remarks apply to two other modifications of the gable ornament which are equally familiar, in which the arc of a circle is used: sometimes broken at the center and sometimes unbroken. The unbroken arc appears in the Paris Opera House (6). Once more it may be observed that such a curved line would not naturally appear at the ends of a building as the result of the construction of its roof; and that it is a purely ornamental modification of the original constructive triangular shape. It sometimes happens, however, that buildings have the ornamental variations noticed, built on to their own roof construction, rising above it or covering it up. Such buildings are also Renaissance in style; but

* A cornice is the horizontal molding or series of moldings crowning the top of a building or of the walls of a room. The words "architrave" and "frieze" are technically applied to distinguish the lower and upper beams of the classic orders, but the word "architrave" may also mean any line of beams, and the word "frieze" also means a horizontal band of sculptured ornament in any use or position.

these are instances where the ornamental style has reacted on the construction and disguised it.

We will now apply the distinction between Greek style and Renaissance, as to use of the similar forms in each, to the cornice and double line of beams. In 3, 4, and similar examples, the cornice is seen to be the decorated projecting line or edge of the roof (which continues also in a straight line under the gable angle). The lines of beams are portions of the portico and essential parts of it. If they were removed, a part of the building would fall down. On the other hand, compare the double line of beams with connected cornice as they appear in 5 and 6, and on other examples of the Renaissance, as found in all modern cities. Here they are seen to be decorative imitations, connected with the columns or pilasters, which are also imitative. Such columns attached to a wall surface for a decorative purpose, without constructive necessity, are sometimes called "engaged" columns. In Example 5 of Renaissance herewith, the jutting back and forth of the beam lines is seen to be the result of the fact that the columns or pilasters are not employed for uses of support, in which latter case the beams, running above them, would be necessarily straight. Thus the jutting or "breaking" back and forth of such lines is also a trait of Renaissance style, as distinguished from the Greek. (The term pilaster generally applies to the projected imitation of a square pillar, but is also sometimes used of "engaged" rounded columns. Both forms are seen in 5.)

Order in which the Historic Styles were Revived.—Although the three architectural styles just specified are found at present in contemporaneous examples, they did not all come into use at the same time. For several centuries the Renaissance was used exclusively. This was the first of the modern styles. It first appeared in architectural examples about and soon after the middle of the 15th century in Italy. It spread thence quite rapidly to all countries of Northern Europe, about the beginning of the 16th century, and soon after the beginning of the 16th century was universally and exclusively employed in all European countries. This universal and exclusive use continued till about the middle of the 18th century; after which the first examples of the Greek Temple style began to appear. This largely supplanted, although it by no means entirely replaced, the Renaissance style, during the last quarter of the 18th

5. CITY HALL, BOSTON.

6. NEW OPERA HOUSE, PARIS.

century and the first quarter of the 19th century. In its turn the Greek Temple style was then largely supplanted, especially in churches, by the buttressed Gothic, which (with some extremely rare and local exceptions) had not been previously used since the close of the Middle Ages.

This **succession of styles** corresponds to certain phases of modern literary and historic study, and was occasioned by it. As far as the Renaissance style is concerned, its appearance is also related to the broadest and most general aspects of modern history—those which relate to its Italian origin and first development. At the close of the Middle Ages a civilization had developed in Italy which, spreading thence, replaced the medieval and became the modern. The word "Renaissance," in its broadest sense, applies to this movement of history and civilization, and is used with the meaning that it was connected with a re-birth or revival of the ancient Greek and Roman culture. In matters of literature and art, especially, the Italians of the period in question were profoundly sensible of their debt to the ancients and copied them in every possible way. The word "Renaissance" is thus, in the next narrower sense, applied to the revival of letters, which at this time was distinctly dependent on the studies of the ancient authors. The word is, then, also applied to the general art of the period—which was that of Raphael, Michael Angelo, and contemporaries, and the other great Italian artists who preceded and followed them. Finally it is applied to the architectural style of the period. This plainly reflects the general character of the movement in letters and civilization—being a copy of the ornamental details of the Roman ruins. Hence the use of the Greek forms in the Renaissance already illustrated. These had been adopted by the Romans from the Greeks with the modifications pointed out, *and were copied from them*. The Renaissance style is simply a revival of the Roman ornamental style, and the distinctions made between Renaissance and Greek style are also the distinctions between Greek and Roman. The Renaissance style is thus of peculiar historical interest by its relations to the origins and beginnings of modern history and modern civilization in general.

The Italians of the 15th and 16th centuries were more enthusiastic than critical in their historical and literary studies, and were not themselves at all attentive to the existence of Greek elements and influences in the Roman art and literature. They took these last as they found them, without inquiring into their derivation. National patriotism led them to exalt their own country as having been the center and motive power of the Roman Empire. The derivation of their own language from the Latin made its study especially easy and natural for them.

The Roman Imperial period was the latest period of antiquity, and the earlier Greek culture had been so absorbed and assimilated by it as to have lost the apparent evidences of its own independent and earlier character. At the time of the Renaissance the Turks were in possession of the Greek territories. Travel in them was rarely undertaken, and never for purposes of historical study. Many learned Italians were acquainted with the Greek language, but still the relations of Greek and Roman civilization were not critically studied.

All these points serve to explain why the copies of the Greek Temple style which began to be made in the last half of the 18th century had not been made before. It was not until this time that the prejudice in favor of the study of Latin in preference to the study of Greek was overthrown, and that the disposition to regard all relics of antiquity found on Italian soil as relics of Roman civilization was abandoned. Meantime, from the beginning of the 16th century to the middle of the 18th century, all Europe had been controlled by the Italian taste and fashions, and by the prejudices and peculiar historical misconception just explained.

The beginning of the Greek movement, as distinguished from the Renaissance, dates from the Prussian John Winckelmann and his studies, made at Rome after 1756, in ancient sculpture. The statues, then so abundant in Rome, were first proven by him to be in general copies of Greek originals. But this discovery reacted at once on questions of literature and history. If the Roman sculpture had been Greek in its influences and subjects, it was apparent that the Roman literature must have the same dependence. So far, literary taste in Europe had been unanimous (at least in the 17th and 18th centuries) in pronouncing the Latin authors superior to the Greek.* But the absurdity of considering a copy superior to an original was apparent. Hence a revolution in taste, from which the 19th century art and literature took their inspiration. The study of Greek authors, Greek art, and Greek history became the fashion, and the first systematic journeys for purposes of study were undertaken in the Greek territories.

Many other manifestations of the Greek movement might be pointed out besides that one with which we are immediately concerned, in the copies of Greek Temple architecture. The most important was the liberation of Greece from Turkish rule in 1829 and the foundation of the modern independent kingdom of Greece. This was due to the sympathies and support of European diplomatists under the influence of the favorable sentiments awakened by the studies of Greek antiquity. An interesting instance of the enthusiasm of the time is offered by the poet Lord Byron, who went to Greece to take part in the war against the Turkish rule, but died soon after.

Another important phase of this movement is found in German literature as developed by Lessing, Goethe, Schiller, and their contemporaries. This is universally known to have had as inspiration the Greek studies inaugurated by Winckelmann.

In female dress, the style known as that of the Directory or of Martha Washington was again an effort to return to Greek simplicity. In music, the operas of Gluck are glorious examples of a revival of the Greek spirit.

As regards the general relation of the Greek architectural revival to these other phases of interest in ancient Greek history and literature, it may be noticed that travel in Greek countries for purposes of study was first undertaken as a result of this general interest. Until travel for such purposes was thus undertaken, no publications had been made as to the Athenian or other Greek ruins, and there was no general knowledge about them. An interesting evidence of this ignorance is offered by an incident in the life of Winckelmann. During his residence in Rome, it was proposed that he should undertake a journey with Italian friends around the coasts of Southern Italy to inspect the Greek ruins which were supposed to be there. It was not known in Rome in the middle of

* Compare Macaulay's Essay on Addison.

the 18th century that no Greek ruins were to be found in Southern Italy, excepting those already known at Paestum.

If explorations on the site of ancient Greek settlements were thus backward even in Italy, it may be argued how little was known then of the ruins in Sicily and in Greece.

Since the "Greek Revival" was especially vigorous in the last quarter of the 18th century and in the early 19th century, and since this period is the first to which early American buildings of importance now standing belong—the Greek style is the oldest apparent in American public buildings. It is represented by numerous examples in cities like Philadelphia, which were of great national importance in the Revolution and the period following—and in Washington, where the traditions of this period have continued to influence the later buildings. The Greek revival was, in fact, very closely connected with the movement which caused the American Revolution and the French Revolution. Both revolutions were very largely inspired by republican ideals drawn from the study of "Plutarch's Lives." This work was universally read at the time, under the influence of the newly-rising studies of Greek authors.

It appears from the foregoing matter that the revival of Greek Temple architecture was the result of a literary impulse, and of historical studies, which showed the Greeks to be the real originators of that Roman civilization which had so filled men's minds in the earlier Renaissance or Italian stage of modern history. The Italians having set the fashion of copying ancient buildings, the habit continued—Greek ruins, instead of Roman, being taken as models. The study of the original Greek monuments of architecture showed that the columns, capitals, and other details were of much greater beauty, in general, than the Roman copies of the same. The proportions of the original Greek monuments were more refined and the execution of the details was more vigorous. It was still further observed that in Greek architecture each part had a structural meaning and a necessary constructive function. The gable was the expression of the roof lines; the cornice was a similar expression; the beams were a necessary portion of the portico; the columns were structural supports; the capital and base were structural elements at the points of support and pressure. It was observed that the ornamental diversion of these structural forms from their natural meaning and use was a departure from the Greek ideal of relation between form and design, ornament and construction.

The Gothic Revival.—Toward the close of the first quarter of the 19th century a new reaction, however, set in, which found its expression in the buttressed Gothic. The word "Gothic" was first used by the Italians of the Renaissance as applied to architecture, and they used the word, as we still do when we speak of the "Goths and Vandals" as barbarian; of "the act of a Vandal," etc. The Italians applied the word "Gothic" to all North European architecture, meaning that it was a barbaric style. As the buttressed Gothic was the latest of the medieval styles, and most numerously represented by existing structures, the word Gothic became attached to it especially.

It was the spread of Italian Renaissance civilization over Northern Europe in the 16th century which stopped the work on the old medieval cathedrals of which so many—for instance, the Cologne cathedral—were left unfinished. The same Italian influence, which carried with itself the Renaissance architecture, carried with itself the prejudice against the earlier style as being ugly and barbaric.

Thus, in the diary of the English author Evelyn, who traveled through France and Italy in the 17th century, we find him constantly noting of such and such a building, that it was "only Gothic." This prejudice continued in the 18th century.

The copies of medieval buildings which began in the 19th century with revivals of the buttressed Gothic were like the preceding copies of Greek temples, the result and expression of a newly-developed historic study. The standards of taste which had been drawn from the Greeks, being those of nature and of natural vigor, proved effectual in vindicating the greatness of art and of civilization in the Middle Ages. The movement began with the revival of interest in Shakespeare, who, though not medieval in point of fact, had been so regarded by the 18th century. Contempt for Shakespeare as a barbarian was the almost universal verdict of the 18th century—for instance, of the English King George the Third, of the Prussian King Frederick the Great, etc. The German Lessing was the first in the 18th century to insist on Shakespeare's greatness and to critically demonstrate it (*Hamburgische Dramaturgie*), and in this line he was followed and supported by the German poet Goethe. With both these critics, by whom especially, next to Winckelmann, the taste of the earlier 18th century was overthrown, the standards of Greek taste had been the inspiration. From the appreciation of Shakespeare, attention turned to the still earlier time of the Middle Ages proper. In England the medieval movement appears especially in the novels of Sir Walter Scott. The popularity of these novels, when published, was due as much to their novelty of subject as to their artistic merits. So we find that Goethe's first dramatic success, the "Goetz von Berlichingen," owed its fabulous success to its choice of a medieval subject. The translation of this drama into English was the first literary work of Sir Walter Scott. From the attention which was thus devoted to the history, literature, and art of the Middle Ages, which had been so long despised under the Renaissance influences, the buttressed Gothic dates its rise as a modern architectural style.

Mixture of Renaissance and Greek Temple Styles.—Although it is apparent from the foregoing explanations that the Greek Temple style was originally a reaction against the Renaissance, it has since its rise been very frequently mixed with it. We may always separate the two elements, when found in one building, by understanding that the forms are Greek if used structurally in the dimensions of the whole of any one part of a building. Thus in the White House at Washington, the projecting portico shows the Greek influence, and the sides of the building itself are in Renaissance style. Such cases are every-where to be observed.

It is true that this mixture was also found in the Roman buildings, and that the forms of the Greek Temple construction proper, also continued in use in the ancient Roman period. But as far as the ruins in Rome and Italy are concerned, there were no remains of this construction which attracted the general attention of the Renaissance imitators, and the combination in question, with rare exceptions in the old Italian Renaissance, is not found in modern times, until after the time of the Greek revival. In the old Italian Renaissance style, structural colonnades and porticos are common, but almost invariably in the minor dimensions of the individual stories of the building, and the columns frequently support arches, which they never do in the Greek Temple construction, or in the Roman style, where arches are always supported by masses of masonry (piers).

Examples of Renaissance.—The old Italian Renaissance, of which the 19th century Renaissance in America is a continuation, through the later European copies, will be illustrated and explained in a later historical section. Some examples of the 19th century Renaissance in America may now be noted. In *New York*, one of the best artistic examples is the old City Hall; the most pretentious examples are the new Post-office and the new City Hall. Most of the "brown-stone fronts," and a very large proportion of the business buildings of New York, are in this style. In *Philadelphia*, the new "Public Buildings" and the new Post-office are pretentious examples of Renaissance; in *Chicago*, the new City Hall; in *Boston*, the City Hall; in *Brooklyn*, the City Hall; in *Montreal*, the Cathedral, are of the same style. A large proportion of the business structures in most American cities belong to it. In *Europe*, the new Opera Houses of *Paris* and *Vienna* are noted and conspicuous examples of the 19th century period.

Critical Notes on the 19th Century Renaissance.—Although the Renaissance has outlived the reactions of the Greek and Gothic revivals, as apparent in the recent dates of the structures named, it has no hold on the best artistic taste of the day. Some critical reasons for this decline in favor will be noted in the later historical account of the style, but it may be at once said that the 19th century examples (*of this style*) do not remotely approach the excellence of the older Italian and other older Renaissance European buildings. The 19th century examples are generally over-ornamented, uneasy in effect and mechanical in detail—wanting in large proportions and simplicity of composition. The Vanderbilt mansions in New York may, however, be quoted as notable exceptions to this general rule, and there are, of course, other exceptions.

Critical Notes on the Modern Greek Style.—In the early days of the Greek Temple copies, the presumption existed that they were to be considered as true revivals of Greek art, and that the imitation of Greek art was the true mission of the modern. A more dispassionate and later attitude of taste has concluded that the best imitation of Greek art is that which strives for a similar fidelity to the surrounding conditions of time, place, and civilization—that the only way for the moderns to rival the Greeks is to be equally true to themselves. In other words, the Greek art is now studied for its own independent beauty and as a means to general principles rather than as offering examples for imitative repetition. The later modern studies in Greek Temple architecture have also resulted in discoveries which show that the modern copies are, and must of necessity be, lacking in most important peculiarities of the originals. The examination of these differences will be one aim of the historic sketch of the old Greek temples in subsequent pages. It can not be denied, on the other hand, that the modern Greek Temple copies are interesting and effective buildings; *i. e.*, those of the late 18th and early 19th century. Their simplicity of taste is not affected. It really existed in the time which produced them, and the sympathy with Greek art which they represented, though less scientific and less well-informed than our own, was in its way, perhaps, more thoroughly genuine. With the general diffusion of the studies and discoveries of the Greek revival, the impulse which had produced the temple copies died away —especially as the style of the Greek temples was by no means adapted to the general uses and necessities of the modern buildings which took on their guise. They were also thrown into the background by the later fashions of the Gothic revival.

Examples of the Greek Temple Style.—The Rush Library, in *Philadelphia*, is a rare instance of a fine recent construction in this style. Aside from the common-place porticoes of Renaissance public buildings, constructions of the Greek Temple style will generally date earlier than 1850 or 1840. Among the examples in *New York*, are the Custom-house, Sub-treasury, the old St. Paul's, the façade of the old Columbia Law School in Lafayette Place, and a number of old churches. Among the examples in *Philadelphia* are the Rush Library, the old Post-office, the Mint, and Girard College. In *Washington*, the Capitol, White House, and other public buildings are examples with more or less Renaissance mixture. In *Boston*, the Custom-house is an example; in *New Haven*, the old State House and many of the older private dwellings. In *Europe*, the British Museum, Bank of England, and Church of St. Pancras, *London*—the Church of the Madeleine, *Paris*; the Museum, *Berlin*; and the Bank of Ireland, *Dublin*—may be mentioned as among important examples. Other fine examples in *Munich*.

Critical Notes on the Modern Buttressed Gothic.—As a revolt against the absurdity of making Christian churches in the likeness of pagan Greek temples, the Gothic revival did good work, and its influence has been much more wide-spread in ecclesiastical than in secular architecture. In this last field, the buttress construction is rarely convenient. As compared with the old cathedrals, whose style is imitated, there are many inferiorities in the modern copies. These are all a result of the one fact that the most independent art is the best, and that attention to the style of an old building is apt to withdraw attention from the conditions and necessities of a modern construction. In the opening of the Gothic revival, the same slavish subservience to the theory that modern buildings must of necessity exhibit a "style," which had so long been prevalent, was apparent.

The historic study of the old Gothic buildings is especially valuable by reason of the light thrown on their methods as being those of common sense and constructive necessity in their own time. Thus, for instance, these studies have shown that the buttress construction was originally designed to withstand the thrust of a stone or brick vaulting (an arched interior roofing), and that the "flying" buttress especially had this use and necessity. As in our own time, so in the Middle Ages, but less frequently than now, the buttress was subsequently used to strengthen a wall which had not this upper pressure of a vaulting to resist. Although there is no objection to a buttress construction for the purpose of strengthening a wall, the modern copies frequently imitate that use which was intended for vaulted buildings, and which is otherwise unnecessary.

The criticism of the modern buttressed Gothic depends on the special example, and the best standard of criticism is found in the study of the old examples—the modern building being judged, not by the faithfulness of imitation, but by similar adherence to constructive necessities. The changed conditions and arrangements of modern churches will naturally involve important departures from the older style. The freedom and independence with which this style is employed, rather than literal exactness of imitation, are the test of excellence.

Examples of the Modern Buttressed Gothic.—These are so universal in modern church architecture that special mention is unnecessary. In *Europe*, the most noted example is the Votive Church at *Vienna*. Among important secular buildings of the buttressed Gothic style may be mentioned the Houses of Parliament in *London*. The Memorial Hall of *Harvard University* is a fine American example. As an example of the Gothic without buttresses, the church of the Paulist Fathers in *New York* is a fine example, and within the observation and personal tastes of the author, this church and Trinity Church, *Boston* (the latter not Gothic), are the finest modern examples of ecclesiastical architecture, especially as regards interiors.

7. Masonic Temple, Philadelphia.

9. All Souls' Church, New York.

9. BOSTON MUSEUM OF FINE ARTS.

The Romanesque.—About 1850, and since the middle of our century, the influence of the historic styles began to exhibit greater freedom. Certain new styles were affected which were themselves more directly available for modern construction, and these styles have been used with modifications, and in combinations, of distinctly modern character. One of these was the Romanesque.

It was natural, when attention had been first turned to the medieval buildings, that the great Gothic cathedrals should have attracted attention first, and that earlier and consequently less numerous constructions should only have been taken as models subsequently. But this natural movement of the copying habit happened to coincide with the tendency to greater freedom in modern constructions, for reasons to be presently noted.

Ornamental Traits of the Modern Romanesque.—The old Romanesque period, preceding the Gothic, will be explained as to name and character in the proper historical section. Its modern copies, as indicated by Illustrations 7 and 8, the Masonic Temple in Philadelphia, and All Souls' Church in New York, show certain ornamental traits, which are thoroughly available for modern constructions—plain masonry pilasters, a cornice ornament of small round arches, and galleries or arcades of columns and round arches.*

The Italian Gothic, introduced after the same date, falls in the same category with the Romanesque as to modern availability. The old Italian Gothic, also to be treated and explained in its proper historical place, had very little about it of a really Gothic character, and is especially distinguished by absence (generally) of the buttress construction. Its modern ornamental traits are, the use of pointed arches in doors and windows, frequently in masonry of alternating white and black, or other colors, the use of horizontal masonry courses of various colors, and the occasional imitation of the old Italian Gothic portals. The Boston Museum of Fine Arts (9), and the New York Academy of Design (10) have been chosen as illustrations. Their general appearance will suggest many other examples; for instance, the building of the Y. M. C. A., Academy of Fine Arts, and Penn. R. R. Station in Philadelphia.

* Medieval Romanesque columns and their modern imitations are easily distinguished from the classic, when a little attention has been paid to the old buildings. They are generally short and of thickset proportion, and always without the fluted surface. In the old Italian and Pisan Romanesque, where the columns were largely taken from ancient buildings, distinctions are not so clear, but may always be found in the capitals.

Criticism of the Modern Romanesque and Italian Gothic.—The traits of these styles are combined, variously omitted, or developed in such modern and original ways that they offer in this respect a peculiar contrast to the three styles first considered. Another distinction from the three styles first considered lies in the examples which grade over toward buildings which show little or no influence of historic style. These last are as praiseworthy as any, frequently the best. The great value of a critical education in such matters, is to free the judgment from the supposition that the building is to be judged by conformity to an old model. The exact contrary is the case.

Criticism of Architecture Distinct from the Question of "Style."—The true critical stand-point in modern building will become apparent, when we remember that the essential feature of a building is the use of its interior apartments. The building is the shell or envelope of an interior. Study of the old styles will show that they are all exhibitions of work in which this shell or envelope was the expression and result of the interior construction, or intimately related to it. We may as well esteem a person for the ornaments or for the clothing worn, as judge a building solely by the exterior ornament, and this is all there is of "style" in modern Romanesque and modern Italian Gothic. Thus the modern Romanesque and Italian Gothic buildings are to be critically considered, according to the feeling apparent in their construction for the construction itself. The introduction of these styles marks an advance in taste, simply because the ornament used is at least susceptible of this constructional relation. As in dress, so in buildings, the best taste is often apparent in the quietest and simplest appearance. Buildings may have the greatest artistic value, in which only plain brick or rough stone surface is employed. The Italian Gothic and the Romanesque exhibit a return to plain surface (as regards projections), in opposition to the expensive and decoratively overloaded buildings of the modern Renaissance. Thus, it is rather for their want of "style," as compared with the three styles first mentioned, than for any thing else that the modern Romanesque and modern Italian Gothic deserve praise.

"Queen Anne."—The modern prejudice in favor of historic styles has frequently led decorators and artists to employ names or designations, to which they themselves are really indifferent or superior, and the influence of fashion has often created or spread a designation, and attached it to many objects to which it really does not belong at all. This has been the case with the so-called style of "Queen Anne." The early 18th century (the time of Queen Anne) is, in the architecture and decoration, both of England and the Continent of Europe, part of the Renaissance period; but very many domestic buildings were made which had little or no Renaissance ornament. In many cases where the Renaissance form appeared, it was in the window-gable or roof-gable only, not in the columnar ornaments. The old "Queen Anne" buildings in question, i. e., those which gave rise to the modern designation, were of brick or of wood, and hence not adapted to the columnar surface ornaments

10. NEW YORK ACADEMY OF DESIGN

This building was taken down in 1915 and replaced by the building of the Metropolitan Life Insurance Company

11. "Queen Anne" Building, Newport, R. I.

12. "Queen Anne" Country House, Lawrence, L. I.

which were used in the same period for pretentious stone structures. From the imitation of these brick or wooden structures, frequently without any ornament whatever, and only distinguished by picturesque irregularity of construction, has grown the modern style of "Queen Anne," and also the modern habit of calling every thing "Queen Anne" which is new and picturesque. Hundreds of buildings are termed "Queen Anne" by the public for which the architects themselves would refuse to give the name of any style as designation. The so-called "Queen Anne" is only a further development (but more especially in domestic and country-house architecture) of the tendencies which Romanesque and Italian Gothic first exhibited in public and city buildings—of the tendency toward modern freedom and modern independence. Illustrations 11 and 12 may serve to indicate the class of buildings in question.

Criticism of the "Queen Anne" Style.—Queen Anne buildings are therefore to be judged not by resemblance to any set type, but by the common sense and good taste shown in the exhibition of the construction, and by the correspondence of the building in outer forms to its interior arrangements. The influence of fashion has led many builders to adopt the "Queen Anne" style from the outside, so to speak, and to force the interior arrangement to correspond to preconceived and manufactured picturesque effects of the outside. This is an exact contradiction of the true spirit of the Queen Anne movement. Irregular arrangements, giving a picturesque effect, are always artistic when they spring from necessities of construction, or from later additions to an earlier plan. If the irregular arrangements are manufactured purposely, they are almost certain to do violence to convenience, and to betray a want of structural feeling in the design.

Summary of the Matter Relating to Historic Styles in Modern Architecture.

—It appears from the foregoing brief sketch, that some acquaintance with the old historic buildings is essential to a knowledge of the merits and demerits of the modern copies; that many modern buildings may be supposed to derive their value from imitation of an old model, when their merit really lies in independence of it—that the latest and best tendency of modern taste is toward complete modern independence; but that this tendency is often disguised under names like "Queen Anne," "Italian Gothic," etc.

What has been said of the constructional stand-point in criticism, implies that a person, passing an opinion on the artistic merits of a building, should have some knowledge of its uses and purpose, and some perception as to the necessary interior arrangements connected therewith. This knowledge or perception must be largely confined to persons of mature years. But this does not invalidate the position that art education in such matters is desirable for young people. They are not expected to exercise an independent taste at the beginning of their studies, but to learn such matter of fact about the history of styles as will guard them from a mistaken stand-point when they reach years of discretion.

Principles or Stand-points of Criticism in Architecture.—These are entirely independent of the question whether fidelity to a historic style has been observed, and in each particular case the use and nature of the building must be considered. It is not, therefore, easy or desirable to define abstract principles apart from good examples, which are abundantly found, both in modern and in old historic structures. Some hints as to criticism may, however, be indicated. For instance, in applying the stand-point of interior construction to the exterior ornament and appearance, it is not necessary to confine one's self to the physical facts, but these may be ideally indicated also. In a stone building the lines of the divisions of the stories do not appear on the outside, but these may be indicated by a "string-course"* of another color or by a projected molding, and this would still be a case of constructional decoration—an ideal indication of the construction. To take another example from old palaces in Florence; for instance, the Riccardi, Pitti (front view), and Strozzi palaces—these do not derive any greater security of construction from the fact that the blocks of stone are largest and roughest in the lower story. But the appearance of strength thus given is an ideal expression of the actual facts; viz., that the lowest story carries the greatest weight, and must be of corresponding strength. (A similar grading and distinction may be observed in comparing the second story with the third in the palaces named.) In other cases, the actual construction may give of itself an ornamental aspect; for instance, in brick buildings where a wooden frame-work is used, this frame-work may be made apparent. So in wooden buildings the frame-work of the beams may be a decorative element.

Much artistic effect may be obtained from rough or unpolished surfaces—which are generally, or very often, preferable to smoother ones of the given texture. The very general absence of large and undecorated surfaces in modern architecture, has tended to make us somewhat unrestful in taste, and to find in buildings which exhibit them an appearance of gloom and heaviness. Good taste is, however, not at all averse to large effects of undecorated or rough surface in building. (A fine example is the Tiffany mansion in New York.) In the old Roman ruins, and in all periods of historic buildings, these effects may be abundantly studied. It does not, however, follow that the same taste would not take pleasure in a profusion of surface ornament, such as is found in Moresque decoration. The same lady may wear on one occasion a plain tailor-cut dress; on another, a ball-dress covered with lace, and the same taste may find pleasure in both. As regards plainness of construction in modern architecture, it may, however, be noted that good criticism ranks among the best productions of modern art, its great engineering construc-

* A "string-course," or "course," is a horizontal line of masonry, distinguished by material or color from the general wall surface. It may, or may not, have projection.

tions, railway bridges, suspension bridges, and other works, where the simple engineering construction is the only element of effect.

The "Decorative Art" Movement corresponds in time and in its inspiration to the rise of the modern Romanesque, Italian Gothic, and Queen Anne "styles." In the so-called "Eastlake" and "Queen Anne" furniture, there is the same tendency to emphasize the lines of natural construction and develop the ornament in connection with them. But here, as in the architectural "styles" in question, the influence of fashion has often led to external imitations which lack the merits and idea of the original designs.

The Modern Moresque Style.—The Arab styles of ornament and building were introduced into Spain by the Arab Mohammedan Conquest in the 8th century, A.D. The Moors of North Africa had become amalgamated with the Arabs; had adopted their religion and culture at this time, and participated in this invasion. Hence the word Moresque is often applied to the Arab style in Spain.

Of all modern imitations of historic styles, the imitations of the Arab or Moresque have been hitherto the least important in number and influence. The copies confine themselves to a revival in ornamental use of the horseshoe arch, and of the peculiar columns and capitals of Arab style (especially those used in the Alhambra Palace of Granada, in Spain, dating from the 14th century), and to imitations of the "Arabesque" surface decoration, of which abundant illustration may be found in all works or photographs relating to modern Egypt, a prominent seat of Arab civilization from the 7th century on (see especially views from Cairo). The climate and civilization in which the Arab style developed render modern imitations of Arab construction almost impossible. The modern copies are scarcely worthy of serious consideration, if considered as copies. In all cases the modern character is predominant, and some slight ornamental influence is all that really allows the use of the word "Moresque" or "Arab" in relation to them.

Criticism of the Modern Moresque.—Such buildings are to be judged on independent grounds, and without any reference to fidelity of imitation. The slender proportions in the Arab and Moresque columns make them especially available for free reproduction in iron. In modern terra-cotta or brick decoration, Arab or Moresque motives have been very successfully employed. The "Casino," in New York, is a fine example of this use. The interior of the Synagogue in New York is an example of modern Moresque especially distinguished by the color effects.

NOTES ON THE ILLUSTRATIONS FOR MODERN ARCHITECTURE.*

(1-12, inclusive.)

Nos. 1 and 2 are illustrations for the buttressed, or Northern Gothic, style, as revived in the 19th century from buildings of the 12th, 13th, 14th, and 15th centuries. Compare 56–63, inclusive.

Nos. 3 and 4 are illustrations of the revival of the Greek Temple style, whose best ancient examples are of the 5th century B.C. Compare 22. The active period of modern revival was in the late 18th and early 19th centuries, and preceded the modern Gothic.

Nos. 5 and 6 are illustrations of the 19th century Renaissance. This is the continuation of the Italian revival of the decorative style of the Roman ruins

* Rehearsing and summarizing points of the foregoing text.

which began in Italy in the 15th century, spread over Northern Europe in the
16th century, and has since continued there, as well as in all colonies of European
States since and during the same time. Compare 66-69, inclusive.

Each of the three styles in question has been illustrated by two buildings, of
which one is in Europe and one in America, in order to show the correspondence
between the two continents in matters of architectural style.

Nos. 7, 8, represent the modern revival of decorative traits borrowed from
Medieval Romanesque. Compare 50-55, inclusive. The buildings of the Medieval
period belong to the 11th, 12th, and 13th centuries. The modern revival succeeded
that of the buttressed Gothic about and after the middle of the 19th century.
Nos. 8, 10, represent the modern revival of decorative traits of "Italian Gothic."
Compare p. 116. Old buildings of the Italian Gothic belong to the 13th, 14th,
and early 15th centuries. The modern revival is somewhat later than the Romanesque (and later than the buttressed Gothic), and has been especially active about
and since 1870. Nos. 11, 12, illustrate the later activity of the so-called "Queen
Anne." No. 12 represents the present tendencies of country-house architecture,
and a class of buildings to which the term "Queen Anne" is frequently applied
without ground. In No. 11 the curved and pointed door and window gable ornaments do actually repeat the particular forms common in the Renaissance of the
early 18th century, time of Queen Anne; but the significance of the movement in
taste to which this building belongs is really shown in the extent of plain brick
surface.

Court of a Modern Oriental House. Arab Style.

ANCIENT ORIENTAL NATIONS.

Relations to Greek Art.—The matter of foregoing sections will sufficiently explain the use, in our own time, of some historical knowledge of architecture. Although there are no modern copies of the ancient Oriental buildings (the "Tombs," in New York, and the Reservoir, at Forty-second street, in New York, are rare exceptions—both in Egyptian style), these buildings had important influence on the Greeks, and hence some knowledge about them is a necessary introduction to the subject of Greek architecture.

Nations in Question.—By the ancient Oriental nations, we mean those belonging to ancient history, as generally studied—excluding the Chinese and Hindoos.

The Countries in Question are those of the Nile Valley, in Africa (Egypt), and of the Tigris-Euphrates Valley, in Western Asia (Assyria and Chaldea).

Temple Ruins of Egypt.—Among the ancient Oriental nations, as in the East at the present day, the exteriors of the private dwellings had very little architectural pretension or ornament. This same fact holds, also, of the ancient Greeks and Romans. Thus the temples, tombs, and public buildings are mainly in question in a brief account of ancient architecture. The ancient private dwellings were built about an interior court. On the court itself, and the apartments opening on it, the luxury and taste were lavished, but the exterior walls were bare and undecorated, often even without windows opening on the street.

The Most Important Egyptian Temple now standing, as regards purposes of general study, is that of Edfou (illustration 13). The temple of Edfou owes its distinction, not to the fact that it was in ancient times larger or more splendid than many others, but to the fact that it is now the best preserved, and consequently the one through which other ruins may be restored in imagination.

Temple Arrangement.—The priests of Egypt were exclusive guardians of its learning, science, and religion. They belonged to an hered-

itary caste, forming a species of nobility. Even the despotic kings
were subject to their laws. Thus the temples may be considered as
a species of priestly palace, as well as places of worship. They
were, moreover, by the wealth which they contained, peculiarly
exposed to attacks of foreign or domestic foes, and so they also, on
occasion, were actually used as fortresses. Thus we understand the
general arrangement of the Egyptian temple—an exterior high
surrounding wall, for purposes of defense; a gateway (pylon) of
massive proportions, towering above the courts and corridors, to
protect the entrance to them; a series of courts, surrounded by
porticoes, for the comfort and seclusion of the priests, as well as to
receive the processions and gatherings of the worshipers; roofed
apartments alternating with the courts, variously intended for the
images of the gods, for the residence or uses of the priests, for the
preservation of their treasures and the offerings made to them or
the divinity, etc.

Since the despotic power of the king, in alliance with the
priestly caste, was considered essential to the safety and glory of
the nation, he received divine honors during life, and was deified
after death. The temples were erected by the kings, and were covered with carvings and inscriptions commemorating their glory and
victories. They may be considered also, therefore, as royal monuments, significant of the king's devotion to the national religion,
and of his deification by it.

Structural Traits of an Egyptian Temple.*—The Egyptians were
a nation of peculiarly conservative tendencies. Solidity and durability were the ideals which all their art indicates and exhibits. The
temple apartments were roofed with horizontal blocks of stone (see
14, 16, 17, 18), and these were supported by stone beams resting
on perpendicular stone columns. Where these columns face on a
court, there results from this construction a double line of beams
over the columns (16). The first line of beams supports the ends of
the roofing blocks, and these ends are fronted and covered up by a
second line of stone beams. This double line of beams was continued in the Greek architecture (see 22 and 24), and so, through

---

* Although the illustrations opposite are taken from two different temples, they are intended
to represent the front view, side section, and ground plan of any one Egyptian temple—with
proviso that the courts and apartments may be of indefinite number and sequence. The gradual
diminution in the height of the apartments, from the front toward the rear, was probably intended
to impress the entering spectator by artificial exaggeration of the natural perspective diminution.

13. Temple of Edfou.

14. Temple of Khons, Karnak. Longitudinal section.

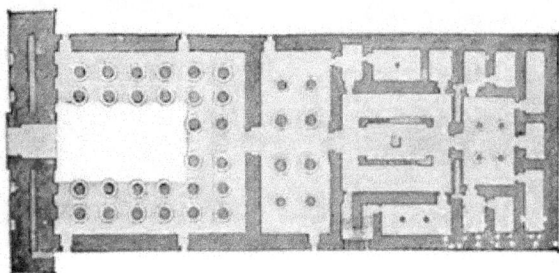

15. Temple of Khons, Karnak. Ground plan.

16. TEMPLE COURT AND APARTMENTS, DENDERAH.

the Roman ornamental copies of Greek forms, passed down to the
Renaissance and to our own modern buildings. (See imitations of the
double beam line in Illustrations 5 and 6.)

The Cornice Construction of the Egyptian ruin (16) just noted
is, however, peculiar to Egypt, and was not transmitted to the
Greeks. This cornice, also seen at the summit of the pylons (Edfou
restoration), has a forward curving profile, below which runs a
rounded horizontal molding.* This form of the cornice was intended
to accent the massive heaviness of effect in the building by the
dark shadow resulting. The molding below accents the shadow by
a line of light caught on the projection.

The Colonnade.—In observing the Egyptian columns, we note
first, that this colonnade architecture, with its upright supports and
horizontal stone beams, was the prototype of the Greek colonnade
style ; second, that the elements of base, shaft, capital, and *abacus*
(the supporting plate of stone between the capital and the beam),
which are observable in Greek architecture, are found in the Egyptian period (14). These various elements are illustrations of the
principle of uniting ornament with structural use. The base is a
transition member uniting the shaft with the supporting surface.
The capital is a transition member uniting the shaft with the supported beam. It avoids an abrupt connection of the round support
with the rectangular *abacus* plate.

Various Forms of the Egyptian Column and Capital are seen in
the illustrations and text-cuts. Of a very ancient period, earlier
than 2500 B.C., are the columns of the rock-cut tombs at Beni
Hassan, famous for their resemblance to the Greek Doric, whose
earliest standing example is more than fourteen hundred years later.
Another form of column and capital found at Beni Hassan, and at
Thebes, of the same early time, imitates a bunch of lotus buds and
stems, bound together. The form at 18 is a later derivative. Forms
of the capital are noticeable in these ruins, resembling an inverted
bell and representing an open lotus flower, the closed lotus bud,
etc., pp. 38-42.

The Period of the existing Egyptian ruins is generally much

* A molding is a line of projected or recessed masonry cutting—generally, i. e., in Greek and
subsequent use, the molding is composed of alternately projected and recessed parts. The
"profile" is the contour of outline or moldings as they would appear if sawn across at right
angles to their length.

later than that of the isolated columns of Beni Hassan just mentioned. Between 1800 B.C. and 1200 B.C., a period of great building activity, were erected most of the temples, now in ruins, at Thebes. These are variously known, from the sites of modern Arab villages erected at various points of the ancient city, as the ruins of Karnak, of Luxor, of Medinet Habou, and of Gourneh.

Important Ruins.—The most famous Egyptian temple ruin is the "Great Hall" of Karnak, built in the 14th century B.C. by the kings Seti I. and Ramses II. (father and son—the mummy of Ramses II. has been discovered and unrolled, and is in the Museum of Gizeh near Cairo).

The temple at Abydus is a construction of Seti I. The "Ramesseum" at Thebes (17) dates from Ramses II. There is a famous rock-cut temple in Nubia at Ipsamboul (80) dating from this last king. On this upper portion of the Nile, above the limits of Egypt proper, there are many other Egyptian ruins.

After the time of the ruin at Medinet Habou, Thebes, about 1270 B.C., many centuries passed of which no remains are now known. The temple of Edfou dates from the Greek rule over Egypt, B.C. 332–B.C. 30. Of the same time are the temple of Denderah (16) and the temples at Philæ. The temples at Esneh and Kom Ambos belong to the period of Roman rule. This rule lasted after 30 B.C. till the Arab conquest in the 7th century A.D. (But pagan temples were not built after the triumph of Christianity in the 4th century, A.D.) Capitals with sculptured leaf decoration, like those at Philæ (19), indicate the Greek or Roman period. The same holds of the capitals with heads of Hathor (Egyptian Venus) (16).

Returning to the Edfou temple as the general type of all others, it is to be observed that the entire wall, roof, beam, and column surface of the temple was covered with carved inscriptions and decorative or pictorial designs; all in brilliant color. Stucco of a very durable quality was laid on the stone surface and received the coloring. If the pylons now destroyed are restored in imagination, the ruins, 16, 17, and 18, may be connected with the typical temple of Edfou for an idea of their original general effect.

The Pyramids.—Of a still older period than any of the temple ruins now standing, and not later than 3800 B.C., are the royal pyramid tombs near Cairo. The largest pyramid, that of Shufu (Cheops [Keeops] as Grecianized in pronunciation), covers nearly thirteen acres of ground, and was once over four hundred and eighty feet high. The adjacent pyramid of King Shafra (Chephren) (both are illustrated at 20) was four hundred and seventy feet. Beside it is the colossal Sphinx, with human head and lion's body, possibly of still more ancient date, now buried to the shoulders in sand, sixty-five feet high, and one hundred and forty-two feet long. This Sphinx is an emblem of the Egyptian Divinity Horus, one of the forms of the Sun-god.

The religion of the Egyptians taught or admitted the existence of a Supreme Being (disguised under various forms and attributes, and giving rise to a variety of subordinate personifications, which were also worshiped as correlated divinities). It taught the immortality of the soul and a state of rewards and punishments after death. The immense size of the royal pyramid tombs was connected with a general habit of emphasizing the importance of the tomb, which, in the case of the king,

17. The Ramesseum, Thebes.

18. Ruins of Hermopolis.

19. RUINS ON THE ISLAND OF PHILAE.

found an extraordinary development. The Egyptian idea of the future life conceived of the continued existence of the soul and of the "vital spark," and also of a spectral shadow or essence of the body, maintaining its guise. This spectre, at least in the earliest period known, was conceived to depend for its well-being and activity, on a corporeal form to which it might attach itself. Hence, one reason for the embalmment of the mummy, and in many cases for the placing of statues in the tomb to which the spirit might attach itself. Such statues (Nos. 77 and 79) are found in many tombs near the pyramids, though not in the pyramids themselves. Great care was taken to avoid the possibility of destruction, and to conceal them in deep wells which formed part of the tomb. The galleries leading to the tomb chambers, within the pyramids, which contained the stone coffins and mummies, were closed at the entrance by immense blocks of stone.

Chaldean and Assyrian Architecture. —The various ancient Empires of the Tigris-Euphrates Valley, Chaldean, Assyrian, Babylonian, and Persian, were successive governmental forms controlling one single civilization, which changed in the course of successive centuries in many ways, but which still retained its unity in spite of the change of rulers implied by the above succession of empires.

On account of the material used in the Chaldean and Assyrian constructions, which was brick, whereas the Egyptians used stone for their most important buildings, the ruins are now so shapeless that only ground plans and restorations can be used for illustration. The older (Chaldean) period is distinguished by immense heaps of bricks, which are the ruins of its temples. These were built in fashion of high platforms ascended by winding staircases on the outside. At the summit was the altar for sacrifice and the space on which the priests made their astronomical and astrological observations. Many of the Chaldean ruins date before 2000 B.C.

In the later (Assyrian) period, the ruins of palaces predominate over those of temples. These are also reduced to shapeless heaps and mounds. Laborious excavations are required to reproduce the plan and construction of the original monuments.

The Babylonian Empire divided the spoils and territories of the Assyrian state with the Medes after 625 B.C. The Persian Empire reunited these territories about 550 B.C., and added Egypt to them about twenty-five years later. The Persian conquests extended to the Indus on the east and to the shores of Asia Minor. The great capitals of this state, Persepolis and Parsagada, lay east of the Tigris-Euphrates Valley, in the province of Persia proper, and here palaces were erected by the Persian monarchs, whose ruins show that the Eastern world was already beginning to feel the influence of Greek art. This Greek influence became ascendant after Alexander the Great's conquest of the Persian Empire, about 330 B.C., and continued ascendant over Western Asia till the rise of the Mohammedan Arabs in the 7th century A.D.

Egypt alone maintained her independent art forms in this Greek period after Alexander's conquest (which included Egypt). In speaking of the ascendancy of Greek civilization as continuing till the time of the Arab conquests, it is to be remembered that the rule of the Roman Empire over the Oriental Mediterranean countries, which began shortly before the Christian Era, did not change their civilization. The Greek Oriental culture rather became that of the Romans.

The Practical Influence of Chaldean and Assyrian Architecture on the Greek was mainly in ornamental forms and designs. The use of the arch was practiced in Chaldea and Assyria. In Egypt, it was also used, though not in temples. It appears very probable that the vaulting (roofing) arch and the dome were also employed in the former countries. It has long been known that the arch did not originate with the Romans of Italy, who obtained it from the Etruscans. The theory which derives the Etruscans of Italy, or a portion of them, from Asia Minor, where Assyrian influence was much felt, is held by good authorities. Or the arch may have passed to Italy by Phœnician transmission, since the Phœnicians of the Syrian coast were in active intercourse with both Egypt and Assyria.

Enameled tiles were used in elaborate compositions of beautiful color effects, especially for the exteriors of the buildings. The most remarkable known examples of this architectural tile-work (placed in the Louvre Museum, 1886) are from Susa. (Persian period; lifesize procession of the royal guard, known as the "Immortals," and other subjects.) The tile decoration of the Arabs and Saracens is undoubtedly a continuation of this art, and the art of our own enameled tiles descends in various channels from the same original source.

NOTES ON THE ILLUSTRATIONS FOR EGYPTIAN ARCHITECTURE.*

(13-21, inclusive.)

Nos. 13, 14, and 15 offer in combination typical examples of the front exterior view, side section, and ground plan of an Egyptian temple. Different buildings vary as to the number of courts and apartments, but correspond as to general

Temple of Khons, Karnak.

plan and arrangement. All the ruins represented at 16, 17, 18, 19, may be restored in imagination by the assistance of the first three typical views, and connected with some portion of the general plan of a temple as there shown. Obelisks or statues were frequently placed in pairs flanking the entrances of the pylons.

20. THE PYRAMID FIELD OF GIZEH.

21. PALACE OF THE ASSYRIAN KING SARGON, KHORSABAD. Restoration by Fergusson.

The interior Court of the Temple of Khons (text-cut, p. 38) should be compared with the plan, 15, and section, 14.* The relation of the view from Denderah, 16, to the original entire building will thus also become apparent. It is designed to show in larger dimensions the Egyptian system of construction as regards the column, capital, roofing blocks, lines of beams in exterior view, and cornice.

Nos. 17 and 18 will now be understood as fragments of constructions similar to the text-cut, p. 38, or to Fig. 16, and as having a similar relation to an entire temple as indicated by the typical views 13, 14, 15. Finally, Fig. 19 illustrates the general appearance of Egyptian ruins in their relation to the surrounding landscape.

Rock Tombs of Beni Hassan.

No. 20 shows part of the "Pyramid field" of Gizeh, near Cairo, with the two largest pyramids of the IVth Dynasty, which antedate by many centuries any temple ruins known at present. They are probably not later than 4000 B.C. To the same period of the "Ancient Empire" (as contrasted with the "New Empire" beginning about 1800 B.C.) belong the rock-tombs of Beni Hassan, XIIth Dynasty (text-cut, p. 41). The architectural details, columns, and capital, here illustrated, have been noted in text.

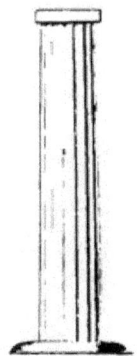

Proto-Doric Column, Beni Hassan.

The walls between the columns, as found at Denderah (16), are not typical for early Egyptian monuments, and are only found in the period of decadence, during the rule of the Greeks and Romans. The true Egyptian feeling admits either an open colonnade or a solid entire wall, but no compromise between the two. Imitation gateways, with side pilasters inserted against columns, as seen at 16 and 18, are also confined to the period of decadence. The original Egyptian construction does not tolerate any break in the outline of the column.

The shattered pilaster figures in 17 are representations of the God Osiris (the Sun during the night conceived as God of the dead and of the Lower World, and thus having the form of a mummy). Similar "Osirid" pillars are frequently found in Egyptian construction. The capitals in 16 show heads of the Goddess Hathor, a double or counterpart of Isis, the spouse of Osiris and personification of the fertile earth. The winged disk seen over the portal at Denderah, and generally found in corresponding positions elsewhere (see Court of the Temple of

Lotus-bud Capital Beni Hassan.

Khons), is one of the forms of the God Horus (the Rising Sun, child of Osiris and Isis). The sun has the wings of a hawk to indicate the swiftness of its course.

* Khons is a Theban form of the God Horus (the Rising Sun).

Fig. 21 is an imaginary restored view, by the English architect and critic, Fergusson, of the Assyrian palace at Khorsabad, near Nineveh. The arrangement of the lower line of relief slabs is based on actual remains. The open colonnades above are borrowed by the artist from later ruins found at Persepolis. The palace was built in the 8th century and destroyed in the 7th century B.C.

Ruins of the Great Hall of Karnak, Thebes.

ARCHITECTURE OF THE GREEKS.

General Type of the Greek Temples.—The most perfectly preserved of these, is the Temple of Theseus at Athens, built about 460 B.C. It has been used as an art museum. Of the outer portion only the roof is new. The illustration of this building (22) may be used with the following matter. For reasons explained (p. 29), and on account of the destruction of the public buildings other than temples, the study of Greek architecture is almost entirely confined to these.

The Ruins.—The earliest Greek Temple ruins now in existence date from the 6th century B.C., or can not be positively fixed as belonging to an earlier time. Among these are several in Sicily (where the Greek colonies then controlled the Island): one, at least, of the ruins at Pæstum, in Lower Italy, in which country there were many Greek colonies, and one at Corinth. The most important Greek Temple ruins are at Athens, and belong to the 5th century B.C. Subsequently, the leading temples were those built in the Oriental Greek countries. Asia Minor, Syria, Alexandria in Eygpt, etc., but these have mainly disappeared, aside from foundations and scattered fragments, like the earlier temples of Delphi, Olympia, and Ephesus. The destruction of temples of an earlier date than the 6th century B.C. is probably owing to the fact that they were generally built wholly or partly of wood.

Temple Construction.—In the earliest stone structures standing, there is already found the fixed and completely developed type of the Greek temple. This type shows in its columnar elements of structure an Egyptian origin, but in form and arrangement a complete independence of foreign influence. Its most striking feature is the exterior portico, whose colonnade, surrounding a wall without windows, supports, above its double line of beams, a gabled roof. The plan of the Egyptian temple admitted an indefinite extent and series of apartments and courts. The room specially dedicated to the statue or statues of the divinity, was often only one of many. On the other hand, the Greek temple is essentially only a shrine **for**

the statue, with the surrounding wall and colonnade. To this main apartment was generally added another, which was used as a treasury for the State funds or for the more valuable offerings made to the shrine.

In the greatest period of Greek art, the 5th and 4th century B.C., the temple statues of special fame were made of plates of ivory and gold (supported by an interior skeleton frame of wood), and were of colossal size. An interior colonnade, of two series of columns, superimposed, supported the roof and divided the apartment of the statue into a middle nave and two side aisles. It is not certain whether or no the aisles were covered by a gallery, overlooking the statue.

Lighting of the Temples.—As opposed to the Egyptian temple, whose roof was flat and entirely of stone, the Greeks used wooden beams for the interior roof, which was covered with stone or terracotta slabs outside. On account of the decay of the wooden portions, none of these roofs have been preserved, so that the method of lighting the buildings is not certainly known. The absence of windows on the sides was probably intended to avoid the effect of cross lights, and to throw the statue into relief by the light falling on it directly from above. Some temples were lighted by a direct opening in the roof, but it is not likely that any of those containing the gold and ivory statues were among the number. (The difficulty of devising a construction by which the lighting was obtained in other cases has led also to the theory that artificial light was used.)

The Colonnade.—There was no exclusiveness about the rites of Greek worship, which consisted mainly of choral hymns and rhythmic dances, executed by the citizens themselves. The priests were not the guardians of mysterious learning or masters of a written hieroglyphic language, which could not be read by the uninitiated. The priestly office was hereditary in certain families, but the priests were ordinary citizens who engaged in public affairs, and lived like their neighbors. This publicity of rites in the religious system finds a counterpart in the portico, by which the temple was surrounded. The citizens were invited by it to approach the building and to enjoy its protection, although the shrine itself could not, on account of its size, admit a large number at once. Moreover, to increase the size of the shrine within would have tended to diminish the effect of the colossal statue. Thus, in the natural tendency to increase the size of new temples, as the Greek States increased in

22. Temple of Theseus, Athens. Present condition.   23. Acropolis at Athens, Present condition.
24. Parthenon, Athens. Present condition.

65. INTERIOR OF THE PARTHENON. Restored.

size and wealth, the development was, so to speak, on the outside. Hence, one explanation of the exterior colonnade. The colonnade may also be understood as the screen or decoration, relieving the blank surface of the wall of the building, which, we have seen, was unbroken by windows.

The Greek Religion was intimately connected with the idea of duty and devotion to the State. The deities were conceived as the patrons and guardians of the city which affected their worship. Thus, the public life as soldiers and citizens was a part of the religion, and the temples were public buildings, whose porticoes were open to the commerce and every-day life of the people. The open colonnades, which are the distinctive feature of all Greek public architecture, both in temples and otherwise, were a peculiar outgrowth at once of the climate and of the civilization of the people. This civilization, unlike the great despotisms of the Nile and Tigris-Euphrates valleys, was one of small and independent civic communities, united by language, by a sense of superiority to surrounding nations, by religion, and by the great gymnastic festivals; but otherwise as distinct from one another as the various nations of modern Europe. The development of Greek art had thus, at once, a civic and religious origin.

With regard to the religion itself, and to the ideas which were associated with the temple statues, some words are necessary. The statues were not idols which were directly worshiped, but were symbols of a spiritual divinity. The more serious Greeks of the best period had risen to the notion of a single God. Others, in earlier times, worshiped their national patron deity as a distinct spiritual power, without questioning the existence of other gods. After the early part of the 4th century B.C., skepticism as to the actual existence of the mythological divinities was very general; but these were still conceived as personifications of various virtues and ideal qualities.

Distinction between the Doric and Ionic Orders.—The plan and use of the Greek temple have been sketched, and we now proceed to consider the different styles in which the general plan was carried out, known as the Greek "Orders."

There are really only two Greek orders, as specified above. The Corinthian is often specified as a third order, but it is really Ionic, with a more elaborate capital and more elaborate ornamentation. The distinction between the orders lies in their proportions, and these proportions are essentially the same in the Ionic and Corinthian.

The "Tuscan" is sometimes distinguished as a separate order, but it is only a degraded form of the Doric which was used in Italy by the Etruscans, and then by the Romans. The "Composite" order, sometimes specified as distinct, is simply a Roman and degraded form of the Corinthian capital.

The differences between the Doric and Ionic temples (compare

27 with 28) represent the distinctions between the two Greek tribes, from which the names are borrowed. The Doric temple was originally that of the Doric Greeks, and in its massive solidity of appearance and construction reflects the simplicity and sternness of their character and taste. The Ionic temple shows in its light and elegant construction the more refined and effeminate nature of the Ionians. In the ruin which is the original of 27, the gable is wanting and has been restored by the artist.

According to the division generally mentioned in Greek histories, there were three tribes of Greeks, the third named being the Æolian. As a matter of fact, however, the Æolic Greeks represent a survival and continuation, in some localities, of the dialect and peculiarities of the early Greeks which were universal before the separation into the Doric and Ionic divisions had become apparent. (A somewhat similar instance might be found in the present well-known differences between North and South Germans, as compared with the Icelanders, whose isolated position explains the fact that they continued to represent an early stage of Germanic life, similar to that from which both North and South Germans sprang, long after this division had taken place.)

The Doric Character and the Doric Order.—Recorded or written Greek history, as distinct from knowledge drawn from the study of language and from archæologic remains, begins about 1100 B.C., with the account of the "Doric Migration." At this time there existed a civilization in Southern Greece of a fairly developed character. Dr. Schliemann's excavations at Tiryns and Mycenæ have revealed something of its jewelry, pottery, and other ornamental art. Aside from this, there are, at various points in Greece, especially at the places above named, massive citadel walls and fortifications of the same period. This prehistoric Greek civilization, of which there are no written records, was overthrown by the Doric migration. The population which possessed it was dispersed or subjugated.

The Dorians were mountaineers from Northern Greece. The little province of Doris, in North Central Greece, is named after them, but does not by any means represent the extent of territory over which they were spread. Owing to the peculiar topography of Eastern Europe, with vast plains unbroken by mountains, sweeping down toward the south, the climate of Northern Greece corresponds to that of the north of Europe, and its early population was of a hardy and relatively barbarous character. Southern Greece, on the other hand, has the climate of Southern Europe, on account of the warm winds from the Southern Mediterranean, and here had consequently developed the earliest Greek culture.

Of these hardy Dorian invaders, some settled in extreme Southern Greece, in and about the town of *Sparta*. These became the Spartans. They had taken from the earlier population all the most fertile lands of the Eurotas Valley, but this population was not expelled. It was reduced to slavery or to a state of political dependence and insignificance. The Spartans were very much outnumbered by this conquered population, and could only preserve their ascendancy by the development of a rigid military system of education, to which they were all subjected without distinction. A part of this military system was constant gymnastic exercise.

26. INTERIOR OF THE JUPITER TEMPLE AT OLYMPIA. Restored.

27. Temple of the "Wingless Victory," Athenian Acropolis.

28. Temple of Neptune, Paestum.

As time went on the military power of the Spartan State proved itself superior to every other in Greece, and its institutions were accordingly respected and imitated. These institutions, in which every citizen was held subject to military service without pay, at the call of the State, and in which the gymnastic education of the citizen was compulsory, were not confined to the Doric Greeks, but they were generally imitated. Thus we have explained the fact that the Doric order of architecture was not confined to the Doric Greeks. It reflects the influence on the general Greek character of their tastes and institutions under the influence especially of the Spartans. For several centuries (until 430 B.C.) the Doric order was universally employed in the mother country and in most of the colonies, aside from those of Ionia proper.

The Ionic Character and the Ionic Order.—In the movement of population caused by the Doric migration, some of the islands of the Ægean Sea and part of the coast of Asia Minor had been settled by the fugitives. The name of the middle part of this coast, "Ionia," gives the name to the tribe in general. The most quoted Ionic population remaining in Greece proper was that of the peninsula of Attica, capital Athens, reaching out toward the islands and the Asiatic coast. The Ionians were thus settled in maritime Greece, or on islands or shores directly bordered by the sea. They became the characteristic sailor Greeks, just as the Dorians were the characteristic soldiers. To the vivacity and versatility of nature, which is proverbial for a maritime population, they added the somewhat effeminate and luxurious tastes which the influence of the farther East on the coast of Asia Minor naturally favored. On this coast developed the first great commercial cities of the Greeks, among them Smyrna and Ephesus, and here rose the school of poetry, about or after 1000 B.C., represented by the Homeric poems. The most famous temple of Ionia, that of Diana at Ephesus, built in the 6th century B.C., was destroyed by fire two hundred years later. The foundations of the later Temple of Diana at Ephesus have lately been excavated by the English architect, Mr. Wood.

The Parthenon.—The Athenians, although Ionians by blood, had for centuries been ruled by Doric institutions, and produced the most famous monument of Doric architecture just before the decline of this style. This was the Parthenon (21), the temple of the Virgin Goddess Minerva (Greek, Athené), finished in 438 B.C. The supervising director of this building was the sculptor Phidias, who designed its sculpture decorations now known as the "Elgin Marbles," and himself constructed for the interior a colossal gold and ivory Minerva, long since destroyed. The present ruined condition of this building is the result of a gunpowder explosion in the 17th century. At this time Greece and Athens were in the hands of the Turks. During a war with the Venetians, the Turks used the building as a powder magazine, and this was exploded by a bomb thrown by the Venetian attacking force.

The Propylæa, or entrance gates to the Acropolis (Citadel Hill), on which the Parthenon stood, were a scarcely less famous structure (30). They were completed, also under the direction of Phidias, between 437 and 430 B.C. On account of the extra height required for the columns of the passage-way, these were made of the Ionic order, whose proportions are more slender than the Doric. This is a rare case of mixture of the orders, which, in the Greek period, were usually confined to distinct buildings. Even in the case of distinct buildings, the orders were not in general use simultaneously. They represent, on the contrary, successive tendencies of Greek history. The Ionic order appeared in Ionia at an earlier date than elsewhere; and the Doric did not absolutely disappear after the Ionic fashion became general. Still, it is true in the general sense, that these styles, considered as dominant fashions in the mother country, are successive and not contemporaneous. They represent the distinction between the period of conservative tendencies, religious belief, and stern patriotism, and the period of refined luxury, religious skepticism, and political decay.

The Ionic Replaced the Doric in the 5th century B.C. Athens was then the center of Greek life, at once in politics, in literature, and in art, and here was consummated the social revolution through which the Ionic order came into general use, after 430 B.C.

This was the time of the Peloponnesian War (431–404 B.C.), which is universally conceded to have been the turning-point in Greek history, after which patriotic conservatism and the old Doric modes of life were replaced by more refined and effeminate tendencies, which terminated a century later in the downfall of the independent Greek States. Greek history proper ends with the battle of Chæronea, 338 B.C., when Philip of Macedon defeated the Athenians and their allies in the struggle to preserve Greece from Macedonian conquest.

The Period of the Ionic Order, when generally diffused over Greece, is, in round numbers, from 430 to 330 B.C., and this period is the last of Greek history, considered as the history of the old independent Greek States.

The Erechtheium* is the most famous Ionic building and ruin. Also on the Athenian Acropolis; it was constructed between 430 and 400 B.C. Here was preserved a statue of Minerva much more ancient than the building. This had been rescued by the Athenians when

* The view at 29 is taken from drawings made soon after the middle of the 18th century (by Stuart and Revett), when the building was in much better preservation than at present. The Erechtheium also appears at 30, on the left.

29. THE ERECHTHEIUM. North-western view, as it appeared in the 18th Century

30. ACROPOLIS

ATHENS. R ... rc ..

32. Ruins of the Olympian Jupiter Temple, Athens.

31. Choragic Monument of Lysicrates, Athens.

the Persians captured Athens in 480 B.C., and destroyed the old buildings on the Acropolis. The new Erechtheium was thus erected on the site of an older building, whose irregular ground plan was followed in the new structure from a sentiment of reverence and religious tradition. The name of the temple is derived from an Athenian king and hero of the mythical period, whose tomb was beneath the structure.

The Little Temple of Nike Apteros, or "Wingless Victory," generally so called, but now known to have been a temple of Minerva, has been chosen as type of the Ionic in illustration (27) because the small size of the building allows a larger view of its details. It appears in the restored view 30, on the right. This little temple, also on the Acropolis, was built about twenty years before the Erechtheium. Its small dimensions show how modestly the style first made its appearance beside the older Doric at Athens.

Historical Explanation of the Corinthian Order, so called.—The overthrow of Greek independence by the Macedonian King Philip was immediately followed by a Macedonian-Greek conquest of the Persian Empire, under his son, Alexander the Great. This empire, reaching from the shores of Asia Minor and Syria to the Indus (p. 37), and including Egypt, had its center in the home of the old Assyrian and Chaldean States, the Tigris-Euphrates Valley. The conquest had been prepared by a gradual introduction and spread of Greek influence in the Oriental countries, and it was followed by a heavy migration of Greeks into the Eastern world. First as governors and soldiers, then as men of art and science, and men of business, the Greeks spread through the West Oriental countries, founding new independent Greek cities, like Antioch in Syria and Alexandria in Egypt, and also intermarrying and amalgamating with the Oriental populations. Greek States grew up on the ruins of the Persian Empire, which ultimately, a little before the beginning of the Christian era, had nearly all become portions of the Roman Empire. (The Greeks of the Tigris-Euphrates Valley and countries farther East were, however, subdued by the Parthian heirs of the Persians after 100 B.C.)

In this period of Greek history, the mother country was almost depopulated; but the Greek language, art, and science had begun their conquest of the civilized world. Under the Roman rule they were to conquer Italy and the countries of the Western Mediterranean, and then descend to later times mainly under disguise of the Roman name and period. The earlier simplicity and purity of Greek life and taste were, however, replaced by more luxurious tastes, and more corrupt civilization.

These explanations are necessary to an understanding of the word "Corinthian" as applied to the luxurious Ionic order of the Alexandrine time. (From Alexander the Great, and from the great Greek capital of Egypt founded by him, Alexandria, the period is so named.) Corinth, by virtue of its position on the Isthmus, through which passed so much of the Mediterranean commerce, had been a rich and luxurious city in days before the Alexandrine period, and in the time when riches and luxury were the rule, "Corinthian" was the adjective naturally used for the taste of the time. It may be also that a Corinthian architect perfected or beautified the capital so named, but there is evidence to show that it has an Oriental origin.

The Corinthian Capital has a body corresponding to the shape of the column itself, but this is overlaid and concealed by leaves (p. 60). In general proportions and essential details the Corinthian order, as already noted, is simply the Ionic: but generally with ornamental details somewhat more elaborated (text-cut, p. 6).

The Choragic Monument of Lysicrates at Athens (31) is the earliest known, and also the most beautiful example of the Corinthian order, as respects the capitals; but these capitals have been so damaged that restored drawings are necessary to an appreciation of their former beauty. This little building is a round structure, of slender proportions, erected to support a bronze tripod, which has disappeared. The tripod was a form consecrated by sacrificial uses in the Greek religion, and hence was one of the usual prizes in the contests of Greek dramatic choruses. The tripod in question was a prize won by the chorus which was supported by the Athenian Lysicrates. Hence the name "Choragic Monument."

The date (334 B.C.) of this building marks the general introduction of the Corinthian style into Greece and into the Greek countries. It corresponds nearly to the general date for Alexander the Great's conquest of the Persian Empire (about 333 B.C.), and to the date for the battle of Cheronaea, just noted.

Later Architectural Remains of the Corinthian order, between the time of the Choragic Monument and the period of the Roman Empire are almost absolutely unknown, owing to the wholesale destruction of the ancient monuments. This latter period has however, left abundant remains of the Corinthian order, and many of great beauty. These belong to the early centuries of the Christian era. The general use of the Corinthian order in the Roman imperial period, in all countries of the Empire, is one phase of the general fact that the culture of the Roman Empire, which comprised so many countries which had been previously Alexandrine Greek, had also in general an Alexandrine Greek origin.

The Ruins of the Olympian Jupiter Temple at Athens (32), may be mentioned as among these later monuments, dating from the

Roman Emperor Hadrian, and the second century after Christ. Other remains of the Roman period will be noted in the corresponding section.

Details of the Doric and Ionic Orders Compared.—Having considered, first, the general plan and use of the Greek temple, and second, the historical sequence of the Greek orders and their correspondence, as to time and taste, with the broadest facts of Greek history, we may now notice the contrasts of the orders in detail. These orders, as already noted, are essentially only two in number, and the following matter applies equally to the Corinthian and the Ionic, with exception for the capitals alone.

Contrast in Proportions of the Column.—For following matter compare 27 with 24 and 28. (See also text-cut at page 6.) The proportions of the Doric column are heavy, and those of the Ionic are light and slender. This distinction has no reference to the actual size, but to the relations of height and diameter. The average height of the shaft of the Doric column is from 5 to 5½ diameters. The average height of the Ionic shaft is from 8½ to 9½ diameters.

The Doric Order has no Base, and its shaft rests directly on the platform of the structure. This absence of bases enhances the effect of the heavy proportions in the columns, which would gain in height, and therefore in appearance of slenderness, if supported by such a member. The slender proportions of the Ionic shaft are, on the other hand, enhanced by the additional elevation which the base gives to the column.

The Intercolumnar Distances, or spaces between the columns, are narrow in the Doric order, and do not much exceed the diameter of the column itself (average, 1½ diameters). This contributes also to the massive effect of the order. The Ionic columns, although more slender, are also spaced in relatively wider distances (average, 2½ diameters).

Diminution of the Shaft.—All Greek columns diminish slightly in size from the foot toward the neck. In the Doric order this diminution is quite emphatic; the converging sides of the shaft give an effect of steadfastness and security, tending to that seen in the form of the pyramid. The diminution from below upward in proportions of the Ionic shaft is so slight, that the reduced size of a picture will not show it. It is none the less, here as in the Doric, a delicate indication of that natural physical law that pressure increases from above downward, and that physical resistance must also increase from above downward. As in the case of the Florentine palaces noted at page 26, there is no physical necessity for this construction. It is an artistic and æsthetic emphasis for the satisfaction of the eye.

Curves of the Shaft.—The diminution mentioned is not produced by straight lines, but in the outlines of all Greek columns there is a delicate convex curve. This curve is called the *Entasis.* On account of the marked diminution of the Doric shaft, the convex curves in the rising lines of the shaft are most pronounced in the Doric. The curves may be conceived as representing an elastic and vigorous supporting power against the weight above, as opposed to one of dead resistance. It may be that the converging lines of the Greek column were intended to enhance the perspective diminution and consequent appearance of size. The curves would assist this perspective illusion. It has been supposed by some authorities that the curves are intended to correct an optical appearance of inward deflection toward the center in the exterior lines of the shaft.

Flutings of the Column.—All the orders, as far as the Greek monuments are concerned, have fluted columns. That is, the shafts are channeled in the perpendicular direction by a series of curved grooves or furrows. These flutings have partly the purpose of uniting the various "drums" or pieces of the shaft into a single whole, and of preventing the cross-sections of the joints of the various pieces from breaking the effect of perpendicular unity. But in cases where a relatively small size of the shaft allowed it to be quarried in a single block the flutings are also found, so that this could not be the sole explanation. The flutings may then be also understood as a decoration emphasizing the perpendicular line, and pleasing the eye by an agreeable and regular variation of lights and shadows on the surface of the shaft.

Doric Capital, Parthenon.

There is a distinction in the character of the flutings of the two orders. The Doric flutings are wide and shallow, and are separated only by the sharp edges formed by the meeting of two concave curves. The Ionic flutings are narrow and deep, and are separated by intervals of plane surface, forming a series of perpendicular bands. This distinction is explained by its results in the effects of the shadows which the flutings cast. The deep and narrow flutings cast a heavy shadow, and each perpendicular dark line of shadow is emphasized by its distinct separation from the others. The slender effect of the Ionic is much increased by these perpendicular shadow stripings. The shallowness of the Doric flutings is such, that the shadow lines, falling mainly only at the sharp edges of separation, do not essentially detract from its heavy proportions. Thus, too, would be explained the fact that the flutings are more numerous in the Ionic (twenty-eight flutings) and less numerous in the Doric (twenty flutings; in early temples, sixteen). That is, the slender shaft has heavier perpendicular shadows and more of them, while the thick-set shaft has lighter perpendicular shadows and less of them.

Ionic Capital, Erechtheium.

Corinthian Capital, Choragic monument of Lysicrates.

The Doric Capital.—At the neck of the shaft, and just below the capital, the Doric column is cut by one or more incisions horizontally, giving the effect in shadow of a ring about the neck of the shaft. This cut is intended to mark off and distinguish the capital from the shaft. The Doric capital was called by the Greeks the *Echinus*, from its resemblance to a kettle or caldron. Its shape is best described by the illustration of the text-cut, p. 60, or by the columns seen in 25 and 26.

The Ionic Capital is also best described by the text-cut (p. 60). The volutes, which are its distinguishing feature, are derived from the downward curling calyx leaves of a conventional form of lotus used in ancient Oriental decoration, and derived from Egypt. The entire flower is found on Cypriote vases, and on Cypriote tombstones, dating from the 6th and 7th centuries B.C.

The Corinthian Capital has already been described (text-cut, p. 60).

In Greek use, there was much freedom and variety in the treatment and details of the capitals of the various orders. No two buildings of the same order are exactly alike in this, or in any respect.

The Abacus is the square

Scheme of Doric Temple Construction, Parthenon.

plate of stone which rests on the capital and supports the beam above. In the Doric order, the *abacus* is a large and prominent member. In the Ionic, the *abacus* is represented only by a thin plate of stone, or disappears entirely.

The Beams are Distinguished as Architrave and Frieze.—Both taken together, are called the "entablature." The lower line of beams is called the *architrave*. The word *frieze* is applied to the upper line of beams, but the same word is also used to define a horizontal band of decoration in general, whether it be on the inside or outside upper portion of a wall, or elsewhere.

The Architrave has an undecorated surface in the Doric order. The Ionic architrave has three horizontal divisions. Each one of the two upper divisions juts forward a little over the one beneath it. The effect, as seen from the front, is that of a beam divided into three sections by two horizontal lines. The divisions are said to be imitations of the overlapping boards of an ancient style of wooden construction. This resemblance is an assistance to a verbal description of

Acroterium of the Parthenon.

the Ionic architrave, and may explain its origin, but it is not likely that imitation of wooden construction was the motive of this use in the perfected stone Ionic. The motive was, doubtless, to relieve the surface of the beam of a bare appearance, which, on the other hand, was easily tolerated by the spirit of the Doric order. In certain cases, however, the Doric architrave was decorated by affixed gold or gilded shields.

The Doric Frieze is spaced in sections by a series of *triglyphs* (28 and text-cut), arranged, one over each column, and one over each intercolumnar space. Thus the *triglyphs* duplicate the number of the columns. The triglyphs consist of perpendicular bands of stone, three in number, separated by grooves.

The spaces between the triglyphs are called *Metopes*. They are generally decorated with sculpture in relief.

The Cornice has a more elaborate outline in profile, and a more decorative molding, in the Ionic and Corinthian styles; a simpler and heavier character in the Doric. The under surface of the Doric cornice is decorated with a series of *mutules*, flat, rectangular, projected surfaces on which are drops, or *guttae*.

The Pediment or Gable is distinguished in all the Greek orders by its low (wide or obtuse) angle. This angle is more acute in the Roman period (compare the Pantheon, 39). The space within the lines of the gable was decorated with sculpture. Ornaments, called *Acroteria*, were placed on the summit of the gable and at the lower extremities of its sides.

Ionic Entablature, Priene.

Irregularities of Construction.—A remarkable feature of Greek Temple architecture is the general absence of rectilinear and of exactly perpendicular lines. Irregularities in the sizes of corresponding members—columns, capitals, abaci, triglyphs, and metopes, and in the spacings between them, are also general. The peculiar delicacy of the masonry construction has admitted of an examination in detail, which proves that these various irregularities of size, proportion, and alignment were a part of the intended construction. The observation of these peculiarities is comparatively recent, and their purpose is still in debate.

The first noted and most curious of these refinements is that relating to the deviations from rectilinear alignment.

The Horizontal Curves.—It was observed, in 1837, by Mr. Pennethorne, an English architect, that the steps of the substructure (*stylobate*) of the Parthenon, and the substructure itself, are constructed in curved lines rising from the corners toward the center of each side. Corresponding but not exactly parallel curves are found in the upper lines of the building. The amount of the curve on the long sides of the Parthenon is only about four and a half inches in about two hundred and twenty feet. That is to say, this is the amount of deviation upward from an imaginary exactly horizontal line, at the center of the curve. The measurements which demonstrated the intentional construction of these curves were made by the English architect, Mr. Penrose, in 1846. A passage directing the construction of such curves is found in the ancient author, Vitruvius, who wrote a work on architecture in the 1st century of the Christian era, at Rome. Although the work of Vitruvius had been well known to modern students since about 1500 A.D., this passage had attracted no attention before the date of the discovery of the curves in the ruins themselves—another illustration of the very recent origin of the interest in Greek art (see page 8). Vitruvius adds the explanation that the lines of the building would otherwise appear deflected in the downward direction (from the ends toward the center). In the case of a gable, there is no doubt an optical appearance of deflection downward in the straight line under it. As regards the main horizontal lines of the temples, when seen from below and in the neighborhood of the angles, there may be a similar optical effect of downward deflection in the direction away from the angle.* Consequently, it has been supposed by some writers, that the curves were intended to counteract an illusion of this kind, which would have tended to an appearance of sagging downward and weakness in the building. In this connection it may be observed that the Greek temples were generally placed on an elevation, and they were always on a raised platform, so that even the lines of the substructure were frequently above the level of the eye of an approaching spectator.

With other authorities, especially with those inclined to consider the taste and knowledge of the time of Vitruvius as inferior to that of the Greeks in the 5th century B.C., and thus inclined also to consider his explanation as only partially

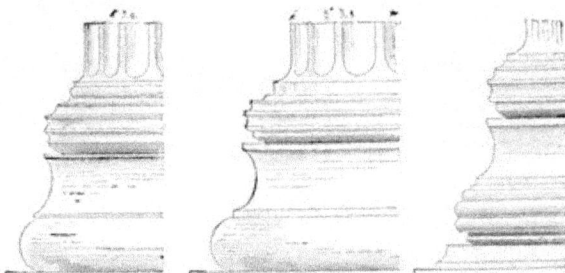

Ionic Columnar bases, Athens.

adequate, various other theories have been advanced. One of these supposes that the curves were intended to enhance the effects of size in the buildings according to the principles of curvilinear perspective. Another view holds that the curves of the substructure were intended to offer an appearance of elastic resistance to the weight resting on them, and that the upper lines were curved to correspond.

* Thiersch, "Optische Täuschungen auf dem Gebiete der Architectur" ("Optical Illusions in Architecture").

Still another theory regards the curves as an expression of Greek distaste for stiff and formal lines, and for exactly mathematical forms, and connects them with the other irregularities above mentioned, which are supposed to indicate, and result from, a similar feeling. It is quite likely that all these different views are correct. It may be, however, that the Greeks themselves were not very distinctly conscious of having any views whatever on the subject. The delicacy of their taste may have led them to prefer the curved lines without formulating any principle or theory about them.

NOTES ON THE ILLUSTRATIONS FOR GREEK TEMPLE ARCHITECTURE.

(22 32, inclusive.)

Illustrations for the Doric Order.—See Nos. 22, 24, 25, 26, 27.

Illustrations for the Ionic Order.—See Nos. 28, 29.

Illustrations for the Corinthian Order.—See Nos. 31, 32.

Restorations.—See Nos. 25, 26, 28, 29, 30. No. 30 shows the Propylæa in front, the Erechtheinm on the left, the Parthenon in the center, and the temple of "Wingless Victory" on the right. The restorations of interiors at 25 and 26 offer suggestions as to mode of lighting the temples, which are not to be considered as conclusive (see p. 44).

The Text-cuts are intended to supplement and illustrate the foregoing matter relating to the details of the orders. The "Egg and Dart" molding herewith in the text-cut is an enlarged view of a common Ionic molding seen on the Ionic

Typical surface ornament in color. Conventional lotuses and "palmettes," and Greek "fret" or "meander." From the Parthenon.

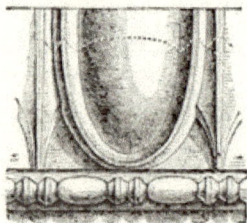

Egg and Dart Molding.

capital and on the Ionic entablature in text-cuts. This molding is also very common in modern decoration, as borrowed from the ancient Greek. Still more familiar in modern surface ornament are the patterns of conventional lotuses and "palmettes," and the ornament known as the Greek "fret," "meander," or "key pattern," herewith in text-cut. Compare the "palmette" in text-cut for the *Acroterium* of the Parthenon, also a typical Greek and modern form.

ROMAN IMPERIAL PERIOD.

Deficiency of Earlier Monuments.—In all aspects of Roman life and history, it is important to separate the views based on existing remains from the facts relating to earlier periods which have left little or nothing to later times. For the history of art, and for studies which are not distinctly archaeological in purpose, the Imperial period is the only one to be considered, as it is also the one which has left by far the largest amount of material for study.

Greek Influence.—Remembering that the Alexandrine Greek history, after 330 B.C. (see page 51), embraces a number of countries which subsequently became portions of the Roman Empire, that Italy had been under mediate Greek influences from an early time, and that the Roman countries of the Western Mediterranean largely owed their civilization to Greek Oriental sources, we shall be prepared to understand that the history of Imperial Roman art is in sequence to the Greek, and describes the continuation of it, and its ultimate mixture with foreign elements.

A Sketch of Italian and Roman History before the Imperial period and the time of existing remains is also essential to exact views of the subject.

Down to the time of Alexander the Great and the close of the history of the Greek republics, the Roman territory was only a small portion of Italy, south of the lower Tiber. The Latin tribe over which the Roman city (founded about 750 B.C.) had extended its rule, and which had also been admitted to Roman privileges and citizenship, was distinguished by great political and practical virtues, and by capacity for military discipline, but in comparison with other Italian nations, was backward in culture and art, and in these respects was dependent on them. Thus, to understand the later Roman art, we have first to understand that of the rest of Italy, especially as the rest of Italy ultimately became Roman in government and name.

Italy did not, for ancient geographers, comprehend the Northern

Po Valley above the Apennines, until shortly before the Christian era. Its most important nations were the Etruscans and Samnites. These may be considered, broadly, as controlling the most fertile parts of Italy above and below the Latin tribe, respectively. Around the South Italian shores was a line of Greek colonial cities of great wealth and importance. Before the date of these Greek settlements (mainly of the 7th and 6th centuries B.C.), the Etruscans and Samnites had been largely dependent on the Oriental civilizations, through the medium of Phœnician commerce. After this time, the same influences continued, but were colored and overlaid by Greek characteristics. Thus, for instance, the Etruscan alphabet was borrowed from the Greek. So intimate were the commercial relations, that the multitude of Greek vases found in Etruscan tombs formerly led to the presumption that the Greek vases were Etruscan.

Conquest of Italy.—In fifty years after the time of Alexander, the Romans had mastered the Etruscan, Samnite, and Greek territories. Their policy was to adopt a portion of the conquered populations into their own political system, and also to spread through the conquered territories colonies of their own citizens, which thus came under the Italian influences of their immediate neighborhood. Thus, for a double reason, the later "Roman" art was that of Italy in general.

The Roman Empire.—Carthage had become mistress of most of the West Mediterranean shores and islands, about 300 B.C., and had controlled parts of them for many centuries before this time. In the third century B.C., the Romans began a contest with Carthage for the possession of Sicily, which finally ended in the Roman control of all the Western Mediterranean, about 200 B.C. At this time, the Phœnician culture and art had already adopted a Greek coloring, and had at least a superficial Greek character. Thus, under "Roman" influences, viz., those of Italy in general, the Western Mediterranean countries continued in that path which they had already entered before the Roman conquest. The extension of Roman government over the Greek States of the East began soon after 200 B.C., and continued until shortly before the time of the Christian era. At this time, under the first Emperor Augustus, the boundaries of the Empire were nearly those of later time.

Roman Art.—In the "Roman" art of the Imperial time, we include the remains of all these various countries. In all of them, the same

33. Hall in the Baths of Caracalla, Rome. Restored view.

34. Ruins of an Aqueduct, near Rome.

RUM. Restored view.

36. The Porta Maggiore, Rome.
37. Basilica of Constantine, Rome.

general character prevails. It would be a mistake to suppose that, in all these cases, this "Roman" art was transported bodily, by Roman intervention, to these countries. The Roman art is that of the countries which became Roman, and this art was a general expression of the civilization in the Mediterranean basin at this time. As Spain, Britain, France, and South Germany were first generally brought within the area of Mediterranean civilization by the Roman conquests, these are the countries in which a distinct "Roman" introduction and dissemination of this civilization took place. But in these countries, also, an earlier Phœnician or Greek influence had prepared the way for the "Romans," and was in no way antagonized or overthrown by the influence which succeeded. It is true, however, for all provinces, Eastern as well as Western, that the Empire had a capital of great importance and far-reaching influence, and that the great force and practical nature of the original Roman blood stamped a certain element of its own character on the remotest portions of its provinces, and on their art.

The General Use of the Arch is a striking feature in remains of "Roman" architecture. In Italy, the remains prove that the arch was used by the Etruscans, at an early date, for city gates, sewers, and drainage constructions, and it was employed probably in buildings as well. The intimate relations of the Etruscans with Egypt and Assyria, through Phœnician commerce, would explain this use. It was from the Etruscans that the early Romans adopted the arch, as well as other elements of art and culture. The great sewer (*Cloaca Maxima*) in Rome is a monument of this early Etruscan influence. Ruins of aqueducts (34) or bridges, in which the arch was employed, are scattered over all former provinces of the Empire. (The earlier Greek aqueducts were tunneled under ground.)

There are apparently no existing remains of arched constructions in the Grecianized Oriental countries positively dating earlier than the roman conquests, aside from those of the earlier Assyrian and Egyptian time; but the later destruction has been so absolutely sweeping in these countries, that negative evidence is of no great value. The probability is, that the arch continued in use in the Oriental world down to its Roman period, without intermission, and that the arched and domed constructions of the Imperial period in the Eastern provinces are simply direct continuations of this earlier use. At least two instances of arch construction are now known in

Greece, dating from the Greek period proper. It is clear that the Greek use was quite limited, but rather from national prejudice than from ignorance of the principles of this construction.

In the Roman Baths (33), both the vaulting or roofing arch and the dome were employed. The bath constructions in the city of Rome were of vast extent, comprising not only bathing accommodations, but also lounging-rooms, reading-rooms, libraries, and gymnasiums. Works of sculpture were so lavishly used in decoration, that the baths were also veritable museums of art.

The Basilicas were the meeting places of the merchants and men of business, and here also were the courts and halls of justice. The most noted remains of a Basilica in which the roof was vaulted, is that known as the Basilica of Constantine, in Rome (37). The ruin has preserved only one side aisle of the original construction. In this case, and quite generally, the vaulting is formed of concrete, which was cast in a mold of plank construction. This was removed when the mass became hard and solid. By this method, the tendency of the arch to thrust the supporting walls outward was avoided. (There were two vaulted apartments in the baths of Caracalla, each as large as the central nave of the Basilica of Constantine.) Another class of Basilicas was constructed with a timber roof, and having the upper walls of the central nave supported by columns. In the ruins of the Basilica Ulpia at Rome, time of Trajan, second century A.D., we can trace the general plan of these constructions. Their arrangements were subsequently copied in one class of early Christian churches, thus named after them.

In the Amphitheaters for the games of the gladiators, the fights of animals, and similar amusements of the populace, Roman engineering skill is again displayed in marvelous ways. The Colosseum at Rome is the most famous example of this class of constructions.

The gladiator games were a phase of the corruption of ancient civilization in the Imperial period, and were unknown at Rome in the early days of Roman republican simplicity. The Greeks never admitted such spectacles. They were a concession to the coarse and cruel tastes of the populace, whose favor was essential to the security of the Emperor's person.

Triumphal Arches (11) marked the avenues through which the triumphal processions, in celebration of foreign conquests, were conducted, and served as memorials of them. The triumphal arches

38. The Maison Carrée, Nimes.

39. The Pantheon, Rome.

40. PORTAL OF ROMAN TEMPLE, BAALBEC, SYRIA.

of the Emperors Titus, Septimius Severus, and Constantine are still standing at Rome.

The Ornamental System.—In all the various Roman constructions so far named (excepting the timber-roofed Basilicas), the arch, arched ceilings, or domes, and supporting piers or walls, are the structural elements; but their ornamental traits have still to be considered. In some cases, the marble casing on which these ornamental details were carved has been destroyed (for instance, in 37), but all Roman buildings affected the same style of ornament. Examination will show that these ornamental traits are Greek, universally, but that, in cases where arches are used, the columns and beam entablatures are not elements of the construction itself, as they are seen to be in the illustrations of the Greek temples. This purely ornamental use of Greek forms, which were originally purely structural, is the distinguishing feature of the Roman style.

Broken Lines of the Ornamental Entablature.—A peculiar feature frequently appears in the lines of the ornamental imitations of the entablature, viz., the projections of the entablature over the columns, making a series of breaks in its lines (41). In the Greek structural use, the lines of the entablature are necessarily straight. A curious exaggeration of these projections is found in the part of the surrounding wall of the Roman Forum, known as the Forum of Nerva, where the columns are really a surface ornament rather than supports of a portico, although they are entirely freed from the wall.

Ornamental Gables.—Another phase of this Roman use of Greek form is found in the ornamental gables which surmount doors, windows, and niches (36). These are imitations in reduced size of the gables of the Greek temples. There are four varieties in the ornamental gable. A curved form was introduced to vary the monotony of the triangle.* Both curve and triangle are occasionally found with a break at the center above or below. In the rock-carved Roman structures of Petra, in Southern Syria, there are remarkably fine illustrations of these various uses. Others may be seen in the Roman ruins of Baalbec, in Syria. The plain, triangular niche gable is seen in the interior of the temple at 40, and on the Porta Maggiore, at Rome, the best preserved of Roman

* Seen at 6 in a modern copy. Many designs in modern furniture show variants of these ornaments

city gateways (36). (Above it are portions of an aqueduct in two sections.)

Use of the Ruins as Quarries.—It has been observed, that brick constructions, like the Baths of Caracalla, were originally decorated with marble casing, in which the Roman-Greek ornamental forms were employed. These casings have been torn off, and burned into lime for mortar in the Middle Ages. In fact, the destruction of ruins for this purpose, and the use of them as quarries, did not cease in Rome till the middle of the 18th century. It still continues in the Oriental countries, which were once Roman provinces. In many Roman provinces, for instance, in Britain, an almost absolute destruction of the ruins has resulted from the habit of using them as quarries. Thus we have explained the singular fact that the most remarkable series of ruined Roman cities is found in Eastern Syria, along the edge of the northern continuation of the Arabian desert. Only in this one portion of the old Roman Empire has the later population spared its remains. The Bedouins, who subsequently occupied the country, live in tents, and hence the ruins have been preserved.

The Roman Temples of early dates imitated those of the Etruscans. No remains of either are preserved. Ancient descriptions show that they had a general resemblance to the Greek temples, without their refinement or beauty of proportions. The Roman temples of the Imperial period (38) are Greek in details and plan. Many of them, however, abandon the surrounding colonnade, only retaining the portico in front. The temple known as the *Maison Carrée* (square house) at Nimes, in Southern France, is a well-preserved example. It thus appears that the distinctive Roman ornamental use of the Greek columns did not exclude the continuation of the Greek structural use.

The Order Generally Employed in the Imperial period is the Corinthian. The Roman preference for this order is an illustration of the origins of the Imperial civilization, which was essentially a continuation of the Alexandrine or Asiatic-Greek (p. 57). When the Doric or Ionic forms are employed, the details are relatively inferior. The so-called "Tuscan" order is an Etruscan modification of the Doric which continued in the Imperial period. The so-called "Composite" order has a capital combining details of the Ionic and Corinthian forms.

41. TRIUMPHAL ARCH OF TRAJAN, BENEVENTO.

42. Ruined houses and colonnades, Pompeii.

43. The Porta Nigra, Trier.

The Domestic Architecture continued as in earlier antiquity, and in modern Oriental countries, without external ornament or archi-

Apartment in a Pompeian House.

tectural pretensions. Dwellings of six and seven stories were built in Rome. Those preserved in Pompeii have only two stories. This town, in the vicinity of Naples, was buried under a shower of ashes from the volcano of Mt. Vesuvius in 79 A.D. The various apartments of a Pompeian house are centered about an open court, into

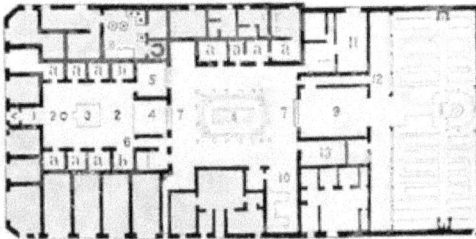

Plan of a Pompeian House.

c, The Vestibulum, or hall ; 1. The Ostium ; 2. The Atrium, off which are six cubicula, or sleeping-rooms ; 3, The Impluvium, before which stands the pedestal, or altar, of the household gods ; 4. The Tablinum, or chief room ; 5. The Pinacotheca, or library and picture gallery ; 6, The Fauces, or corridor ; 7, The Peristylium, or court, with is its central fountain ; 9, The Œcus, or state-room ; 10, The Triclinium ; 11, The kitchen ; 12. The transverse corridor, with garden beyond ; and 13. The Lararium, a receptacle for the more favorite gods, and for statues of illustrious personages.

which they open. The wealth and luxury were exhibited in the interior decoration and domestic furnishing. The walls facing the street are bare ; often even without windows.

The Pantheon.—Of all Roman buildings, the Pantheon at Rome claims precedence by its complete preservation (No. 39). The interior is a single domed apartment, lighted by an opening at the center. The exterior is of brick, with a stone portal in the form of a temple gable and portico. It is generally supposed that the use of this building as a temple for the gods of the conquered nations was not the original destination, and that it was originally part of the plan of a bath construction, subsequently separated during erection from the main building. This has been recently disputed by high authority, but it is at least true that the Pantheon offers a fine illustration of the immense domed apartments which were one feature of the Roman baths.

NOTES ON THE ILLUSTRATIONS FOR ROMAN ARCHITECTURE.
(65-80, inclusive.)

Nos. 33, 34, 37, are chosen as types of the arch construction and of arched vaultings. Nos. 36, 39, 40, 41, 43, show the association of the arch or dome with Greek structure used for decoration. No. 38 illustrates the continuance of the Greek temple form under the Roman Empire.

The Theater of Marcellus, in text-cut showing a section of construction, offers an excellent type of the Roman combination of the arch with Greek forms. The entire building, begun by Cæsar and finished by Augustus, held thirty thousand spectators.

The restored view of the Roman Forum shows several instances of the continuance of the Greek construction proper.

At p. 72 reference is made to the Basilica, or Business Exchange, built by the Emperor Trajan, as belonging to the class of timber-roofed Basilicas. The broken columns of this structure are seen at No. 125 (p. 180) in front of the column erected by the same emperor. The division of nave and aisles, which continued in the Church Basilicas,

Theater of Marcellus, Rome.

as explained in the next section, can be seen in the lines of the broken columns.

ARCHITECTURE OF THE MIDDLE AGES.

BYZANTINE PERIOD, A. D. 300-1000.

In the 5th century of the Christian era, the Western provinces of the Roman Empire were overflowed by an armed migration of German tribes, which had been previously settled in Central and Eastern Europe beyond the Danube and the Rhine. They were a simple agricultural people, of warlike ferocity and unlettered tastes, seeking new homes remote from the pressure of a Mongolian invasion from Asia, which was threatening their own security. In the preceding centuries, contact with Roman traders, or service as soldiers in Roman pay, had partially familiarized the Germanic tribes with the civilization into which they now rudely entered as conquerors and masters. They had already, in general, adopted the Christian faith from Roman missionaries, or became converts soon after the invasion.

During the 4th century, the one preceding the German invasions, Christianity had escaped the persecutions of the first three centuries. Under the Roman Emperor Constantine it was protected and fostered by the State. Under the Roman Emperor Theodosius it became the State religion, and pagan worship was forbidden. Thus in the 5th century the Roman Church became the connecting link between the conquered provinces and their German invaders, the power ruling both. For many centuries the efforts to revive the culture of Western Europe, or to protect that culture which had escaped the wreck of the invasions, were entirely the work of the clergy and of the Church. Thus the continuation of the Roman architecture under new conditions and in new uses may be studied in the early Christian churches.

The Byzantine Empire.—In Eastern Europe, and in the countries of Asia and Africa bordering the Eastern Mediterranean, the Roman Empire continued without any break of continuity or character, aside from those most important changes, introduced by the dominance of the Christian religion. The new name applied, in modern historic usage, to this Eastern portion of the Empire sometimes obscures its identity and the continuity of its existence. The Emperor Constantine had transferred the Imperial residence from Rome to Constantinople. Constantinople was the site of an earlier Greek colony *Byzantium*. Hence the use of the term "Byzantine Empire," as applied to this Eastern continuation of the Roman Empire. It is also called the "East Roman Empire" and the "Greek Empire." The use of this latter term emphasizes the fact that the population of the East Mediterranean countries was Greek in culture and language, and largely Greek in blood after the time of Alexander's conquest of the Persian Empire (p. 37).

Byzantine Architecture.—The best, because the most comprehensive, term for all early Christian architecture is the term Byzantine. This term covers both the Christian churches of the East Roman Empire and of the Germanic States, founded on the ruins of the Roman Empire in Western Europe, because Western Europe, in its backward condition, subsequent to the invasions, was very largely dependent on East Roman art and influences. The name is, however, a matter of indifference, provided a single one is used to comprehend the period, during which the Churches of Western Europe and those of the Byzantine Empire had the same general forms and plan.*

Basilicas and Baptisteries.—There were two types of churches in use during the period in question, one founded on the plan of the timber-roofed Roman Basilica, or Business Exchange, the other founded on the plan of the large-domed apartments of the Roman Baths (No. 39). In both cases, the names *Basilica* and *Baptistery* (*Baptisterium*) were retained.

The Periods of Church Architecture.—The first (Byzantine) period of architecture lasted in Western Europe about seven centuries; from the triumph of Christianity under Constantine to about the beginning of the 11th century. New methods of construction,

---

* Classifications which designate as distinct styles the "Early Christian" and "Byzantine" are confusing because they are not founded on facts. So too are the classifications which introduce the term "Romanesque" in the sense of "debased Roman," as co-extensive with "Early Christian." Such classifications obscure the sense of the word Romanesque, which in architecture implies simply a return to certain Roman features of construction, and leave us without a term for the real Romanesque period, which lies between the Byzantine (or "Early Christian") and the Gothic.

44. BASILICA OF SAN APOLLINARE NUOVO, RAVENNA.

45. Basilica of San Apollinare in Classe, Ravenna.

46. Basilica of San Apollinare in Classe, Ravenna.

to be subsequently specified, were then gradually adopted for the cathedrals and larger churches of the new period, which is designated as the Romanesque, and which lasted till about the close of the 12th century. The style now characterized as the Gothic then succeeded, and lasted till the close of the Middle Ages, about 1500 A.D.

History of the Word "Basilica."—The Basilica, as Christian Church (33, 34, 35, 36), retained the name and mainly retained the plan of the buildings thus previously named (p. 72). The name dates from a very early event in Athenian history—the overthrow of the rule of the king (*Basileus*). His duties were divided among a series of elective officials (*Archons*). One of these Archons retained the title of *Basileus*, and after him was named the building which served for his judicial sessions, and which was devoted to other public uses. The use of the term spread to other Greek cities, and finally became that of the Roman Empire. In the Christian period, the term gained a new meaning, the "Royal House," *i. e.*, the dwelling of the King of Kings.

Early Christian Churches.—For obvious reasons, there was no development of Christian architecture until the close of the persecutions at the opening of the 4th century. The earliest Christian Basilica still in use, is the Church of the Manger at Bethlehem (early 4th century). The two great Roman Basilicas of the 4th century, those of St. Peter and St. Paul, have been destroyed. The St. Peter's Basilica was pulled down in the early 16th century to make place for the new St. Peter's Church. The St. Paul's Basilica was mainly destroyed by fire in 1828. It has been rebuilt on the old plan. Some other early Basilicas in Rome have been transformed by restorations in the taste of later times, so that they have lost their ancient character and effect. The most important ones have suffered the most in this way, but there are still several Roman Basilicas of the 5th and 6th centuries which are substantially intact, aside from the loss of important mosaic decorations.

The City of Ravenna, on the Adriatic shore of Northern Italy, has the most remarkable series of well-preserved early Christian buildings of the 5th and 6th centuries. Ravenna was a place of great importance during the period of the German invasions. Surrounding swamps and lagoons were a protection against the attacks of the Germanic invaders, and its position made it an important

commercial port, and, consequently, a connecting link with the
East Roman countries. On the other hand, it has been isolated, by
the same position, from the march of progress in later times, and
its later poverty has been the real protection of its interesting
monuments. It was not till the 19th century that the dawn of
revived interest in medieval history led to an interest in the preservation of medieval buildings (see page 16), and the early ones
which have been preserved, owe this preservation to isolation or
to chance.

Plan of the Church Basilicas.—As studied in the examples just
mentioned, the early Christian Basilica has an oblong and rectangular plan terminating at one end in an apse or semicircular niche
—the origin of the Choir. This apse was the seat of the magistrate
in the Pagan Basilica, and a portion of the building before it, railed
off by a transverse line of columns, was the court of justice. When
we remember that the clergy were the main supporters of public
order in the period of the invasions, and the mediating power between conquerors and conquered, and that the bishop was generally
the leading city magistrate, it will appear that there was a natural
logic in the arrangement which turned the apse of the Roman
magistrate into the choir of the Christian bishop and the Christian
clergy.

Details of Construction.—In the early monuments this apse, or
choir, corresponds in width to the central nave. The division of
the building into nave and aisles (44, 47) was also a feature of the
Pagan Basilica, and so becomes one important feature of arrangement in all the later cathedrals. This division is connected with
the method of roofing the building. The outer portions, the aisles,
are covered with a separate roofing considerably lower than that of
the nave. The nave rises above the aisles by walls supported on
columns, and these columns form the separation between nave
and aisles.

The Clerestory.—The method of elevating the nave above the
aisles, also found in all the important later cathedrals, where this
upper part of the nave is called the Clerestory, admits of roofing,
with more convenience, a wider space, and it also admits of a
method of lighting by upper windows, which has great advantages
of effect. Large apartments are most successfully lighted from
above. The eye thus enjoys the effects of light illuminating the

47. BASILICA OF ST. PAUL (FUORI LE MURA), ROME.

48. Church of San Vitale, Ravenna. Cross-section showing construction.

49. Mosque of St. Sophia, Constantinople.

building and cast on the objects in it, without being strained by
the glare of direct horizontal rays. It has been noted (page 44)
that the Greek temples were probably lighted from above. The
Pantheon owes its wonderful interior effect to the same method of
lighting.

The Basilica Roofs were of timber (not vaulted), an important
distinction as compared with the important cathedrals of the Romanesque and Gothic times, whose use of the arched ceilings of
brick or stone (vaultings) led to most of the other distinctions from
the early Basilicas.

Columnar Supports as Distinguished from Piers.—Another characteristic is the use of columns, as distinguished from piers or
pillars, as supports for the upper walls of the nave. In Greek and
Roman antiquity, columns were always composed of a single block
of stone as regards the diameter. In the perpendicular line, the
larger columns were generally composed of a series of "drums," or
cylindrical sections. Piers or pillars, on the other hand, are composed of aggregated masonry. They may be of cylindrical shape,
but rarely are. (Compare columnar supports of the Basilica with
the piers of the Romanesque and Gothic, 50, 53, 56.)

The Combination of Column and Arch (as seen at 44, 47), by
which the upper walls of the nave are supported, was one developed into a permanent system by the Christian Basilicas. This
combination appears in some few Pagan structures, for instance,
the palace of the Emperor Diocletian, at Spalatro, in Dalmatia,
which slightly antedate the general period of Church Basilicas, but
is otherwise unknown in ancient architecture. In the Greek construction, either of Greek periods or as copied by the Romans, the
column invariably supports a straight beam, and in Roman use the
arch is supported by a pier. In Roman ornamental use of Greek
forms, the column frequently decorates the front of the pier (see,
for instance, the Theater of Marcellus), but it is always connected
with a projected imitation of the beam entablature above, and has
nothing to do with the structural support of the arch.

Development of Interior Perspective Effects.—The column and
arch construction, as introduced in the Christian Basilicas, has a
considerable influence on their perspective effect, and on the appearance of length in the interior. The eye is arrested at each successive arch in its computation of dimension. The straight beam line

would be detrimental to the appearance of interior size, as the eye
is led by it directly to the extremity of the line. It may be remembered that Greek temple interiors did not affect an appearance of
size. This would have been prejudicial to the effect of size in the
statue. The Greek temple was essentially only the shrine or casket
of the temple statue, not a building for a congregation of worshipers.
In the Christian church, an appearance of size is consonant with
the uses of the building, and the later cathedrals owe much of their
power to the perspective effects introduced by the sequence of
arches, which continued in the later periods, although the columnar
supports were then replaced by piers.

Some few Basilicas in Rome retain the straight beam line of the
ancient columnar style, an interesting illustration of the superior
power of the ancient traditional style in this particular city.

The Interior Decoration of the Basilicas was like that of the
Baptistery churches, and will be noticed after these are described.

The Exterior Appearance was bare and undecorative (45, 46).
The walls are frequently ornamented by arcades in relief (46).
Under roof lines and cornice lines is occasionally found an orna-
mental frieze of small round arches in relief.

The Bell Tower [Italian, *Campanile* (căm pä nee'lä)] was a separate
structure (45, 46). In all medieval periods, the Italians continued
to make a distinct structure of the bell tower (see 54). In the
architecture of the Northern Romanesque, the tower became a portion of the building, sometimes in double, sometimes in quadruple
use (51, 53). The spires of the Gothic (57, 58) are a later development of this use, continued in the modern steeple.

Baptisteries and Baptistery Churches.—It was customary throughout the Middle Ages, in Italy, to construct in each city an especial
building for use as a Baptistery. This custom began in the Byzantine period, which also constructed churches proper on the
same plan.

The Dome Plan.—This plan, adopted from the large domed
apartments of the Roman Baths, and retaining the same name, is
entirely distinct from the Basilica plan. As opposed to the oblong
elongated plan of the Basilica, that of the Baptistery (48, 49)
radiates from a center. (The exterior outline may be octagonal,
round, a combination of circles, or of a circle and half circles; so
that the term of "radiating" plan is the only one that is compre-

hensive.) Corresponding to this aspect of the plan, is the use of a dome, or series of domes, for ceiling and roofing.

The Pantheon (No. 39) has been noted at page 89 as the one building of ancient Roman times, in modern preservation, which gives an idea of the character of these domed constructions in the Pagan *Baptisteria*.

The Word "Baptistery."—The retaining of this word in Christian usage has an interesting relation to the baptismal rites of the Church, the Greek word from which our word "baptism" is taken, meaning originally "to bathe."

Byzantine Preference for the Dome.—Churches of the Baptistery or dome construction, as distinct from Baptisteries proper (for baptizing purposes), were more numerous in the Byzantine provinces than in the countries of Western Europe, where the Basilica type was more generally affected.

Existing Monuments in Western Europe.—In existing remains, there are only three important churches of this type in Western Europe—San Vitale (vee tah'la) at Ravenna (48), St. Mark's at Venice, and the Cathedral of Charlemagne at Aix-la-Chapelle.

Mosques of Omar and of St. Sophia.—Among many notable churches of this type in Eastern Europe, two are specially famed—the Mosque of Omar at Jerusalem, and the Mosque of St. Sophia at Constantinople. The Mosque of Omar was originally a Christian church of the 4th century. The Mosque of St. Sophia was originally a Christian church of the 6th century, and was built by the Emperor Justinian. In their use as mosques, these buildings date respectively from the Arab Mohammedan conquest of Syria in the 7th century and the Turkish Mohammedan conquest of Constantinople in the 15th century.

The Interior Decoration of both Basilicas and Baptistery churches was of the most costly and gorgeous character. Mosaics, marble paneling, and elaborate stucco ornament, were employed. For some additional notice of the mosaics, see the "History of Painting."

Limits of the Byzantine Period.—Before passing to the development of the Romanesque and Gothic cathedrals in Western Europe, it may be observed that this development is quite foreign to the Byzantine world. The limit fixed for the Byzantine period, *i.e.*, about 1000 A.D., has reference only to Western Europe. In the Byzantine provinces, architecture continued to exhibit substantially the same general character till the final overthrow of the Byzantine power in the 15th century. The Turkish conquerors made this architecture their own model. Most of the mosques of Constantinople, for instance, have been based on the plan of the St. Sophia. Russian civilization owes its origin to Byzantine influence, and in Russia, also, Byzantine architecture continued down to recent times. The Church of St. Basil, at Moscow, built by Ivan the Terrible in the 16th century, is a notable example of this fact.

NOTES ON THE ILLUSTRATIONS FOR THE BYZANTINE PERIOD

(44–48, inclusive.)

Nos. 44 and 47 are types of Basilica interiors. Nos. 45 and 46 are types of Basilica exteriors. Nos. 49 and 48 represent, respectively, an exterior and interior of the Baptistery or Dome type. For Byzantine Capitals see pp. 110 and 113.

THE ROMANESQUE PERIOD, A.D. 1000–1200.

The New Features of the Romanesque period (types at 50, 51, 52, 53) are most easily understood by reverting to the description of the Basilica type, noting especially its use of a timber roof and of columnar supports for the walls of the nave. In distinction from these characteristics, the word "Romanesque" has been used to indicate the return, in the second period of Church Architecture, to the Roman elements of the pier, and the vaulting arch.

The Pier, consisting of a mass of aggregated masonry, thus differs from the column in its capacity for indefinite increase of bulk and height. For the "drums" of a column (see p. 89), being monolithic in the diameter, can not be quarried with facility beyond a certain limit.

Substitution of Piers for Columns.—The Basilica period had drawn its supplies of columnar supports mainly from the porticoes and temple colonnades of the Pagan Roman period. The rise of the new style, as regards the use of piers, is mainly a result of the exhaustion of this supply of columns from the ruins. An increase in the average size of the important cathedrals, and the introduction of the vaulting (arched ceiling of brick or stone), were also causes for the use of piers in preference to columns. A column is too slender a support for the heavy walls and ceiling of a vaulted construction. Moreover, the period which, for seven centuries, had

59. CHURCH OF SAN AMBROGIO, MILAN.

51. CATHEDRAL OF SPEYER.

drawn its supplies of columns from the ancient ruins, had lost the habit of quarrying columns of the larger size.

The Vaultings.—Thus the exhaustion of the supply of columns, the increase of average dimensions in the churches, and the introduction of vaulted ceilings, are all causes explaining the use of the pier. The introduction of the vaulting (53) was not instantaneous. It made its appearance gradually. It was used at first in the side aisles of certain churches. Then churches were built in which the nave also was vaulted. Finally, the method became general for all important cathedrals. (Contrast timber construction in 47.)

Use of Vaultings Explained.—The use of vaultings in preference to timber roofs was probably favored by various considerations, among which the superior permanence and non-inflammable character were doubtless the first. As the cities and religious communities of the Middle Age grew in size, power, and wealth, there was a constantly increasing tendency to spare no efforts and stop at no expense which might promote the splendor of the religious edifices. They were shrines of the State, public resorts of the populace for political meetings and other purposes, the buildings devoted to the spectacular representations of the Passion Plays, and Miracle Plays, and even, on occasion, fortresses and treasure houses. The union of roof and wall in one continuous curving line gave the buildings a unity and rhythm of effect which was preferred to the simpler and more rigid interior lines of the Basilica construction.

Basilica Features Retained.—On the other hand, important elements of the Basilica plan were retained: the division of nave and aisles, the extra height of the nave, the perspective effect of the succession of arches, and the choir. The choir began to develop in size in relation to other parts of the building (51).

The Transept.—The plan based on the form of the cross had already appeared in the Basilica period, but it now obtained wider use and greater extension in the individual cases. The form of the cross, as used in the form of the church, had undoubtedly a symbolical reference, but it served to increase interior dimensions and exterior effects of picturesque variety at the same time. The portion of the church at right angles to its main lines, and making the cross form, is called the transept (52).

New Use of the Dome.—Over the junction of the main building and transept a dome was constructed. Such domes, during the

Romanesque period, had an exterior pointed roof; and it is to be noticed, also, that the interior vaultings were likewise covered and protected by exterior gabled roofings. Occasionally, apses or transepts (see 52) were constructed at both ends of the building.

The Towers.—The picturesque and massive effect of the exterior was generally emphasized by heavy square towers with conical or pointed roofs. Sometimes these towers, two in number, formed a portion of the front (façade) of the cathedral. Sometimes four such towers were constructed in the angles formed by the intersection of the double transepts with the main building, or otherwise flanking the two extremities. These towers were a development from the bell tower, which, in the Byzantine period, was generally separate from the building (45, 46). They were used for bells or chimes, but they illustrate the civic pride and rivalry of the medieval communities, and a disposition to build up an imposing exterior effect, which is not generally apparent in the earlier Christian time. They also had reference to the occasional use of the cathedrals as fortresses and treasure houses, which has already been noted, serving as watch-towers, as places of refuge and resistance, and for the storing of valuables.

Exterior Ornamental Traits.—These are the least important aspects of the style, but they are the aspects in which the modern revivals of the Romanesque (see p. 24) are most clearly apparent. In fact, they are generally the only claim of a modern building to be designated as Romanesque. These ornamental traits are—friezes of small round arches under the roof lines, or at the horizontal courses marking the different stories of the towers, etc.; masonry pilasters projected from the wall, but in the same plane with the cornice and plinth lines; and galleries of columns and arches on upper exterior portions of the building (52).

The Round Arch Frieze, or cornice decoration, is also found in the Byzantine (early Christian) period, but not in such elaborate and constant use.

The Perpendicular Masonry Pilasters strengthened the wall and admitted an otherwise thinner construction. They are distinguished from Gothic buttresses (see later matter) by the point just noted, that they do not project beyond the plane of the upper connecting horizontal cornice, or the horizontal plinth line at the base of the

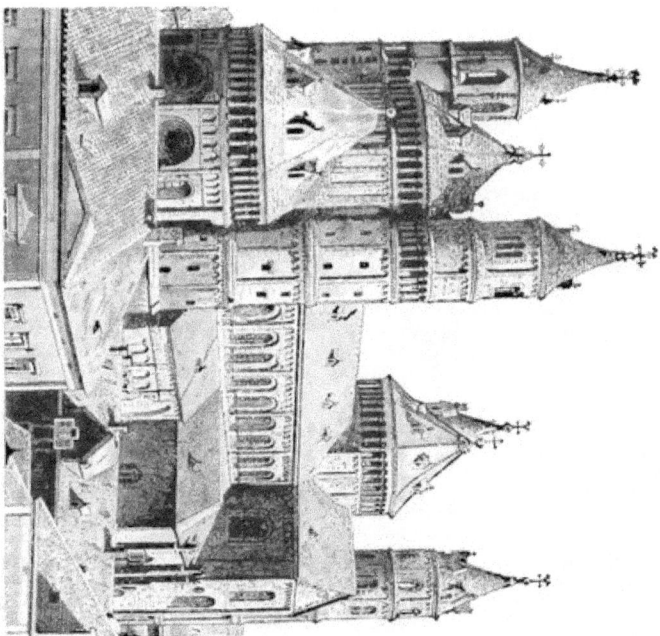

52. Cathedral of Worms.

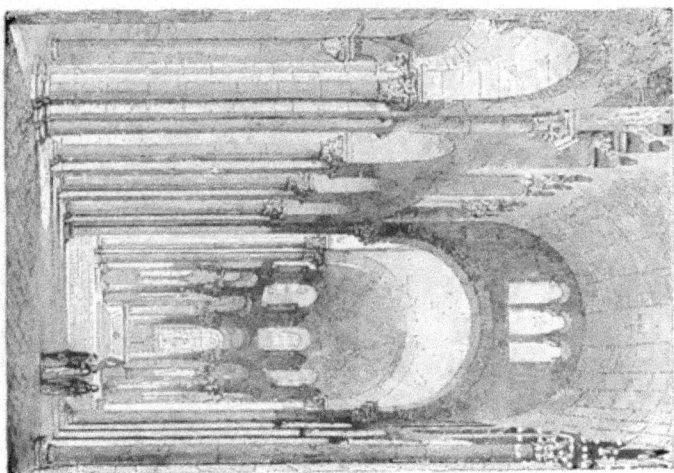

53. Notre Dame du Port, Clermont.

54. Cathedral of Pisa.
55. Cathedral of Pisa.

wall,* and they have no capitals or bases in the Northern style. These pilasters are found, also, in the Byzantine period, but in this period they usually terminate in round arches, forming with these a series of blind arcades. In the Romanesque period, they generally connect with an upper straight horizontal band, or frieze, of small round arches. These flat pilasters are to be distinguished from the columnar pilasters, also found as surface ornaments in the same time (54). Flat pilasters terminating in capitals, and having also a base profile, are also found, especially in Italy.

The Galleries of Columns and Round Arches used on the upper portions of the exterior (51, 54) show the continuation of the structure which was used in the earlier Basilica interiors, now converted to semi-ornamental uses. Of course, these exterior galleries may also be conceived as structural adjuncts of the building.

Medieval "Styles" Determined by Construction.—A descriptive summary of the distinctions between the different medieval periods is of special value in breaking down the prejudices on the subject of styles which have been considered at pages 5-28. Such summaries show that the general changes in "style" were changes in structure for which definite reasons can generally be given now, and which always existed originally. Ornamental traits may be more profuse and elaborate at one time than at another, but they generally reflect, imitate, or assist the structural uses. From this point of view, it will be understood that the words "Byzantine," "Romanesque," "Gothic," indicate certain broad distinctions as to constructions and periods, and it will also be understood that there are many local or special exceptions to the facts indicated by this use of words.

Vaultings Used before the Romanesque Period.—One of these exceptions relates to the use of arched vaultings earlier than the date fixed for the Romanesque. Especially is this use demonstrated for certain early Christian constructions in Syria (now in ruins, and in districts which at present are almost inaccessible on account of banditti, Bedouins, or Mohammedan prejudice).

Timber Roofs Used in the Romanesque Period.—Another exception relates to the Romanesque period itself. It has been already implied that the new methods of construction (that is, new for the Middle Ages) indicated by the term Romanesque, hold of the larger and more important cathedrals. Timber roofs were always the rule for humble churches, and the Basilica construction and arrangement long survived, in some localities, the date fixed for the Romanesque. This is especially true in Italy.

The "Italian Romanesque" (54, 55) very generally continued to prefer the Basilica construction of columns, arches, and timber ceilings, as opposed to piers and vaultings, throughout the Roman-

* A plinth is either a block of stone placed under the base of a column, or pier, or a line of foundation masonry projecting slightly beyond the wall which it supports.

esque period. The reason was, at least partly, that the supplies of ancient columns from the Roman ruins held out longer in Italy. Thus, also, the "Italian Romanesque" frequently lacks (on account of the absence of interior vaultings, or from a difference of taste) the massive towers and generally heavy appearance of the Northern Romanesque. On the other hand, it carried the decorative traits of the Romanesque to an unusual degree of elaboration and profusion. Thus, the "Italian Romanesque" frequently showed Basilica construction combined with Romanesque decoration.

·These Exceptions assume their proper place when the examination of a number of cathedrals makes it clear that the individual distinctions of one from another are even more interesting than the points of correspondence. For purposes of classification, we need systems and terms, but the exercise of a free individual taste, by the artisans and builders, in the various parts of single medieval buildings, was alone sufficient to constitute a never-ending variety as between different buildings.

Picturesque Variations in corresponding parts, both of ornament and construction, are a general rule. It is clear that exact symmetrical regularity was often neglected, because it was not conceived of as necessary--also clear that symmetrical regularity was frequently avoided by preference. It is probable that the conscious study of picturesque effects in architecture is apt to lead to mannerisms and eccentricities; but in contrast to such conscious striving after the picturesque, the medieval builders had a happy preference for variety in ornamental details, and a thorough independence of the prejudice that regularity is a necessary standard of taste in construction.

The So-called Norman Style. —The Romanesque period corresponds to that of the so-called "Norman" style. Mr. Freeman, the standard English historian of the "Norman Conquest" in England, never speaks of "Norman" architecture, but always of the Romanesque. The Normans conquered England in the 11th century, during which the Romanesque had become general on the Continent of Europe, and it was they who introduced it into England. Hence many English writers speak of the "Norman" style. There is, however, nothing distinctively Norman about it, and the use of local terms is almost certain to create confusion as to the broad and simple facts controlling the history of medieval architecture. Similar objections apply to the conception of a "Lombard" style, which is simply the Romanesque of North Italy.

The **Finest Examples of Romanesque Cathedrals proper** (as distinct from the Italian variation) are, generally speaking, in Germany, and especially in the Rhine countries. The cathedrals of Speyer. Worms, and Mainz are especially celebrated. The size and grandeur of the German cathedrals of this time indicate the power and ascendency of Germany in Europe in the earlier Middle Age. In the later Middle Age. France took the place of Germany in this respect, and the subsequent ascendency of the Gothic style, which developed in France, throughout the whole of Europe, indicates this fact.

NOTES ON THE ILLUSTRATIONS FOR THE ROMANESQUE PERIOD.

(50-55, inclusive.)

Nos. 50, 53, are types of vaulted Romanesque with piers. Contrast 44, 47. Nos. 51, 52, are types of Northern Romanesque exteriors. Contrast 45, 46. Nos. 54, 55, are types common in Italian Romanesque, showing Basilica construction with Romanesque ornament. For Romanesque Capitals see pp. 113, 114. Distinguish those for columns and for piers. Columns frequently alternate with piers in early Northern Romanesque, and the capitals frequently show Byzantine influence. But it is impossible to understand Gothic construction without considering the pier and vaulting as the essential Romanesque elements.

THE GOTHIC PERIOD, A.D. 1200-1500.

The **Word "Gothic"** was originally used by the Italians of the early Renaissance (see p. 13, and later matter), to indicate their distaste for what they considered the barbaric architecture of Northern Medieval Europe. In this sense, and at the time of the Renaissance, the word "Gothic" was applied indiscriminately to all Northern medieval buildings. This Italian taste and fashion carried with it the Renaissance style (p. 13), and replaced and overthrew the medieval civilization, and the medieval styles of architecture.

First Use of the Word Marks Overthrow of the Style.—Hence, in dependence on this Italian taste, influence, and style, the Northern European nations, after A.D. 1500, adopted this use of the word "Gothic," as applied to their own earlier architecture. The word still had simply the meaning of "barbarian," as we still speak of "Goths and Vandals." It continued to have this meaning, and to be applied indiscriminately to all Northern medieval buildings until the opening of the 19th century.

Modern Revival of the Gothic.—As has been explained at pp. 15, 16, the revival of the medieval styles in the 19th century was due to historic and literary studies which overthrew the Italian Renaissance taste and prejudice of the three preceding centuries. During this movement, as the distinctions between medieval periods became apparent, the word "Gothic" was gradually confined to the latest medieval period and style, which naturally required a distinctive name. The odious signification of the earlier use of the word has, of course, entirely disappeared.

The date 1200 A.D. would be, in round numbers, a fair approximate date for the time when the Gothic had begun to be generally
diffused over Europe. The beginnings of the style in France are of
a somewhat earlier time. The transitions by which the new style
was developed were gradual and tentative; but in explanation it is
best to speak of the ultimate result, without noticing the steps of
transition.

Gothic Cathedrals Compared with Romanesque.—A casual glance
at the illustrations of a Gothic cathedral (56, 57, 58, 63) shows a
remarkable distinction in appearance from the Romanesque. Among
the differences the use of pointed arches is a prominent feature.
As seen in the doors and windows and in the ornamental details,
the pointed arches are only a decorative outgrowth, which began in
the structure of the interior vaulting.

The Pointed Arch is a frequent appearance in Arab and Saracenic buildings, and was thus brought to the attention of the medieval builders during the time of the Crusades. But they used it
from a different motive. In the Arab and Saracenic buildings the
pointed arch was apparently used out of preference for its light
appearance and, so to speak, airy character, which harmonized with
the frequently fragile, or at least highly ornate, appearance and
sometimes flimsy construction of their buildings. The earliest Gothic
buildings were of a plain and severe appearance, and the use of the
pointed arch was apparently only the means to a greater stability
in the vaultings.

Influence of the Crusades.—The opening of the era of the Crusades preceded by
just a century the full development of the Gothic, about 1200. The Crusades had
for their purpose not only the rescue of the Holy Sepulcher in Syria, but also the
pushing back of the Turkish invasion, which was threatening Europe, and the protection of the East Roman (Byzantine) Empire from the Turks. An important
result of the Crusades was the quickening of commercial intercourse with the
Byzantine Empire and with Oriental countries.

Rise of the Communes.—The impulse to commerce reacted on the prosperity and
activity of the civic communities all over Europe. These had always been rivals
and antagonists of the feudal nobility. The same feudal nobility was also antagonized by the power of the kings, whose theoretic control of their kingdoms was
frequently nullified by the superior military and territorial power of their own
barons. This had been especially the case in France, and it is first in France that
we clearly see the alliance between the civic communities and the royal power.
The "communes" contributed money to support the power and the military force
of the kings. These in their turn assisted the communes by charters and by pro-

56. CHURCH OF ST. OUEN, ROUEN.

57. CHURCH OF ST. OUEN, ROUEN.

tecting them from the encroachments of the feudal nobles. The feudal system had created a number of small States within the State. The perpetual warfare and contentions of these feudal States were a standing threat to the prosperity of the merchant class. Hence, the alliance between kings and merchants which so enormously developed the size and prosperity of the medieval communes.

The Communes and the Gothic Style.—It is only by understanding the enormous growth of the civic communities that the Gothic style becomes comprehensible. In the erection of cathedrals, which surpassed in average size those previously undertaken, any structural device contributing to the stability of the vaultings was of supreme importance.

Structural Use of the Pointed Arch.—The pressure of the pointed arch is carried off to the sides by the nature of its construction. The lines of resistance are more directly placed as regards the point of greatest pressure. This undoubtedly explains the rapid introduction of pointed arch vaultings.

Decorative Use of the Pointed Arch.—The use of the pointed arch in doors, windows, and ornamental tracery, is a decorative imitation of a structural necessity. When the style was once introduced, the decorative habit naturally spread to the buildings which continued to employ the timber roofs. But these timber roofs were almost unknown for large cathedrals, outside of England. A certain number of the English Gothic cathedrals have timber ceilings, but the style of the buildings is otherwise derived from the vaulted cathedrals of the continent, and can only be explained through these.

The Lofty Elevation of the Nave is another Gothic peculiarity (56, 63). This elevation has a tendency to dwarf the spectator, and to increase by contrast the effect of magnitude beyond the point which any mere expansion of area could attain.

The Gothic Pier.*—The intention of this construction is made apparent in the treatment of the Gothic pier (No. 56). This differs from the Romanesque pier in the character of its ribbings, which are produced by vertical channels or furrows. The heavy shadows resulting, emphasize the rising line and tend to exaggerate the already disproportionate height. The related ribbings of the Romanesque pier are pilaster-like additions to its exterior mass (53).

---

* A variety of piers used in the early Gothic period do not come under the description given. Various modifications of construction show the development from, and the connection with, the Romanesque pier. The description given applies to examples of the fully-developed Gothic.

The Gothic Windows.—In this difference between the Romanesque and Gothic piers may be noticed a tendency, which marks the Gothic period, to avoid the use or appearance of unnecessary weight and matter. The furrowed pier affords the same amount of resistance with less material, and with less appearance of weight and mass of material. From this characteristic, another feature of the Gothic cathedrals becomes comprehensible, viz.: the enormous development of the size of the windows (57, 60). In the most typical Gothic cathedrals, the entire wall surface is given up to windows (aside from the spaces corresponding to the exterior buttresses, to be noted presently).

The Use of Stained Glass.—This extension of the space devoted to windows has been attributed to the use of stained glass and the wish to increase the space devoted to it. It may be observed that the use of stained glass would have been made necessary by the amount of window space in question: otherwise, the interior light would have been too great. But, in either point of view, the same disposition to avoid the use and weight of masonry as far as possible is apparent.

The Exterior Buttress.[*]—If the interior of the Gothic cathedral be observed, it appears that the wall surfaces are mainly devoted to stained glass windows, and that the vaulted ceiling exercises a heavy pressure which requires a suitable resistance. The vaulting is constructed in such a way that its pressure converges on the ribs or frame-work of the vault, and these carry the pressure to the piers. The resistance to this pressure is furnished by the exterior buttresses, which correspond in position to the piers within (63). The buttress, as its name implies, is a vertical projection of the wall, which gives it the necessary strength at the necessary points.

The Flying Buttress.—The buttress rises above the lower side aisle of the cathedral, and is connected by the "flying buttress" with the upper walls of the nave.

The Pinnacles, which surmount the buttress, increase its weight and power of solid resistance, and also emphasize, ornamentally, its use and importance.

The Window Tracery of the Gothic style assumes an infinite

---

[*] "A buttress is a piece of wall set athwart the main wall, usually projecting considerably at the base, and diminished by successive reductions of its mass as it approaches the top, and so placed as to counteract the thrust of some arch or vault inside."

58. CATHEDRAL OF RHEIMS.

59. Type of Gothic Sculptured Ornament.
60. Gothic Window, St. Chapelle, Paris.
61. Typical Gothic Crocket.
62. Typical Gothic Finial.

variety of geometrical forms and combinations. These increase in variety and complexity as the style develops from the earlier and simpler constructions to those which are more elaborate and more profusely ornamented.

The Surface Tracery.—In this gradual development of a more ornamented style from the heavier and simpler construction of the early Gothic, the surfaces of the buttresses and of the walls are gradually relieved and lightened in effect by an expansion of the plans of the window tracery over the solid surfaces (58). With this use is combined the development of sculpture decoration—in the portals, and also on the wall surfaces, especially of the facades.*

Significance of Gothic Sculpture and Tracery.—In this use of tracery and sculptured decoration on the wall surfaces, may be observed a tendency to idealize and spiritualize the dead matter of which they are composed—a tendency analogous to that which avoids as far as possible the appearance or use of unnecessary material.

Divisions of the English Gothic.—Special works devoted to the English Gothic have created a series of subdivisions—"Early English," "Decorated," and "Perpendicular," which have no distinct boundaries, and which are, in reality, only the English local phases of the general tendency of the Gothic style to develop from simpler ornamental forms to those which are more elaborate.

Fine Examples of Gothic Cathedrals are numerous in every European country. Many of the best examples are in France. Among the most quoted, are those of Paris, Chartres, Amiens, Rheims, and Rouen. In other European countries, the cathedrals of Canterbury in England, of Cologne in Germany, of Burgos in Spain, and of Milan in Italy, are especially renowned.

The Italian Gothic offers peculiar exceptions to the above description of Gothic traits, and corresponds to the Italian Romanesque in its eccentric position as far as classifications are concerned. Vaultings were not generally introduced into Italy until toward the close of the Romanesque period elsewhere, and the Italians continued, through the Gothic period, to adhere to the low proportions and solid walls of the Romanesque period, often using an elaborate surface decoration, or casing, in black and white marble (p. 116).

* The facade (*façade*) is the exterior front of a building.

The Examples of the "Italian Gothic" are of astounding variety and individual independence. They are only alike in rejecting the traits which distinguish the Northern Gothic. The following points of negative similarity may be observed. The windows are small; the buttresses are generally wanting, or merely rudimentary reminiscences of Northern influence; the interior proportions have not the Gothic exaggeration of height. Even the pointed arches are sometimes absent. The exterior decoration above noticed, of casing in black and white marbles, was arranged in segment patterns or in horizontal stripes quite incompatible with the accented rising lines of the Northern Gothic.

Important Italian Cathedrals (p. 116).—The Cathedrals of Florence, Siena, and Orvieto, illustrate the individual divergence of Italian Gothic cathedrals, one from the other, as well as the absence of Gothic traits. The Cathedral of Milan is a nearer approach to the Northern examples, but also shows marked divergences from the Northern Gothic type.

NOTES ON THE ILLUSTRATIONS FOR THE GOTHIC PERIOD AND FOR MEDIEVAL ARCHITECTURE.

(Nos. 56 65, inclusive.)

Byzantine Capital. Ravenna. 6th Century.

Byzantine Period.—Compare 44 with 53 for the Basilica column as contrasted with the Romanesque pier, remembering that the pier does not immediately or entirely replace the column in the Romanesque period, but that it does ultimately, and generally (outside of Italy). Compare 44 with 55 for the general continuance of the Basilica column in Italy during the Romanesque period.

Compare 47 with 53 for distinction between timber roof and ceiling of the Basilica and the round arch vaulted ceiling of the Romanesque; remembering that timber ceilings continued during the Romanesque period, but were rarely used for important cathedrals outside of Italy.

Compare 47 and 48 for distinction between the plans and arrangement of a Basilica and a Baptistery.

Compare 45, 46, with 51, 52, for

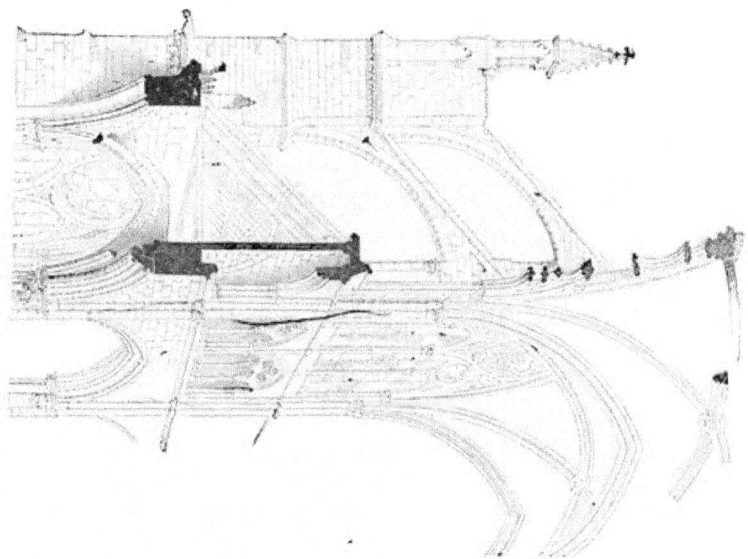

63. Cathedral of Amiens. Cross-section.

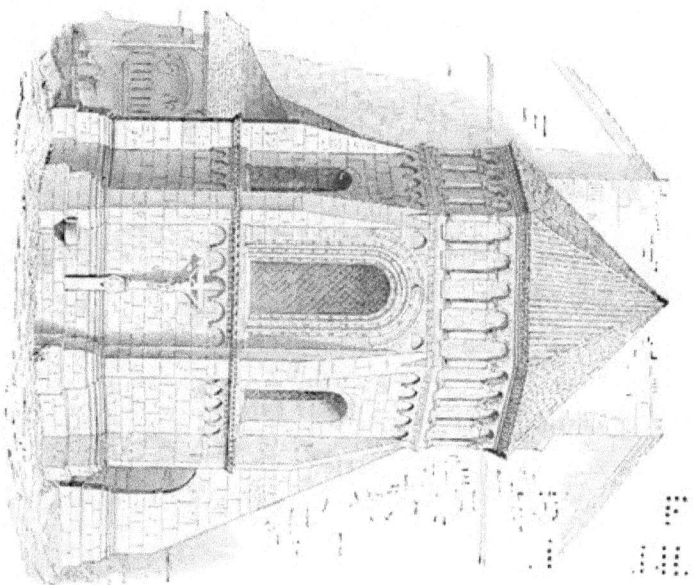

64. Church Choir, Pfaffenheim.

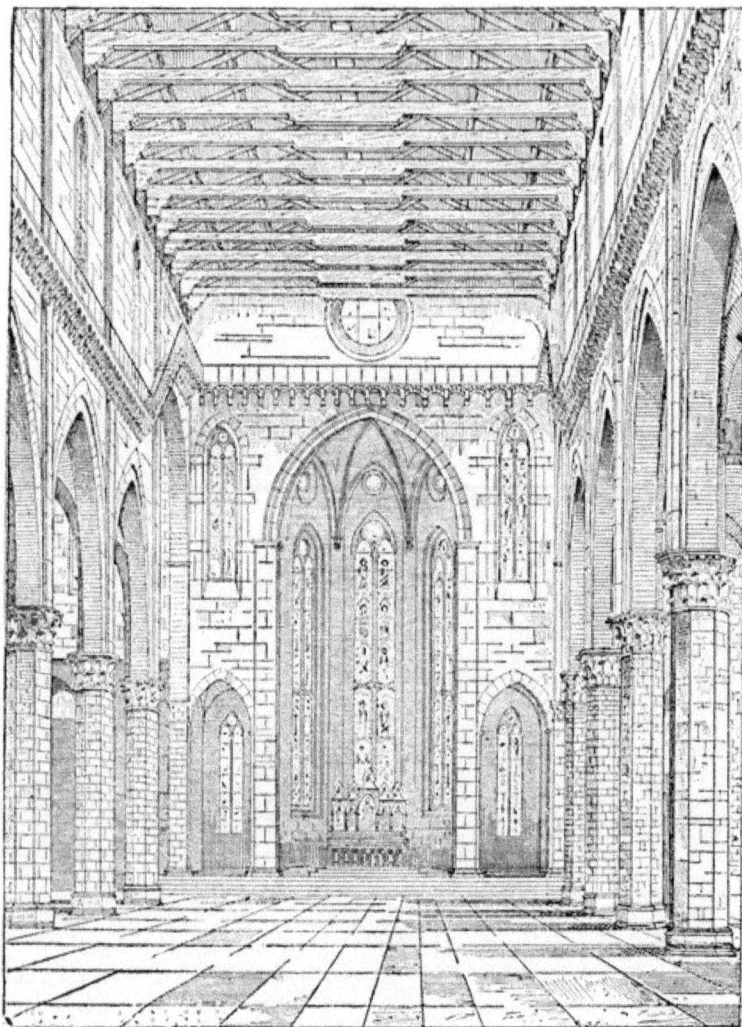

CHURCH OF SANTA CROCE, FLORENCE.

contrast in exterior appearance of a Basilica and a Romanesque Cathedral.

Note the text-cuts illustrating types of Byzantine capitals.

Romanesque Period.—Compare 50, 53, with 56 for distinction between Romanesque and Gothic vaulting.

Compare 50, 53, with 56 for distinction between Romanesque and Gothic piers.

Compare 51, 52, with 57, 58, for contrast of Romanesque and Gothic exteriors.

Compare 52, 54, with 60-63, for contrast of ornamental details.

Compare 55 with 50, 53, for contrast of Italian and Northern Romanesque interiors.

Compare 54 with 52, for contrast of Italian and Northern Romanesque exteriors.

Byzantine Capital, Ravenna, 5th Century.

Romanesque Capitals, Limburg.

Compare 46 and 52, for the Romanesque development of the transept.

Note the text-cuts illustrating types of Romanesque capitals. Such capitals as those from Limburg (Germany) are developments from earlier Byzantine forms.

Type of Romanesque Cube Capital.

Romanesque Pier Capital, Gernrode.

Romanesque Pier Capital, Hacklingen.

Contrast the capitals for piers (Gernrode, Hacklingen, in Germany, and North-ampton).

Romanesque Pier Capitals, Northampton.

Gothic Period.—Note the development of the Gothic tower over the union of transept and nave (57) from the dome at corresponding points in 52 or 51. This dome in the north is always covered originally by a pointed roof. The dome roofs of 51, with convex lines, belong to the 18th century.

Compare the Gothic choir in 57 with the Romanesque choir (51) and the Basinea choir (46).

No. 63 is a highly important illustration for the scheme or skeleton of a Gothic vaulted construction and the connection between the exterior buttress and "flying buttress" and the interior arched ceiling. Observe, as illustrated by the side aisle, how the vaulting is always protected by a timber roof. In this view the ribs of the vaulted ceiling are apparent. The vaulting between the ribs is so arched as to bring the pressure upon them. These carry the pressure to the pier,

Typical Gothic Capital, Esslingen.

and this is held up by the outside buttress. Notice here and in other Gothic cathedrals the origin of the system of nave and aisles, and of the higher elevation of the nave, as shown in 44, 45, 46.

For details of Gothic ornament in windows, gables, finials, crockets, and curved borders, see Nos. 59–62.

No. 64 illustrates the frequent mixtures of styles which are formed in buildings of the transition periods, and in cases where an older building has been subsequently restored and reconstructed. The illustrations have been otherwise confined to central types in order to avoid confusion as to the principles and sequence of construction. In actual fact the instances of transition and mixture are quite as frequent as cases corresponding to the illustrations offered and no less beautiful. In 64 we see the Gothic buttress construction connected with the Romanesque round arch and Romanesque arcades—a building of the transition period.

Typical Gothic Capital, Cologne.

No. 65 illustrates the occasional or frequent use of timber ceilings during the Gothic period, even for large churches; but this use as regards Cathedral churches was confined to England.

The Florence Cathedral, text-cut, p. 116, illustrates the rudimentary buttress, small windows, and paneled ornamentation, generally characteristic of the Italian Gothic. Contrast with 57.

Typical Gothic Capital, Rheims.

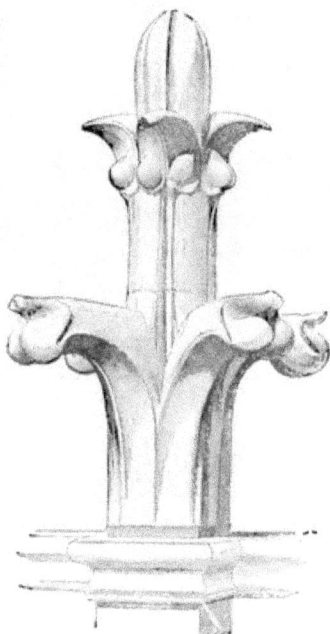

Typical Gothic Finial, Troyes.

Compare types of Gothic capitals in text-cuts with Romanesque and Byzantine types. All similar ornament based on natural forms (see also 59–62) was abandoned by the Renaissance, to be next considered, which returned to the use of the classic details, as illustrated at pp. 60–64.

The Cathedral of Florence.

PERIOD OF THE RENAISSANCE.

A.D. 1450-19TH CENTURY.

The Absence of Gothic Traits in the so-called Italian Gothic (p. 109) shows a growing national divergence in Italy from the styles and influences of Northern medieval civilization. Italy was about to experience a resurrection of her ancient past as far as the enthusiasms and studies of her people could make this possible. The feudal system of territorial baronial independence had never taken deep root in this country. The civic communities had absorbed these feudal territorial rights and powers at an early day. Italy was thus divided in the later Middle Age into a series of civic republics, or of States headed by important cities, in which the rulers, however apparently despotic, represented the interests and advantage of the commercial class. In these States, nearly connected as they had been with the more ancient civilization of the Byzantine Empire (conquered by the Turks, 1453), modern civilization took its rise.

Influence of Antiquity.—During the 15th century, patriotism led the Italians to cultivate with enthusiasm the language and literature of their ancient past. The remains of ancient art began likewise, and in no less degree, to attract attention. Excavations of buried ancient statues were not undertaken till the 16th century, but the ornamental forms of ancient Roman ruins were already copied by architectural students in the middle of the 15th century.

This Italian "Renaissance" (rebirth), also known as the time of the "Revival of Letters," was contemporaneous with the great maritime discoveries and first colonial settlements in America and India, with the invention and use of printing, with the general application of gunpowder to artillery and firearms, and the related rise of the modern military system. It was also contemporaneous with the development in Northern Europe of the modern national States, which were welded together by the power of the kings from the chaotic territorial elements of the feudal period.

The Style of the Renaissance in architecture (67, 68, 5, 6) is easily comprehended by noting the peculiarities of the Roman architecture, which it revived and copied (pp. 65, 80, and related illustrations), and by observing that the decorative forms of the Romans were copied from the Greeks. As has been explained in related sections, the Roman ornament was Greek structure.

Details of the Style.—The engaged classic columns (p. 75), surface imitations of the Greek entablature (p. 75), and the various forms of the decorative gable (p. 75), applied by the Romans over doors, niches, etc., and derived by them from the gable of the Greek temple, are the still familiar traits of the Renaissance style. This style still continues in modern use, not as a revival, as in the case of the Greek temples and Gothic cathedrals, but as a direct continuation of the Italian style.

19th Century Renaissance.—An account of the 19th century Renaissance, and of the late revivals and movements in opposition to it, has been given at pp. 6–13.

The Corinthian Greek Forms are those commonly used, although the Tuscan Doric (p. 76) and the debased Roman Ionic are also found. The prevalence of Corinthian Greek forms during the Roman Imperial period has been explained (pp. 58, 76). This accounts for their prevalent use in the modern Renaissance.

Absence of Structural Characteristics.—The Italian Renaissance style has no distinctive structural characteristics. It is purely a style of ornament, not a style of construction.

St. Peter's at Rome (No. 66) is the largest and most elaborate example of the style. Its date (begun in 1506) indicates the time at which the style had become general throughout Italy. There are, however, many examples of the Renaissance which have more vigorous and more spirited ornamental details. The building was not completed till the 17th century, when the ornamental style had already stiffened into conventional forms. The engineering talent displayed in the construction of the famous dome is worthy of all admiration. The name of Michael Angelo is connected with this achievement, although he did not live to see it completed.

The Rapid Diffusion of the Renaissance Style over the rest of Europe, during and after the first quarter of the 16th century, is a notable illustration of the equally rapid spread of all other Italian tastes and fashions at the same time. The overthrow of the Gothic by the Renaissance was rapid and complete, but the change of architectural style was only one phase of a sweeping revolution in European civilization.

The Elizabethan period of English literature, in the later 16th century, the literature of France, as represented by Corneille, Racine, and Molière, in the 17th century, are derivatives of this same Italian movement. The culture of Milton, of Addison, and of Samuel Johnson has the same common origin. Not till the times of Winckelmann (p. 14) and the revival of Greek studies in the

66. ST. PETER'S CHURCH, ROME

67. COURT OF THE FARNESE PALACE, ROME.

later 18th century, did Europe experience a new artistic and literary impulse.

Important Buildings of the Renaissance Style in Northern Europe.—Among these may be mentioned the Louvre in Paris (16th century); the Palace of the Escurial near Madrid, in Spain (16th century); the Castle Façades at Heidelberg, in Germany (16th century); St. Paul's Cathedral, London, and Temple Bar (text-cut p. 126); the Palace of Versailles near Paris (17th century); and the Palace of Frederick the Great at Potsdam, near Berlin (18th century). As the style became rapidly universal, it is apparent that individual mention would be almost without limits.

The **"Elizabethan"** and **"Queen Anne"** styles, so-called, are simply phases of the English Renaissance and not distinct styles. As has been explained at p. 22, many buildings of the time of Queen Anne, as at all other times, were of an unpretentious character and not distinguished by ornament. Such buildings have sometimes served as models for the so-called "Queen Anne" of our own times, which is essentially an effort toward modern independence. In the historic Queen Anne buildings, the ornamental details are Renaissance, if there are any. Such ornamental details, when found, are generally confined to the Renaissance gable-shaped ornaments. (See No. 11, p. 24.)

The Renaissance Decadence.—An important point in the history of the Renaissance style is the distinction between the early examples, whether in Italy or in northern countries, and those of the time of decadence. This decadence began to show itself soon after the first quarter of the 16th century, and developed in a degree corresponding generally to the order of time. Generally speaking, Renaissance buildings of the 19th century are inferior to those of the 18th century; the 18th century examples are generally inferior to those of the 17th century, and so on. The early Renaissance was distinguished by remarkably vigorous and spirited ornamental details, borrowed in general outlines from the Antique, but developed with independence and individuality.

Traits of the Decadence.—The early decline of the style is marked by cold, formal, and conventional ornamentations, which are external imitations of the Antique patterns, lacking their vigorous beauty; by a tendency to arbitrary and broken lines in construction, and by the increase of projections and broken surfaces. The later Renaissance decadence of our own century shows finally a diminution of dimensions as regards the relation of parts to the whole and an overloading of details, *i.e.*, a weakness of composition, scarcely found in the most "Rococo" Italian examples.* Comparison of the Church of St. John Lateran at Rome (68) with countless examples of 19th century Renaissance, will illustrate the difference in proportions just indicated. The rapid deterioration of the early Italian Renaissance is connected with the elemental criticism to which the Roman-Greek ornamental style is open, viz.: that it has no structural significance. Wherever ornamental forms grow out of structure or relate to it, decided and characteristic effects and bold proportions are a necessary result. In the Roman period, these were, however, rarely lacking, notwithstanding the absence of a necessary connection between structural forms and ornament. The Arch of Titus, shown in the text-cut, may serve to mark this fact, as well as to illustrate once more the ornamental system which the Italians revived from the Roman ruins. The original use of the Greek forms is shown by contrast at pp. 45-64.

THE ARCH OF TITUS.

The Increase of Projections and Broken Surfaces which characterizes the Renaissance decadence is connected with this fact, that the Greco-Roman or Renaissance ornamental style has no structural character. It was only a question of individual taste how much projection should be given to the engaged columns, entablatures, and gables, and how many repetitions of breaks in the entablature should be introduced. The decline of taste carried with it an ever-increasing excess in this direction.

These Various Traits of the Renaissance decadence are all re-

* "Rococo" is an adjective applied to the 18th century Renaissance decadence. There is no distinct "Rococo" style. The word simply indicates the excessively arbitrary and broken outlines of this period of the Renaissance style. See, for example, the Dresden "Zwinger."

68. CHURCH OF ST. JOHN, LATERAN, ROME.

69. WINDOW OF THE PITTI PALACE, FLORENCE.

lated to general historic causes, and to the decline of taste in Italy, which immediately followed the greatest period of Italian painting and sculpture in the first quarter of the 16th century. This was owing to social revolutions in Italy, and to the overthrow by foreign European nations of the independence of the Italian Civic States and Republics, and the establishment of foreign ascendencies and dynasties over most of them. This political revolution is, on the other hand, an indication of the perfection of the Italian civilization which preceded this subjugation, as showing that foreign countries wished to possess themselves of the wealth and resources of Italy. The general spread of Italian taste and culture over Northern Europe, which was a natural result, was naturally attended by deterioration of its original force and quality.

Principle for Comparative Study.—As regards the difference between late and early Renaissance ornamental patterns and details, illustrative comparisons may be based in personal study on the comparison of dates, and the general rule that designs after 1530 are inferior to those which are earlier.

The **Influence of the Renaissance Style on Furniture** and the late effort to overthrow this influence have special interest for students of decorative art. Down to 1870, the furniture designs of Europe, and hence of America, had been based on Renaissance patterns for over three centuries, with slight breaks during the Greek and Gothic revivals. Examples to be studied in most modern houses, show derivations from the ornamental gables, which are still familiar to all of us. The deterioration of design induced by the use of machinery for carved patterns, and by the consequent decline of the art of wood-carving, had brought these motives * to the lowest depth of debasement in the years just preceding the "Eastlake" and "Queen Anne" revivals.

The **Rise of the "Eastlake" Style** was due simply to the large sale of Mr. Charles Eastlake's book on "Household Taste," a highly valuable and commendable work. Mr. Eastlake had supplied some original designs in this work to show that economy in furnishing was compatible with good taste. The extremely simple forms used to emphasize this point became the rage, and were copied by the furniture trade in general. They were frequently misunderstood as a freak of fashion, and were often caricatured, in consequence, by the supposed copies.

The **So-called "Queen Anne" Style** in furniture may be considered, as in architecture (p. 22), simply as an effort to be structural and straightforward in design, but this effort has disguised itself under the name of a style because the public is in the habit of asking for one.

Explanation of the Reaction toward Straight Lines. — Both "Eastlake" and "Queen Anne" may be summarized as efforts to design furniture simply, conse-

---

* A "motive" is the fundamental or elementary scheme of a pattern, its basis, or typical idea.

quently in straight lines and in dependence on the frame-work and skeleton of the natural construction. They are, moreover, reactions against the wild extravagance of arbitrary lines which has characterized the death agonies of the Renaissance style. The deterioration in workmanship and solidity which went hand in hand with the decline of ornamental design, is also an element explaining the severe outlines of the new taste in furniture, because the expense of good workmanship was such as to preclude any great amount of decoration.

These explanations may serve to vindicate the good sense of the original "Eastlake" and "Queen Anne" designs, but also to show that a more elaborate ornamental style is compatible with good taste, provided wood-carvers and hand-workers are not fettered by the competition with machinery, and by formulas of the fossilized Italian style. On the other hand, some of the most beautiful decorative work of the late art revival has been inspired by the ornament of the early Renaissance.

NOTES ON THE ILLUSTRATIONS. (66-69, inclusive.)

Compare 66-69, inclusive, with 5 and 6 of the same style. All of these relate to 33-43, inclusive, for method of using the ornament, and to 22-32, inclusive, for the forms of the ornament. The architectural details at pp. 60-64 are especially in point, if it be understood that the distinctive Roman and Italian use is to divorce them from the original structural relation and significance. The façade of St. John Lateran dates from the 18th century, although it is characteristic, as regards composition, for the virtues of an earlier time. Temple Bar was taken down some years since as an impediment to traffic. It dates from the 17th century. The window of the Pitti Palace has been chosen as type of the Renaissance gable, derived through Roman copy from the Greek temple form 27, 28. Temple Bar shows the alternating curved variant. Compare p. 75 and p. 9.

Temple Bar, London.

SCULPTURE.

INTRODUCTION.

Elementary Instruction in the Criticism of Sculpture is at present almost inseparable from a historic review of the subject. Individual genius, armed by hard study in original design, may be superior to any such instruction, but the related historic knowledge is a valuable thing for the most gifted talent. In cases where the interested person is not an educated artist in design, the standards obtained from a historic review of the subject are absolutely essential. They will, at least, promote modesty in the formation, and reticence in the expression, of opinions. Respect for the superior technical knowledge in which the least successful professional artist must always excel the most cultivated amateur, is the first step toward independence of opinion in matters of subject and conception. In these matters the professional artist should be the minister and agent of a cultivated public taste, which has no necessary relation with a purely technical knowledge of design.

Modern Sculpture as Influenced by the Antique.—An additional reason which makes some historic knowledge essential to the criticism of modern sculpture, is found in the fact that this sculpture has been largely inspired by the Antique art, and has been in many ways dependent on it. In fact, the modern school of taste in literature and art owes its origin to the same studies of Greek art and literature which have been already mentioned in connection with the revival of the Greek forms of architecture (pp. 5–18). It has been explained that this revival was not infallible in its conceptions of what was appropriate in modern architecture (p. 17), and it is also true that the influence of the Antique in sculpture has by no means been an unmixed good. This only makes the review of its influence the more necessary. Thus a sketch of the rise of modern interest in Antique Greek art is a natural introduction to the subject.

Casts from the Antique are generally found in Art Institutions. Collections of such casts are already widely distributed in this country. For this reason, also, some acquaintance with the history of sculpture is a matter of necessary popular education.

Antique Collections Enumerated.—There are, at present, seven especially important centers in Western Europe for the study of Antique originals—London, Paris, Munich, Berlin, Florence, Naples, and Rome.

Before the Middle of the 18th Century, Rome was, strictly speaking, the only center for Antique studies. The collections of the British Museum in London, of the Louvre Museum in Paris, and of the Glyptothek (glyp'tō take) in Munich, were first formed in the late 18th and early 19th centuries. Most of the important Antique originals owned by the Berlin Museum are of very recent acquisition. The leading statues of the Florence collection in the palace of the Uffizi (yoo feet' see) were transported from the Medici (méd'e chee) Villa at Rome toward the close of the 18th century. (Hence the name of the Medici Venus in Florence.) The Museum of Naples owes its important statues to two sources. Some pieces, like the Farnese (far nee z' or far nä' sä) Hercules, Farnese Bull Group, Farnese Flora, etc., were transported to Naples from the Farnese Palace at Rome toward the close of the 18th century. The remainder came from excavations at Pompeii (pom pä'ee) and Herculaneum. These excavations had begun a little before the middle of the 18th century, but no results had been made public at that time, and the statues found had not been exhibited.

Roman Collections before 1750.—Thus it appears that Rome was in reality the only point at this time where studies of the Antique art were possible. Collections of casts were still unknown, and individual casts were a rarity in Northern Europe.* Excavations, and even journeys of scientific observation, had not yet been undertaken in Greek territories (p. 14).

Roman Collections Enumerated.—The collections of statues in Rome were not then conceived of from the stand-point of Museums. Three of the five present great collections in Rome are Villa collections—those of the Albani (al bah'nē), Borghese (bor ghay'sä), and Ludovisi (loo do vee'sē) Villas. The collections now arranged in apartments of these villas, were then scattered through their grounds. The collection of the Capitol Museum, then recently founded, had been the original collection of the Albani Villa. After its sale, the present Albani Villa collection was begun. Finally, the Vatican Museum had for its starting-point the collection known as the Belvedere, from the Belvedere Garden of the Vatican Palace, where these statues were exposed down to the beginning of the 18th century. After this time they were protected by sheds, but not till after 1750 were they removed to a gallery in the Vatican Palace.

Errors of Italian Students.—By understanding that at this time Antique statues were almost exclusively known as scattered through the gardens of Roman palaces and villas, it will be apparent from what stand-point they were viewed and studied. Italian patriotic pride in the ancient glories of the Roman Empire led to the natural presumption that objects found on the soil of Rome were of Roman creation as regards subject and origin. That these objects were generally ancient copies or importations of works of Greek art, was absolutely unknown (p. 13). The interpretations and designations were a series of errors based on the erroneous hypothesis of a Roman origin, and were derived from Latin literature and Roman history.

Artistic Appreciation.—As regards the artistic appreciation of the Antique sculpture, that had still, on the whole, to be developed. The general prejudice and presumption were that the sculpture of the 18th century was superior to the Antique. Certain ancient statues had, from the time of Michael Angelo (16th century), been much admired, but the general superiority of modern art to the ancient was supposed to be axiomatic. The ancient statues were valued and studied rather as local relics than as works of art. It was at this time (1756),

---

* It is a disputed point whether the German critic Lessing had ever seen a cast of the Laocoön Group when he wrote his famous essay on it.

that a poor German student came to Rome, who was destined to revolutionize the ruling conceptions of ancient history, and the ruling taste in literature, and to create the criticism and history of art.

John Winckelmann was born at Stendal, in Brandenburg (Prussia), in 1717, at a time when Germany was in a most backward condition of culture as compared with France, England, Spain, or Italy, of the same date. The German culture of this period was borrowed from the French, but North Germany in general, and the province where Winckelmann was born in particular, were especially rude and uncultivated. Winckelmann's origin was humble, and his early career was harassed by extreme poverty. He studied, as a young man, successively, theology, medicine, and mathematics. He made his living first as a tutor, then as teacher of a village school; finally as private librarian and secretary to a gentleman of rank. He had reached the age of thirty-eight without having even seen the few ancient statues then in Dresden, near which place he was then residing. He was equally devoid of acquaintance with works of paintings, but he had always been an enthusiastic student of Greek literature. As explained at pp. 13, 14, Greek studies had been for some centuries much neglected, and Winckelmann had been unable to secure a footing through his proficiency in this direction.

Winckelmann in Dresden.—Contact with an artist named Oeser, who valued his genius and erudition, taught Winckelmann to appreciate the virtues of Raphael. The Sistine Madonna by Raphael had just then been purchased for the Dresden Gallery. The same painter taught Winckelmann the artistic worth of the ancient statues above mentioned. These statues had come from Herculaneum by way of Vienna, and formed a rare exception to the general absence of Antique statues in Northern Europe, in the 18th century. The ruling taste of the time was for theatrical and extravagant art. The virtues of repose and simplicity which distinguish Raphael among artists, and which characterized the Antique in contrast with the emotional sculpture of the 18th century, appealed to Winckelmann's native good taste as soon as they were pointed out to him. Thus was prompted a pamphlet "On the Imitation of the Ancient Greeks," which found approbation with the King of Saxony, and procured Winckelmann a pension which enabled him to go to Rome.

Winckelmann in Rome.—Winckelmann lived thirteen years in Rome, till his death in 1768. He published in 1763 the famous "History of Art," which is still the basis of modern art studies and art criticism. Originally deficient in all detail knowledge of the subject which he made his own, his Greek erudition, and the tenacity with which he exalted the ideal of "Repose" as the true standard of taste, gave him success. The latter principle appealed to the good-breeding of society, which saw that the theatrical and sentimental behavior shunned by well-bred individuals was equally out of taste in sculpture. His Greek erudition enabled him to overthrow, one by one, the interpretations and designations which had been suggested by the false theory of the Roman origin of Antique art.

Distinction between the Roman Portraits and Greek Antiques.—One class of works was proven by Winckelmann's indication of the Greek subjects to be distinctively Roman—viz., the Roman portrait-busts and statues. Thus, for the first time the ideality of the Antique Greek art was established by the elimination of the Roman portraits. Its sentiment for beauty was now also, for the first time, apparent. For as long as the realistic works of Roman portraiture were considered as an integral part of Antique art as a whole, this sentiment could not be distinguished.

The Periods of Greek Art.—Finally the standards of simplicity and repose were demonstrated for the Greeks by a curious revelation of historic insight. The statues which had, since Michael Angelo's time, been most admired were proven to be works of the Greek decadence. Individual pieces of ancient sculpture had been admired before the time of Winckelmann, but always those which tended toward the pathetic, theatrical, or realistic tendencies of the 18th century. Winckelmann was thus the first, not only to indicate the existence of an independent Greek art, but also to demonstrate the divisions of periods and styles within its general limits. These periods are still divided according to the outlines which he indicated.

The First Direct Result of Winckelmann's Career was the reversal of the taste which had so far pronounced the Latin literature to be superior to the Greek. It was impossible to assert the superiority of a copy as against an original. The Roman sculpture had been proven (aside from its portraits) to be copy from the Greek, and this involved the whole Roman literature and Roman civilization in the same argument. Hence that sudden expansion of interest in Greek literature, Greek history, and Greek territories which still continues (p. 17). A temporary influence on the styles of modern architecture has been already indicated (p. 6, and Nos. 3, 4).

In Modern Sculpture the names of the Italian Canova, and of the Dane Thorwaldsen (resident in Rome) are the external landmarks of what may be called the Winckelmann revival. Winckelmann himself did not exercise a direct personal influence on modern sculpture. The tendency to affect an imitation of the Greek art was rather a result of the Greek literary and historic studies which were prompted by his discoveries.

Influence of the Greek Revival.—From the time of the artists named (late 18th and early 19th centuries), modern sculpture has been, till recently, almost exclusively controlled by an external imitation of the Antique, either in form or subject. At present, corresponding to the art revival in other directions, already mentioned in architecture and decoration, a parallel and praiseworthy tendency to modern freedom and modern independence is apparent in sculpture. But while the imitation of Greek forms and subjects must be ephemeral, the standards of taste drawn from Greek sculpture must always remain authoritative. Hence the great importance of this subject for students. It is not as works of sculpture alone, but as standards of taste, that the Greek statues are valuable. Casts of these statues are universally employed by schools of design as models of exercise for technical instruction. This fact alone would make some knowledge of the history of ancient art a matter of necessary and useful information.

The Greek Sculpture Developed from the Oriental.—This, then, must be first briefly considered both as a matter of history, for the understanding of Greek art, and for its own independent interest.

ANCIENT ORIENTAL NATIONS.

CHALDEAN AND ASSYRIAN SCULPTURE.

Chaldean Sculpture.—As a matter of archæologic interest, certain recent discoveries of ancient Chaldean statues have great value. They demonstrate a fact which has also recently been made known as to Egyptian art, viz.: that the oldest known works are the best; possessing qualities of verisimilitude and faithful science which have not been previously credited to the ancient Oriental art. The later, more schematic and conventional, works of the ancient Orientals were those first known to modern discoverers. The statues in question are of high antiquity (about 3800 B.C.). Nos. 70 and 71 are specimens of this sculpture. The few Assyrian statues known, of much later time, but derived from the early Chaldean, have no great importance or interest.

The Assyrian Sculpture, as known to us, was almost entirely in relief, on the stone slabs with which the walls of the Royal palaces (p. 37) were decorated (No. 21). The scenes from the lives and wars of the kings are frequently designed with great vigor and fidelity to nature. As befitting a style of architectural surface design, perspective was ignored. The Oriental taste regarded art rather as a means to symbolize ideas or facts than as a literal imitation of nature. It was pictorial writing rather than pictorial art. Large numbers of the slabs in question are in the British Museum. The best designs belong to the 7th century B.C. The later Babylonian and Persian periods of sculpture were continuations of the Assyrian as regards historic derivation (74, 75).

EGYPTIAN SCULPTURE.

The Earliest Known Egyptian Statues have been found in hidden well-like recesses connected with tombs (76, 78, and p. 37). They are portraits of the deceased persons buried in these tombs, or of attendants, the latter represented occasionally in various menial occupations. These figures belong to a stage of the Egyptian belief in immortality which conceived of a spiritual "double," which was dependent on the preservation of the mummy, or on an effigy in default of this preservation, for well-being in its spiritual existence. The statues of attendants represent the assistants whom this "double" existence was supposed to need, according to the station held in life. This early class of statues has been known for a comparatively short time only. The first examples were shown in Europe, at Paris, in 1867, and most of them are at present in the Boulak Museum, near Cairo.

Characteristics of Early Egyptian Sculpture.—These statues exhibit frequently a supple and highly realistic art absolutely foreign to the generally preconceived opinions of Egyptian sculpture. Compare "The Scribe" (p. 136) with 79, as typical for later periods of Egyptian art. Although the chronology of the remoter periods of Egyptian history is not definitely settled, the date of the latest of this particular class is at least earlier than 2300 B.C.

The Later Egyptian Sculpture after 1800 B.C. (example at 79) is far from lacking science and the sentiment of realism, but its attitudes are conventional and the outward formalism is such that the distinctions between superior and inferior work require exact attention and some sympathy with Egyptian types of art. This sympathy depends again on comprehension of the character of the people and of their history, but this comprehension is easily acquired from the works of art themselves, if they be viewed as expressions of character. The attitude which regards all expressions of art of novel aspect simply as targets for criticism and ridicule, is as fatal to independence in modern art as it is to comprehension of any other.

The Formal Attitudes of this later and more generally known Egyptian sculpture mainly exhibit the figure standing erect with pendant arms and the left leg advanced, or seated, with body faced exactly to the front and stiffly posed, the arms and hands resting on the knees. The portrait statues of the kings are the most numerous, and the statues are otherwise portraits or representations of divinities. The illustration, 79, offers a better idea of the peculiarities of the Egyptian style than description conveys. Once observed, the general resemblances are unmistakable and in singular contrast with the freedom and realism of the earlier statues mentioned.

70. Chaldean Statue, Louvre.

71. Chaldean Sculpture, Louvre.

72. Tiglath Pileser II. besieging a town. Assyrian relief from Nineveh. British Museum.

75. **King Darius and Attendants.**
Persian relief. Persepolis.

74. **Mythical subject.**
Persian relief. Palace of Darius, Persepolis.

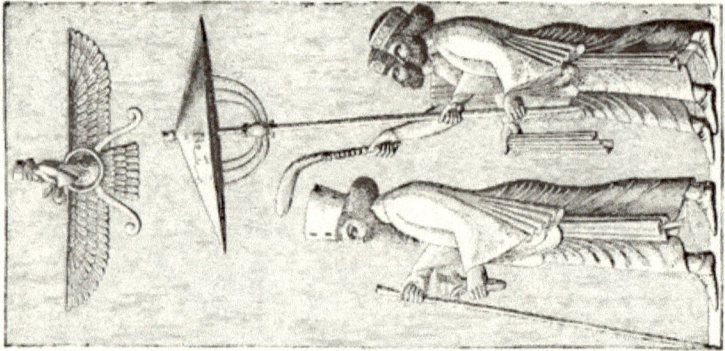

73. **King Sargon.**
Assyrian relief. Berlin.

Explanation of the Conventional Egyptian Style.—It is clear that the representations of kings and divinities were the all-important ones, and that a style was gradually created for these which reacted on all other statues. The effort was to present the king or divinity in a solemn and imposing manner, unaffected by the transient emotions and momentary gestures and attitudes of daily life. The ideal of unapproachability, of authority, of dignity, was conveyed by the fixed attitude and the magisterial pose. The relation between the style of temple architecture (pp. 29–42) and the style of sculpture is unmistakable. The same conditions created both.

Influence of the Priests.—Much stress has been laid on the prescriptions and formulas of the priests as confining Egyptian sculpture to certain fixed proportions, methods, and attitudes. This influence of the priests is doubtless to be admitted, but it is also clear that the tendencies of national character and national history created the priestly caste and determined its general administration. The conservative nature of the Egyptians, their tenacious regard for the external conditions of solidity and durability, both of aspect and of the material itself, their reverence for tradition, and their indifference to casual and accidental aspects of nature, are all apparent in their later sculpture. They chose to represent the general rather than the particular, and their art is clearly monumental in its mission. Its greatest interest is the light which it throws on the Egyptians themselves.

The Period of Ramses II., about 1350 B.C., was the most prolific in monumental art, and at this time the enormous amount of production is thought to have promoted a superficial and conventional execution, wanting that mastery of details (within the limits of the conventional style) which characterizes earlier statues.

The Decline in historic force and vitality which appears in Egypt after 1200 B.C., undoubtedly is reflected in the character of the later sculpture as regards its minor details; but the general resemblances and general character of Egyptian art remained absolutely unchanged throughout the Persian, Greek, and Roman conquests (pp. 37, 57, 66). In the Roman Imperial period the style of its Egyptian province penetrated even to the capital of the Empire, and distinguishes some of the latest efforts of the Greco-Roman sculpture.

NOTES ON THE ILLUSTRATIONS FOR CHALLEAN, ASSYRIAN, AND EGYPTIAN SCULPTURE.

(70 79, inclusive.)

The specimens of early Chaldean art at 70, 71 are from excavations at Tello, carried on by M. De Sarzec, the French Consul at Bagdad, between and since the years 1877-1881. Nos. 72, 73, are Assyrian reliefs, and Nos. 74, 75, represent the later Persian continuation of the Assyrian art.

The Scribe, Louvre.

At 76 is shown the celebrated wooden statue of Ra-em-ka, "Governor of Provinces"—time of the Fifth Dynasty. The period of King Shafra (78) was probably about 4000 B.C. (Fourth Dynasty). His pyramid is shown at 20. Both statues were found by the French Egyptologist Mariette. The period of Ramses II. (79) was about 1350 B.C. King Menephthah (77) was his son. The same Egyptian style continued till the 4th century A.D. The statues at Ipsamboul are seventy-five feet high, and flank the entrance to a rock-cut temple one hundred and fifty feet in depth and thirty-five feet high. Statues of even larger size were also cut out in the solid block, and transported hundreds of miles.

An illustration of Egyptian sculpture in relief is shown at 169. King Seti I., whose portrait in relief is there shown, was father of Ramses II., and lived about 1400 B.C. (Nineteenth Dynasty).

Assyrian Human-Headed Winged Bull.

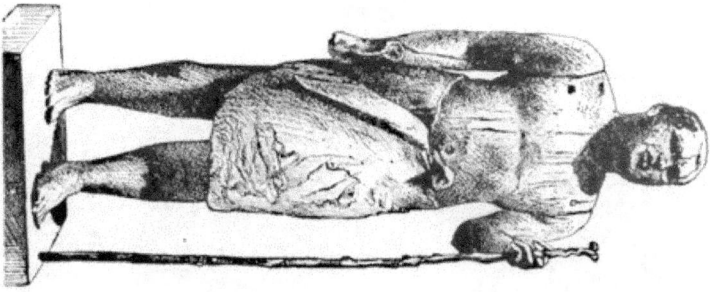

76. The "Wooden Man of Boulak."

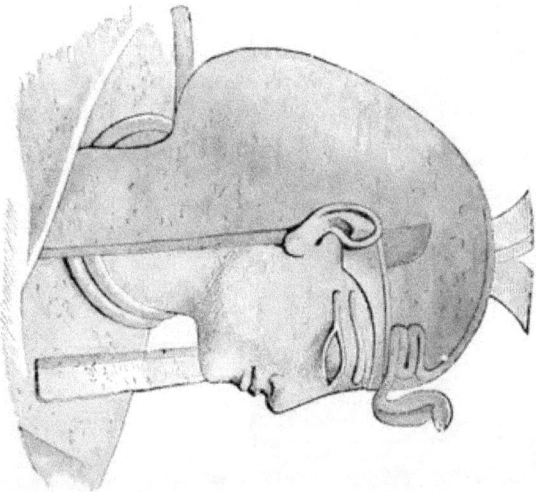

77. Head of Menephtah, Pharaoh of the Exodus.

78. King Shafra. Museum of Boulak.

79. COLOSSAL STATUE OF RAMESES II., IPSAMBOUL

GREECE.

EARLY GREEK SCULPTURE.

Early Period.—There are no dated examples of Greek sculpture earlier than the 6th century B.C., and its finest examples are of the following century. Apparently the Greeks did not generally practice sculpture in stone before the 7th century B.C. The famous "Liongate" of Mycenæ is the only existing work which is definitely ascribed to an earlier time, and this belongs to the prehistoric period before 1100 B.C., and is apparently of foreign (Lycian or Carian) workmanship.

Oriental Influence through Asia Minor.—The eastern and south-eastern provinces of Asia Minor (Phrygia, Lydia, Lycia, Caria, etc.) were among the connecting links between Oriental art and history and that of the Greeks. Greek colonies lined the shores of Asia Minor, and the adjoining Lydian Empire was an Assyrian dependency as regards its civilization. This Empire, in its greatest development (6th and 7th centuries B.C.), comprehended all the provinces just named.

Oriental Influence through Cyprus. — More important, because more direct, points of contact with the Oriental civilizations—Chaldeo-Assyrian and Egyptian—were the Phœnician colonies established on the Greek Islands and around the shore of Greece, in the times before Greek civilization became powerful, but these had been mainly expelled before the date of the development of Greek sculpture. The Island of Cyprus, colonized in various distinct quarters both by Greeks and Phœnicians, was a place where they continued in direct contact during and after this time, and thus was a most important spot for the development of Greek art. A glance at the map of the Eastern Mediterranean will show how the Phœnicians of the Syrian coast naturally amalgamated in their own civilization influences from Egypt on the one hand, and from the Tigris-Euphrates Valley on the other. These influences operated on the Greeks in Cyprus in a most decided manner (80, 81, 82).

Direct Influence from Egypt.—The most important point of contact between the civilizations of the ancient East and the rising culture of the Greeks was in the delta of the Nile, during and after the 8th century B.C. In the decline of the Egyptian Empire at this time, the earlier policy of exclusion was abandoned. Greek mercenaries became the military force of the Egyptian kings. Greek colonies were consequently established in the Nile Delta. The intercourse between these Greeks in Egypt and the mother country was constant and intimate during the 8th, 7th, and 6th centuries B.C. Recent excavations at Naukratis, in the Nile Delta, have substantiated the natural hypothesis of an Egyptian influence on Greek art, spreading from this point.

Cypriote Greek Art.—Among the statues from Cyprus in the Metropolitan Art Museum of New York, are a number illustrating the various stages of transition between Oriental art and the fully developed Greek. It is quite probable (almost positively certain), that even the absolutely Oriental types in this series are Greek works under Oriental influence, and imitating their external appearance (80–82). No. 80 shows Egyptian influence; Nos. 81, 82 show Assyrian influence. Compare 73.

The Style of Greek Sculpture about 500 B.C.—that is, about ten years before the birth of Phidias—is still archaic, and shows palpable reminiscences of Egyptian influence—in the stiff pose, and in a frequent adherence to the Egyptian attitude in erect statues, which places the left leg in advance, etc. In the figures of this period there are also reminiscences and influences of the Greek statues, which preceded the period of the stone figures, and which continued to be reverenced even during the time of fully developed art—viz., the wooden puppets and wooden figures which were dressed in garments, and which served as the earliest temple statues. The garments of these figures were plaited in a set, quaint fashion, which is imitated in the zigzag drapery lines of the early works in stone.

The Subjects of Early Greek Sculpture.—As to the subjects and use of the Greek statues about 500 B.C., it may be said that the most important were those made for temples and shrines. The mythology underlying these statuary subjects is a most important element in the perception of their relation to Greek life and art.

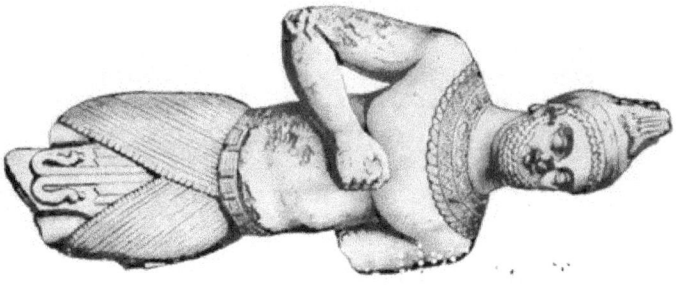

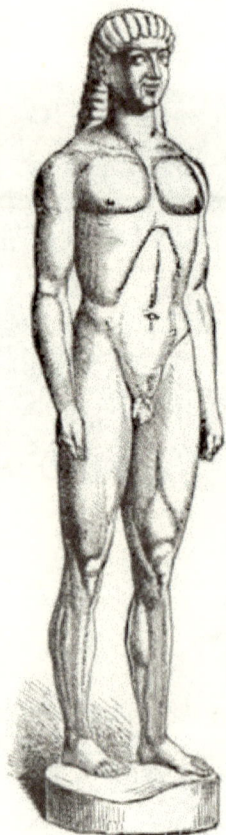

a, Hercules carrying off the Cercopes.

b. Perseus and the Medusa.

84. Apollo of Tenea, Munich.   83, a. b. Metopes Selinus.   85. Tomb-stone of Aristion, Athens.

Probably the study of mythologic art may be made more successfully at first, in connection with examples of the perfected art, and
thus we may, for the moment, overlook this aspect of the subject.

Nos. 83a and b illustrate the rude Greek art of the 6th century
B.C., from the metopes of a temple at Selinus, in Sicily; No. 85 is
an illustration of the style about 500 B.C.—all interesting as contrasts with the developed art which followed.

The Gymnastic Culture of the Greeks, and the connection of this
culture with their military system, had already produced a statuary
type of athletes. The distinction between the early Apollo type
and the early type of athletes is not clear, and it is probable that
the same type served occasionally for either subject (84).

GREEK ARCHITECTURAL SCULPTURE.

Reliefs from Selinus.—The temple architecture had begun to employ sculptured decoration at this time. The metopes from the temple
at Selinus, in Sicily, above referred to (now at Palermo), probably
date from the earlier part of the 6th century B.C.* They are the
only remaining temple architectural sculptures of the 6th century.

Reliefs from Assos.—The style of sculptured temple decoration
soon after 500 B.C., is indicated by the frieze and metopes from the
Temple of Assos, in Asia Minor, which are partly in the Louvre,
partly in the Boston Museum of Fine Arts. These again are a
unique monument of the early 5th century style. As provincial
work, remote from the active progressive movement of Greek art at
this time, these sculptures may, however, individually date as late
as those next mentioned.

The Ægina Marbles.—The style of Greek Temple architectural
sculpture about 470 B.C., is indicated by the noted gable sculptures,
in Munich, from a Temple of Minerva, on the Island of Ægina
(ē gī´ nah), west of Attica, representing combats of Greeks and
Trojans. Certain figures of this series from the angle of one of
these gables are shown at No. 87. The warriors' figures exhibit a
fully developed mastery of technical knowledge and execution in
sculpture, and it must be observed that they are only a quarter of
a century later than the type represented by the illustration for
500 B.C. (85). Although the faces have still an archaic character,
any greater detail or refinement of facial expression would have

* For the location of the metopes in a Greek temple, see p. 61.

been lost at the elevation where the figures were placed, and at the distance from which they were necessarily viewed.

Sculpture of the Jupiter Temple at Olympia.—The next step in the development of architectural sculpture decoration, as far as existing remains are concerned, is found in the gable and metope sculptures from the Jupiter Temple at Olympia. With exception of one or two metopes in the Louvre, these have been excavated since 1875, and are still at the site of discovery. Their date is about twenty years later than the Ægina figures, i.e., about 450 B.C. The tinge of archaic influence coloring the style of the Ægina sculpture has disappeared in these works.

Elgin Marbles.—A final landmark in the development of Greek sculpture is the work of the Parthenon frieze and Parthenon gables (p. 51). The metope sculptures of the Parthenon have an analogous but not quite equal importance. The general date may be fixed in round numbers as 440 B.C. The Parthenon was finished in 438. The well-known masterpieces of this series, now in the British Museum of London, are named from the English Minister to Turkey, who procured their removal from Athens, at the beginning of the 19th century—the "Elgin Marbles" (illustrations at 88–90). The scientific and technical perfection of these works is characterized by a simple dignity and unaffected grace, peculiar to all original statues of the great Greek periods.

Subjects Represented.—The subject of the group to which the figure 90 belonged, was the birth of Minerva from the brain of Jupiter. The figures preserved represent divinities and heroes of the Greek mythical series. The designations are uncertain, but the usually quoted names are sufficient for specification. The absence of expression in the face of the "Theseus" befits the distance from which the gable was necessarily viewed. The sharp cutting of drapery folds in other figures, and the generally bold and vigorous methods of execution, are all related to the effects of distance and of elevation.

The Parthenon Frieze.—The location of the frieze was at the top of the exterior temple wall under the portico ceiling. Its subject, as generally interpreted, is the Panathenaic Procession, which every fifth year celebrated the gift of a new mantle to the ancient wooden Minerva statue of the Erechtheium (p. 52). The treatment of the frieze is decorative, without details, and in sympathy

86. Gable Sculpture of Ægina. Restored view.

87. Gable Sculpture from Ægina, Munich.

88. Section of the Parthenon Frieze, British Museum.

89. Metope Sculpture from the Parthenon, British Museum.
90. Theseus of the Parthenon Gable, British Museum.

with the architectural purpose. In its design, vigor and vitality of feeling are combined with simplicity. Illustration 88 shows a small portion of this frieze.

Parthenon Metopes.—The subjects of the Parthenon metopes are mainly combats of Greeks with Centaurs. These again must be studied with reference to their architectural location and effect (89).

Balustrade Reliefs of the Temple of "Wingless Victory."—In the order of time, as regards the most important existing remains, the balustrade reliefs of the so-called Wingless Victory Temple (p. 57 and No. 27) come next, dating about 400 B.C. The temple s built on a projecting spur of the Acropolis, and the balustrade was a solid wall of marble slabs decorated with reliefs. The best preserved figures are two "Victories," one loosening her sandal (92), now kept inside the little temple. The comparison of this celebrated figure with 89 and 90 shows a difference of style analogous to the distinction between the Doric and Ionic orders, which reflects the same changes in taste and history (p. 52).

Reliefs from Halicarnassus.—The same distinction appears, by contrast with the Parthenon frieze, in the more rapid movement of the frieze reliefs (combats of Greeks with Amazons) from the tomb monument of the Carian ruler, Mausolus—the "Mausoleum," located in South-western Asia Minor, and dating from the 4th century B.C. These are in the British Museum.*

Reliefs from the Lysicrates Monument.—The related contrast between the tastes of the Doric and Ionic periods, appears once more in the frieze reliefs of the Choragic Monument of Lysicrates (p. 58 and No. 31), still in position. The subject is the transformation into dolphins of pirates assailing the train of Bacchus.

Reliefs from Pergamus.—A more violent and extravagant art appears in the immense frieze relief from which the best fragments are now in Berlin, and which decorated the great altar of Zeus (Jupiter) at Pergamus, in Asia Minor. The subject of the largest frieze is the combat of the gods and giants. The change of style again indicates a succession in time, otherwise attested (2d century B.C.), and is related to the general development and subsequent decadence of the Greek sculpture, presently to be sketched. No. 93 is a fragment of this frieze. (Restoration of the altar at 94.)

* As remarked in the Preface, the Soule photographs offer cheap and easily obtainable illustrations of all objects mentioned in text without illustration.

The Foregoing List presents, in sequence of time, most of the fairly well preserved and important works of Greek architectural sculptured decoration which have been so far made known to students. The subjects constantly reappearing in Greek art of the combats of the gods and giants, combats of Greeks and Amazons, combats of Greeks and Centaurs, etc., all relate to that contest between brutal elemental forces and civilization, which was so prominent an aspect of life to the delicate cultivation of the Greeks.

Dates of Excavation or Discovery.—Without exception, the works mentioned have only come under the close attention of students since the opening of the present century, and they have added many new conceptions to the views of Greek art propounded by Winckelmann, but they have been especially of value in verifying the position taken by him as to the distinction between original Greek works and those copies of the Roman Imperial period which had been almost the only Greek statues previously known. In this sense, Winckelmann was the prophet of these later discoveries of the original Greek sculptures, which were unknown to him. On the other hand, the colder and more mechanical work of the Roman Imperial period had influenced the types of imitative modern art before the superior vitality and vigor of the original Greek art had been appreciated, and this influence was not easily supplanted. If the history of art had no other value for modern sculpture, it would be something to show that the modern Antique art, dating from Canova and Thorwaldsen, had drawn its Antique aspects rather from the colder and more formal art of the Roman copying period than from Greek originals.

ROMAN COPIES AND GREEK ORIGINALS.

Distinction between Ancient Originals and Ancient Copies.—The attentive study of the Greek architectural sculpture, and of the qualities of original Greek execution, has led to the identification of various original Greek statues scattered through European museums, which had been imported into Italy from Greek countries during or just before the time of the Roman Empire. Others have been discovered, of late years, on Greek soil. Two of these, the "Victory" by Pæonius (95) and the Mercury by Praxiteles (96), are especially famous. See also the Milo Venus (106). Again, the number of these original Greek statues is considerable, though (as far as remains are concerned) not considerable in relation to the immense number of copies made in the Roman Imperial time. It is thus highly important to understand the distinction between certain famous statues which are admired for the motive,* pose, conception, and because they are known to be copies of famous lost originals— and others which are admired not only for such traits, but, also, for the qualities of original Greek execution. The Apollo Belve-

---

* *I.e.*, the action or aspect of the subject chosen.

91. "Victory," Athenian Acropolis.

92. "Victory," Athenian Acropolis.

93. From the Battle of the Gods and Giants at Pergamus, Berlin.

94. ALTAR OF JUPITER, PERGAMUS, WITH FRIEZE OF THE BATTLE OF GODS AND GIANTS. Restored view.

dere (118) and the so-called Marble Faun (113) may be mentioned as types of the first class; the Theseus, Milo Venus, "Victory" by Paeonius, and Mercury by Praxiteles are types of the second.

Another Distinction to be made is that between original Greek statues by unknown artists, and those to which the name of a famous Greek artist can be definitely fixed. The Mercury and "Victory" are, so far, the only works known of the latter class, dating from the originating periods of Greek art, aside from some architectural sculptures. The "Elgin Marbles" are works of the school of Phidias, not actually creations of his chisel.

Typical Subjects.—In architectural sculptures the subjects were restricted to the Greek myths, and in all statues that character of Greek art must be especially noted which led it to be content with the constant repetition of a certain series of types. These represent the well-known mythological personifications of Greek belief, and only in exceptional cases did Greek art go outside of or beyond them. Statues of athletes are the only important additional class. In this sense, the Greek sculpture appears as the expression either of the gymnastic life or of the religious beliefs of the people, and is especially interesting for this relation to them. Belief in the gods as spiritual beings, generally ceased, or seriously declined, in the 4th century B.C., but the statues of them continued to be made as ideal personifications of the qualities, virtues, and activities which they had previously symbolized.

Enumeration of Certain Types.—Thus, statues of Vulcan as the artificer, of Venus (106 and 120) and Cupid (108) as personifications of the passion of love, of Bacchus (109) as harvest divinity, of the Fauns (107, 113) as types of a natural animal existence in the woods and fields, were equally significant for Greek feeling, whether the actual belief in the divinity had, or had not, disappeared. From this point of view, an enumeration of some other Greek types is of value. The Hercules ideal (117) represented physical energy devoted to the cause of civilization. The Amazon statues (102) were personifications of heroism and martial valor. The Jupiters (100) and Junos (101) personified the power of the will. The Apollos (111, 112, 118) were types of musical and gymnastic cultivation. The Mercuries (96) also personified gymnastic cultivation. The Dianas (119) were types of female chastity. The Minervas (98, 99) symbolized intellectual enlightenment, etc.

Repetitions of Typical Subjects.—Each one of these types was reproduced in hundreds and thousands of examples. The individual statues varied, one from the other, in attitude or in motive (compare 98 with 99, 107 with 113, 106 with 120), yet each conception was stamped by certain simple attributes and peculiarities. Thus, the Venus is the only female type which is represented undraped, a curious contrast to the multitude of nude female statues in modern art. The Amazon is indicated by the attire and the weapons, etc. A very slight familiarity with the statues is sufficient to the distinction of the various types.

Repetitions of Individual Statues.—Aside from the variations within a given type, we must also note the cases in which a given famous original was reproduced individually in hundreds of subsequent repetitions. The so-called Marble Faun (113) of the Capitol Museum in Rome is a statue in point. In the middle of the 18th century there were already thirty-two statues in Rome of the same attitude, all copies of a lost original, probably by Praxiteles. As these statues were found by chance, and as the destruction of Antiques has been incomparably greater than the preservation, this argues a much larger number of copies of this one original as having existed in ancient Rome alone, to say nothing of other cities. In the same way, there are a number of repetitions of the "Apollo with the Lizard" (112) in various museums. The Belvedere Apollo is known in three repetitions—a head in Basle, which once belonged to an entire statue, and a bronze in St. Petersburg, beside the statue in Rome (118).

Exceptions to the Typical Character of Greek Sculpture, and to its tendency to free repetition of the same mythological subjects, are mainly of the period of decadence, after the overthrow of the independent Greek States (p. 57). Of this class are statues like the so-called Dying Gladiator in Rome (122). These exceptional cases as to subject are generally characterized by remarkable science of execution, but of a more minute and pretentious character than that usual in earlier Greek art.

Designations of the Greek Divinities. When the Romans came under the influence of the Greek art and culture, their divinities were assimilated with those of the Greeks, and Latin designations were applied to them. It is by these Latin designations that the Greek deities and statues of deities have been currently known in modern use. The Greek name of Vulcan was Hephaestus; of Venus—Aphrodite; of Cupid—Eros; of Bacchus—Dionysus; of Jupiter—Zeus; of Juno—Hera; of Mercury—Hermes; of Diana—Artemis; of Minerva—Athené. Apollo and Hercules were known by these names to the Greeks (with slightly different spelling).

95. "VICTORY" BY PÆONIUS, OLYMPIA.

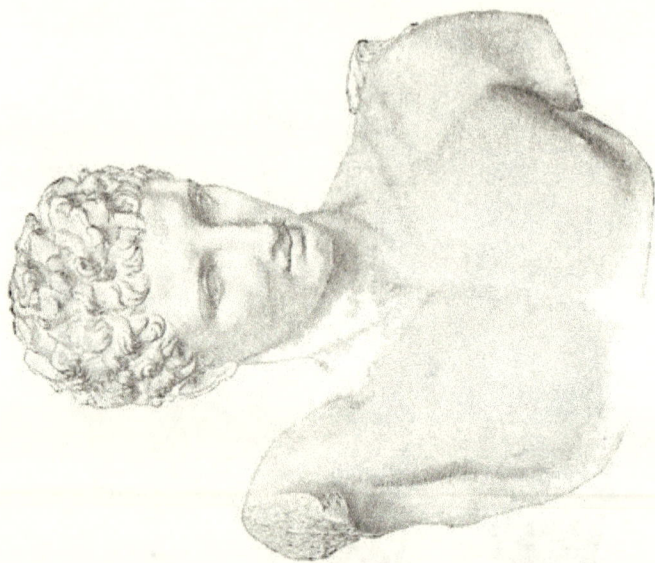

97. Head of the same.

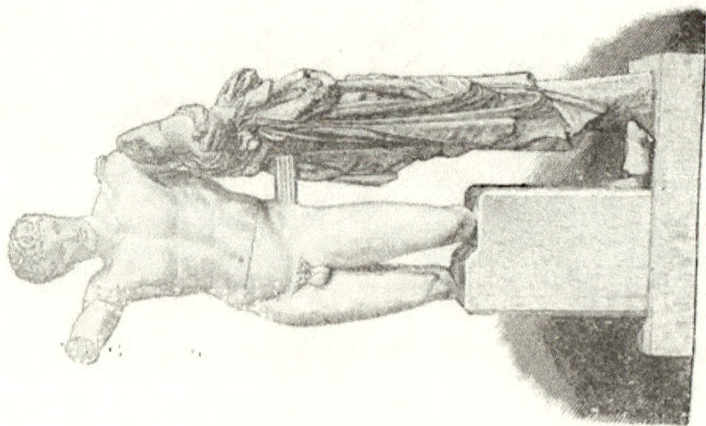

96. Mercury with the Infant Bacchus, by Praxiteles, Olympia.

TYPES OF THE FIFTH CENTURY B.C.

Historical Review.—We are now prepared to follow a summary historical review of the most quoted Greek sculptors and their works, as known by later copies. The value of these later copies for this review, as repetitions of lost originals, is apparent. The periods in question correspond to those already indicated for the orders of Greek Architecture, to which periods reference should now be made (p. 52).

The Rapid Development of the perfect Greek art in the 5th century B.C. has been already apparent in the contrast between the art dating about 500 B.C. and that of thirty years later. The perfection of this art had its parallel in Greek literature and its cause in Greek civilization. The victories of the Persian wars, dating 490–480 B.C., made the Greeks fully conscious of their own superiority to the Eastern civilization, from which their earlier art had borrowed so much, and promoted an independent national art expression.

Athens, as the leading Greek State of this period, was the center of political activity and of greatest wealth. The native artistic tendencies of its population were headed by the genius of Phidias and supported by the favorable disposition of the statesman Pericles.

Works of Phidias.—Beside the sculptures of the Parthenon already noted—probably the works of scholars after models by this artist—the especially famous works of Phidias were his colossal Jupiter in the temple at Olympia and his colossal Minerva in the Parthenon. Both were "Chryselephantine," that is, works in gold and ivory, and these were the usual materials employed at this time in similar temple figures. A wooden scaffolding, or skeleton form, was first erected, on which plates of ivory were laid and joined to represent the flesh. Gold was used for the hair, draperies, and accessories.

Destruction of the Chryselephantine Statues.—No statue of this class survived the devastations of the 5th century A.D. The antagonism of Christianity was as fatal to Greek art at this time as the ravages of the barbarians, and these last were not confined to Western Europe, although they were not as lasting in the East. (See the Restorations at 25 and 26.)

Copies of Works by Phidias.—A statuette recently discovered at Athens (98) appears to be a late copy of the Parthenon Minerva.

The later Minerva type in general, as illustrated by 99, seems to have been founded by this artist. The Jupiter bust of the Vatican, known, from the place of its discovery, as the "Otricoli Jupiter" (100), is not thought to be an exact copy of the head of the Olympian statue, but it is the finest example of the large number of Jupiter types which date their general conception from the Jupiter of Phidias.

Works of Polycletus.—A famous contemporary of Phidias was Polycletus. The greatest work of this artist was a colossal gold and ivory Juno (Hera), made for the temple at Argos, in the Peloponnesus. The bust named the Ludovisi Juno, from its location in the Ludovisi Villa at Rome, is thought to be a later copy from this work (101). The later Juno type in general is related to the epoch-making original.

The Type of the Amazon in several variations dates from the same period of Greek art. The Temple of Diana at Ephesus instituted a contest between seven Greek sculptors for the statue of an Amazon. Among the sculptors who entered this contest are named Phidias, Polycletus, and Cresilas. Polycletus is recorded to have been the victor. The Amazon statue of the Capitol Museum in Rome (102) is a noted copy of a work by one of these artists, and there are a number of repetitions in several variations which are ascribed to originals dating from the same contest.

The "Doryphorus" and the "Diadumenus."—Various copies are extant of two statues of athletes by Polycletus, which are quoted by ancient writers—one of a youth bearing a spear, one of a gymnast binding about his head the fillet which was the trophy of victory in a gymnastic contest. The most noted copy of the first-mentioned statue, the "Doryphorus" (spear-bearer), is in Naples. One of the copies of the second work, the "Diadumenus," is in the British Museum.

Myron was a contemporary, but of somewhat earlier date. One of his quoted statues, that of a gymnast throwing the *discus* (a species of quoit), is known in two copies—one till lately in the Palace Massimi at Rome, the other in the Vatican (103).

Another Statue of a Disk-thrower, known in various copies, represents the gymnast as holding the disk in an attitude just before undertaking the throw. These copies are thought to date from an original of the Phidian period.

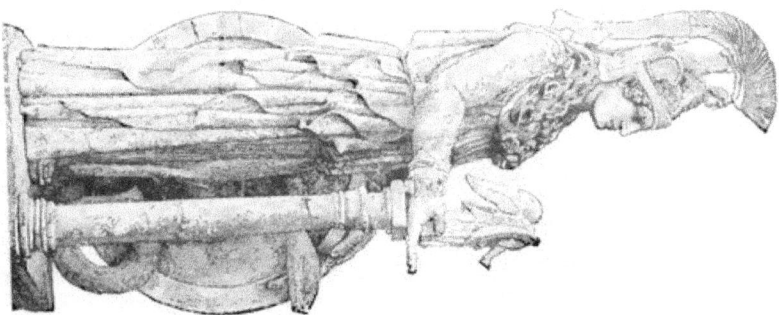

98. Copy of the Phidian Minerva.

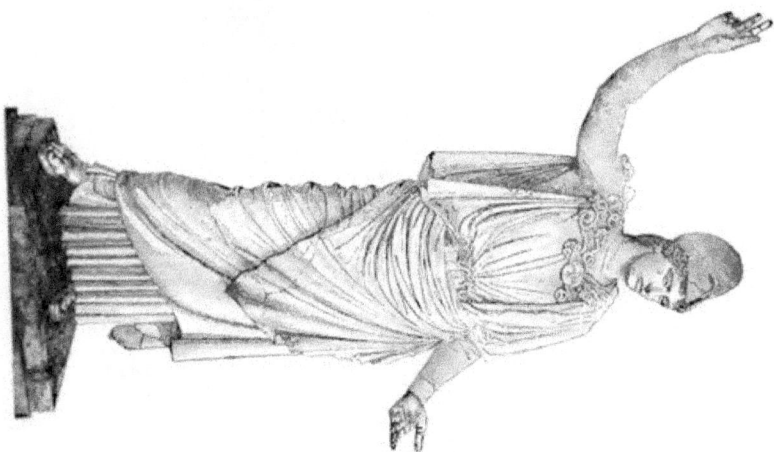

99. Minerva. Vatican.

OTRICOLI JUPITER, VATICAN.

101. JUNO OF THE LUDOVISI VILLA.

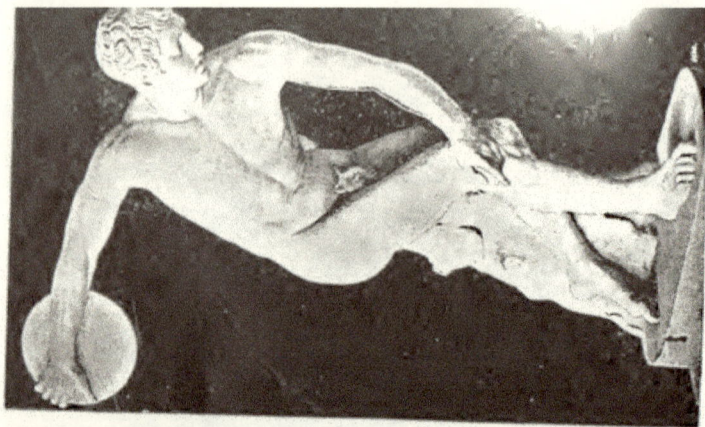

103. Disk-Thrower, Vatican.

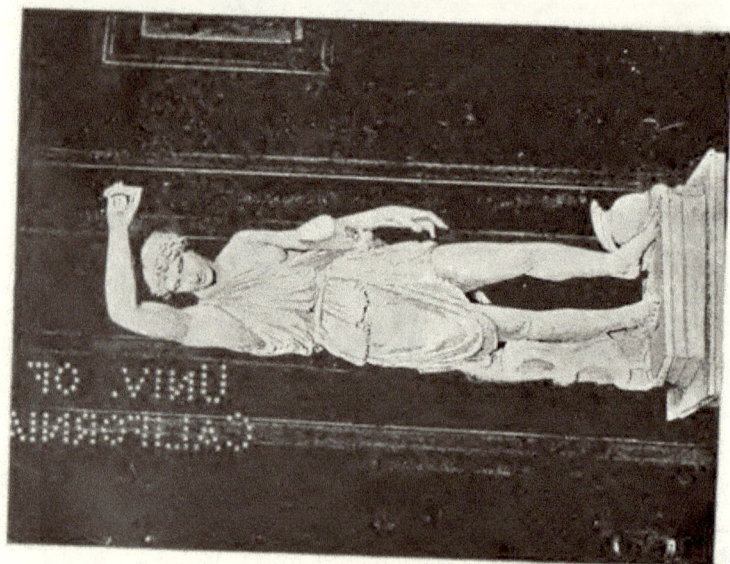

102. Amazon, Capitol Museum.

Traits of Greek Art of the Fifth Century B.C.—A comparison of the copies known to date from originals of the generation of Phidias (5th century B.C.) with one another and with the original architectural works of the same time, shows that they unite in certain qualities of style. All have a serious and earnest tendency. The conceptions especially affected are of the most serious types of Greek Mythology—the Jupiter, Juno, and Minerva. The types of the Amazons and Athletes have the same serious and virile qualities. A related taste appears in the attitudes and styles of the sculptures of the Parthenon and of the Jupiter Temple at Olympia.

TYPES OF THE FOURTH CENTURY B.C.

Style of the 4th Century.—As compared with the above-mentioned statues, the style of the 4th century has a more graceful and less serious character, both in the re-treatment of subjects previously affected and in the choice of new ones. The names of Praxiteles and Scopas are especially famed in this period, and the copies of works ascribed to these artists vary from those just indicated as the Ionic order differs from the Doric. The same general historical causes produced a change of social conditions and of taste which are reflected both in sculpture and in architecture (p. 52).

Works of Praxiteles.—A quoted work by Praxiteles, the Lizard-slaying Apollo (Sauroktonos), is known in a number of copies. The one illustrated is in the Capitol Museum at Rome (112). The playful conception and slender effeminate proportions are characteristic both of the artist and of the period. The relation of the act represented to the character of Apollo is not clear, although the lizard is known to have been associated with soothsaying superstitions, to which the conception of Apollo was also related.

The Venus Type.—Equally significant for the taste of the 4th century, and equally in contrast with the taste of the 5th century, are the types of Venus (Aphrodite), most of which, in the countless later copies, are more or less connected with lost original works by Praxiteles and Scopas. The most quoted example of the Venus type, in the Louvre, is named from the Greek island on which it was discovered in 1816—the Venus of Milo, or Melos (106). It was made by Alexander of Antiocheia on the Meander, 2d century B.C.

The Cupid (Eros) types are equally significant for the taste of this century, in contrast with the style of the Phidian time. Again, the names of both Praxiteles and Scopas are quoted for famous works, by which the numerous Cupids of later antiquity were more or less directly inspired. A Cupid in the Vatican is a well-known illustration (108).

Type of the Faun.—Praxiteles was famed for the statue of a Faun, of which the statue in the Capitol known as the "Marble Faun," is generally conceded to have been a copy (113). Similar graceful and playful tendencies appear in numerous other statues of Fauns. As regards execution, the "Barberini" (bar·be·rē′·nē) Faun, in Munich, and the Faun of the Borghese Villa, are far superior to the so-called "Marble Faun." The names of specific artists are not connected with these works.

The Bacchus (Dionysus) type (109) is also a creation of this period. The multitudes of statues of this class, are only equaled in number by the Fauns. As regards execution, the finest example is a torso* of the Naples Museum. A bronze head of the same Museum has so serious a character that it is incorrectly designated as the philosopher Plato. The head of the Capitol Museum, commonly known as "Ariadne," is also one of Bacchus.† A fine group in Florence, shows the god with his attendant, Ampelus (personification of the Vine).

Works of Scopas.—The "Niobe Group," in Florence (110), belongs to a series of copies, the lost originals of which are generally ascribed to Scopas. The myth of Niobe relates that she had roused the jealousy of Apollo and Diana, and that her children were slain by their arrows. The largest statue is that of Niobe endeavoring to protect her youngest daughter from the impending death. Other statues show her children in attitudes of flight, terror, or suffering. The location of the original group is uncertain, and no satisfactory arrangement to correspond with the natural supposition that this was a temple gable, has been offered. Some arrangement connected with architecture appears certain. The copies were found in Rome. A torso of the Vatican belongs to a similar series, but is of far superior execution; and a work of Greek chisel, possibly belonging to the original group. The pathetic tendencies apparent in this group are not exhibited by the Phidian period.

---

* Torso is the word used to define the broken trunk of a statue without head or limbs.
† See Freiderichs' "Bausteine," and other authorities. An illustration at 135.

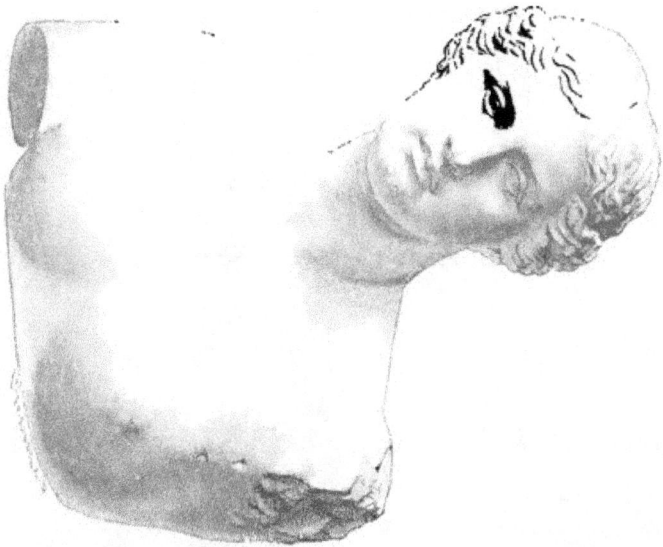

104. Head of the Milo Venus.

105. Head of the Niobe.

106. THE MILO VENUS, LOUVRE.

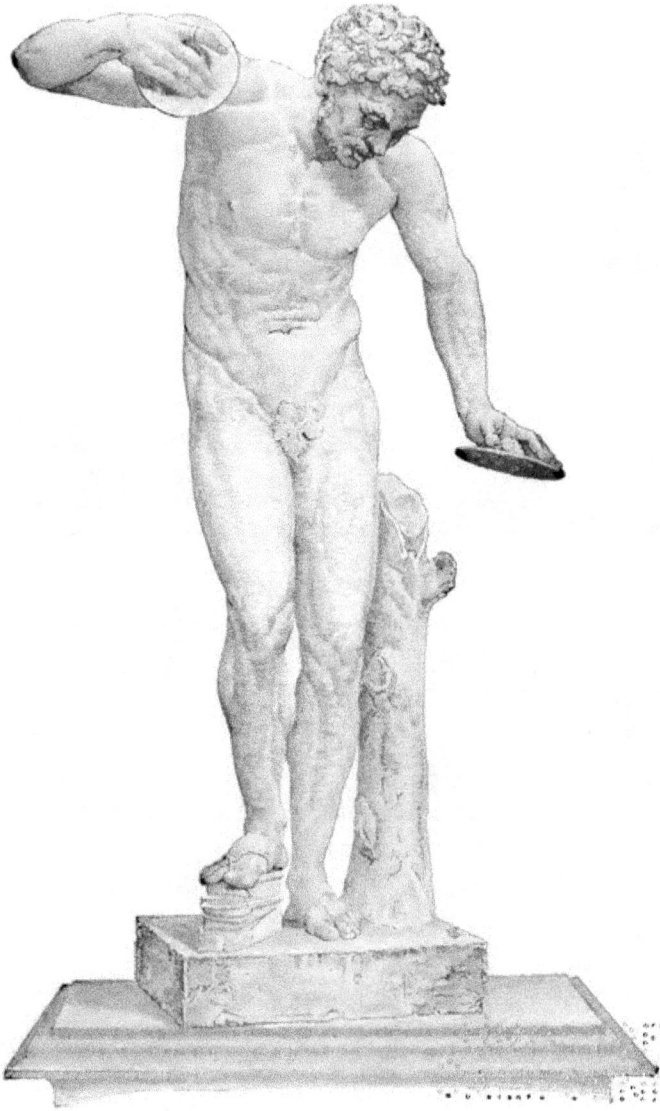

107. DANCING FAUN, FLORENCE.

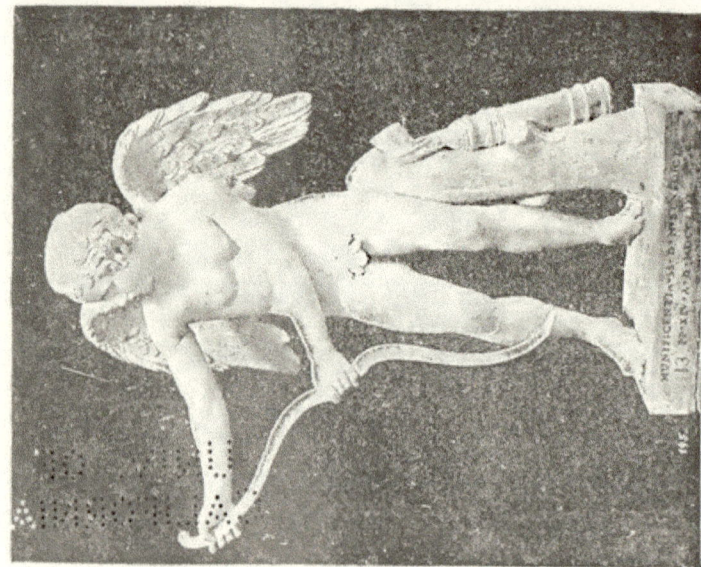

109. Bacchus, Vatican.

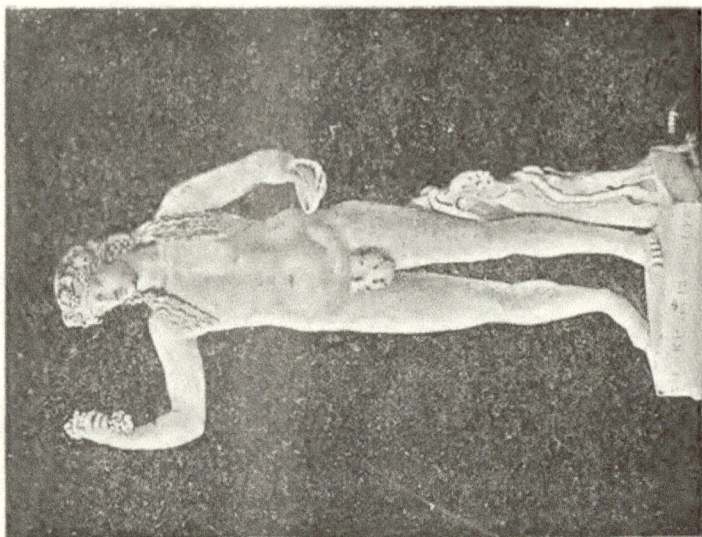

108. Cupid, Vatican.

110. Niobe, Florence.

111. Apollo with the Lyre, Vatican.

213. The "Marble Faun," Capitol Museum.

212. Apollo with the Lizard, Capitol Museum.

An Apollo of the Vatican playing on the lyre, has been classified as the copy of a work by Scopas. The attribution is doubtful (111).

The Mercury (Hermes) of Praxiteles.—In 1875, the German exploring expedition sent to excavate at Olympia, found an authenticated original statue by Praxiteles, of Mercury holding the infant Bacchus on his arm. This statue is still at Olympia. Two views of this figure are shown at 96, 97.

ALEXANDRINE PERIOD OF GREEK SCULPTURE.

Correspondence with the History of Architecture.—The sketch of the history of Greek architecture has noted (p. 57) some of the conditions of Greek culture after the Macedonian overthrow of the independence of the Greek Republics. The Corinthian order has been explained as a continuation of the Ionic, and the general character of its period has been explained as connected with the expansion and diffusion of Greek culture over many foreign countries. For the adjective "Alexandrine," see p. 57.

Characteristics of Alexandrine Art.—It was not a creative time in other respects, and in sculpture its leading claim to attention is that it began to multiply and spread the copies of earlier works or conceptions borrowed from them. Its own independent productions show generally a tendency to elaboration of detail in execution, to the *minutiae* of naturalism generally avoided by the earlier Greek art, sometimes to a relatively pompous or theatrical style, as compared with the extreme simplicity of the earlier Greek works.

Connection with Greco-Roman Sculpture.—There is no distinct separation between the art of the Alexandrine time proper and the Roman-Greek art of the Imperial time. Direct influences of Greek art at Rome were quite pronounced as early as the 2d century B.C. Works of Greek sculpture began to be carried to Rome in great numbers then. The Empire itself, founded at a later time (31 B.C.), simply continued the civilization of the late Republic. This was already that of the Alexandrine Greeks. Side by side with this continuation of the Greek art rose the independent Roman sculpture of portraiture. This, in its turn, spread to Greece and the Oriental Greek countries. All territories of the Empire thus united in producing, side by side, the ideal types of the Greek Antique and the realistic types of "Roman" portraiture.

Works of Lysippus. — The name of Lysippus introduces the new period. He was a contemporary of Alexander. The colossal "Farnese" Hercules of the Naples Museum (117) is considered a later copy of a bronze by this sculptor. Various other typical conceptions of the Hercules do not, as far as known, antedate his time. The Athlete in the Vatican, called the Apoxyomenus, is copy of a work by this artist. The "Mars" of the Ludovisi Villa probably dates, in conception, from his period (116).

The **"Belvedere" Apollo** of the Vatican (118) is considered to be the copy of an Alexandrine work. The pose shows more calculation for striking effect than appears in any statue known to date from an earlier time than that of Alexander. This statue is more celebrated for its striking pose and conception than for its execution. The arms are restored, and the presumption of the restorer that the figure held a bow has been subsequently abandoned.

Correct Restoration of the Belvedere Apollo. — It is probable that the left hand held an Ægis. The Ægis was a shield of goat's skin, to which was affixed the head of the Gorgon or Medusa. As an emblem of the powers of darkness and evil, the Gorgon's head is the trophy of the sun-god who triumphed over them. So terrible that it turned to stone those who gazed upon it, it was conceived also as a weapon of the god. The Ægis is also an attribute of Minerva and of Jupiter, divinities who also personify the triumph of light over darkness. The supposition that the Belvedere Apollo held an Ægis has been suggested by a bronze statuette in St. Petersburg, exactly corresponding in pose to this statue, and holding an object thus interpreted.

The **Diana "of Versailles,"** now in the Louvre, is one of the many fine copies to which no artist's name is attached (119). The character of pose and conception justify an ascription of the original to the Alexandrine art.

The **"Medici" Venus,** in Florence (120), is an original work of the 2d century B.C. Its qualities of execution are far superior to those of the ordinary Roman copies. The conception lacks the ideal nobility and grandeur of the Venus of Milo. The inscription recording Cleomenes of Athens as the artist is a forgery.

The **"Dying Gladiator."** — A similar tendency to realism, but in a different vein, appears in the famous "Dying Gladiator" of the Capitol (122). This statue is probably one of a group which was placed on the Acropolis, at Athens, by an Alexandrine Greek sover-

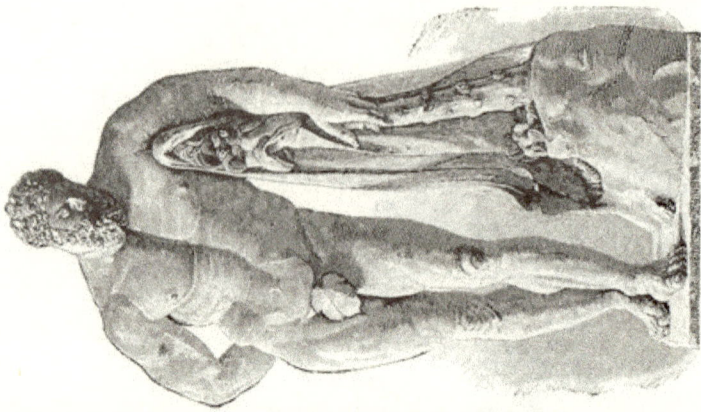

117. "Farnese" Hercules, Naples.

116. Mars of the Ludovisi Villa.

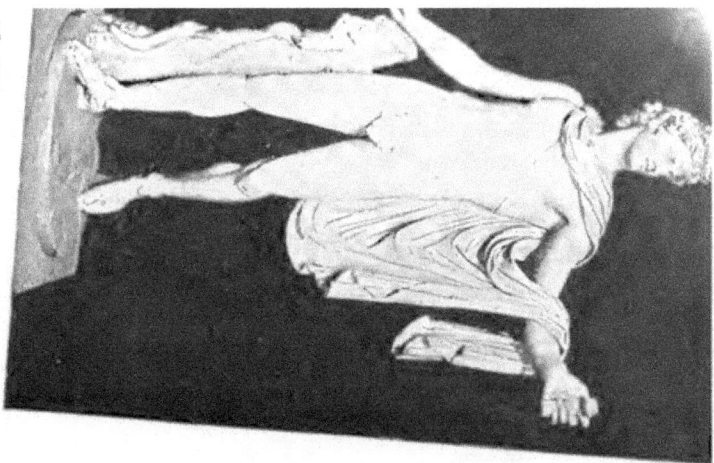

118. "Belvedere" Apollo, Vatican.

119. Diana "of Versailles," Louvre.

115. "MEDICI" VENUS, FLORENCE.

121. The Wrestlers, Florence.

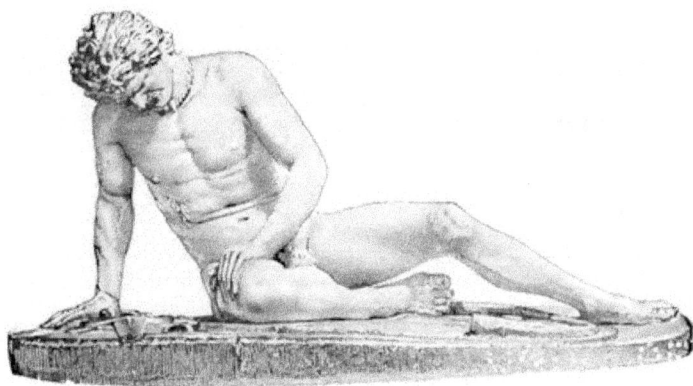

122. The "Dying Gladiator," Capitol Museum.

123. LAOCOÖN GROUP, VATICAN.

eign, Attalus I. of Pergamus. This State, headed by the city of the same name on the shore of Asia Minor, had been involved in wars with the Galatians of interior Asia Minor. These Galatians, or Gauls, were emigrants of Celtic race allied to the ancient inhabitants of France. The group, which was dedicated in commemoration of certain victories, represented dead and dying Gallic warriors. Works like this, of an absolutely tragic realism, were not created by the original Greek art. The elaborated science of the execution also characterizes the period.

The Group of the "Farnese" Bull, in the Naples Museum, shows similar tragic and realistic tendencies (124). The myth in question describes the punishment of a jealous woman by the sons of a mother whom she had designated for a like punishment. Amphion and Zethens bind Dirce to the horns of a bull. Their mother, Antiope, stands in the background. The group was found at Rome, in the Baths of Caracalla. It is ascribed to the Rhodian School of art. (The Island of Rhodes rose to great importance after Alexander, as the center of the grain trade between Egypt and the Western Mediterranean. Its wealth and importance placed it beside Alexandria and Pergamus.)

The Laocoön Group.—To Rhodian artists, the famous group of the Laocoön, in the Vatican, is also attributed (123). The date of this work is in dispute. It is ascribed by some to the 3d century B.C., by others, to the 1st century A.D. The uncertainty illustrates the fact that where exact memoranda are wanting, the differences of style between the Imperial and the Alexandrine periods are not distinctive. The myth represented by the group is an episode of the Second Book of Virgil's "Æneid," and describes the destruction of the Priest Laocoön and of his sons by serpents. This fate befell Laocoön in his effort to forestall the destruction of the city of Troy. The essay on the Laocoön group by the German critic Lessing, has been pronounced by competent authority (Lord Macaulay), "the greatest critical production of the modern time."

The Wrestler Group, in Florence (121), may be compared with the Disk-thrower (103). As both are gymnastic subjects, the complicated composition in the one case, as contrasted with the simple conception in the other, may be fairly considered a significant illustration of the Alexandrine taste, which is known to have produced the Wrestlers.

The Belvedere Torso.—From the large list of famous Antiques, two more may be selected as worthy of especial mention. Both are quoted rather for the benefit of technical students than for a more general interest. The "Belvedere Torso" of the Vatican, the trunk of a seated Hercules, is considered by anatomical experts one of the most astounding works of ancient science. It was the favorite study of Michael Angelo.[*]

The "Boxer," or "Fighting Gladiator" of the Louvre, is a work of similar anatomical tendencies. The real meaning of this piece is not clear. It has been sometimes thought to be a warrior warding off the attack of a mounted soldier, or a copy of one part of a group treating this subject.

Periods of Greek Sculpture Summarized.—The critic Winckelmann (pp 129, 130) was the first to indicate the existence of a sequence of styles in Greek sculpture according to the outlines above indicated, and corresponding to changes of history and national taste. As appears by the grouping of Illustrations 98–103, inclusive, with which 88, 89, 90, 95, should be associated, the style of the 5th century was one of severity, sublimity, and grandeur, or of serious and earnest character. As appears by grouping of Illustrations 104–113, inclusive, with which 91, 92, 96 should be associated, the style of the 4th century was one of beauty, elegance, and grace. The simplicity, dignity, and repose of attitude and conception in both these styles are very apparent. As explained at pp. 129, 130, Winckelmann was the first to call attention by publication to these traits. He was also the first to contrast with this simplicity the more pretentious style, in conception and execution, of certain groups and statues (114–124, inclusive, with which 93 may be associated) of the Alexandrine period, and to show that it marked the relative decadence in taste of this over-opulent and luxurious era. He was also the first to show that the Alexandrine and Greco-Roman art was mainly devoted to the repetition and reproduction of earlier types.

[*] By inscription, the work of Apollonius of Athens, not otherwise known to fame.

For the origin of the titles "Belvedere," "Farnese," and "Medici," applied to various Antiques, see p. 122.

124. "FARNESE" BULL GROUP, NAPLES.

125. THE COLUMN OF TRAJAN, ROME.

ROME.

ROMAN HISTORICAL AND PORTRAIT SCULPTURE.

Historical Subjects, as well as portraits, were generally avoided by the Greeks. In the production of historical reliefs, the Romans thus departed from the habits of the Greek art which they otherwise borrowed and imitated. Some few of these reliefs are especially interesting; for example, those on the inner walls of the Arch of Titus, which represent the "Triumph" of this Emperor after his destruction of Jerusalem. In one of them is represented the "Seven-branched Candlestick," which was carried off from the Jewish temple by the Roman soldiers (127). The spiral relief on the column of the Emperor Trajan, in Rome, gives a pictorial history of his campaigns in Dacia (Southern Hungary). (125.)

Roman Portraits.—In the field of Roman portraits, the list of honorable mention would be as long as the list of Emperors and great men of the Imperial period. Corresponding to the general decline of culture in later antiquity, there is a gradual falling off in qualities of refinement and of careful execution during the 2d century B.C., and yet the latest Roman portraits have value as faithful and characteristic works. The illustrations chosen show the characteristic Roman indifference to ideal beauty, and the blunt rendering of actual appearance, common to all their portraits (128–133).

Roman Copies of Greek Works.—It should not be forgotten that the copies already quoted and illustrated, by which we learn to know the earlier Greek originals, are mainly productions of the Roman Imperial time. See, for instance, 135.

The Antinoüs Type.—During the reign of the Emperor Hadrian (2d century A.D.), a combination of Greek ideality with Roman portrait art is found in the portrait statues of his favorite, Antinoüs. After the death of Antinoüs, the devotion of Hadrian and the adulation of the Emperor's subjects multiplied these portraits in such numbers, that they form a definite type of Antique art (136).

After and during the **Second Century A.D.**, the Antique sculpture declined rapidly. The reliefs (from Greek myths) decorating the stone sarcophagi (coffins) are the most numerous and most interesting works of the 2d and 3d centuries. In the 4th century A.D., the triumph of Christianity, and its then acquired control of the Roman State, gave the last blow to the waning forces of the Antique art.

Meaning of the Word "Roman."—In speaking of "Roman" sculpture, it is well to remember that the word defines the time and territory of the Empire rather than the art of a Roman race or nationality. One half the Imperial territories were countries in which a Greek culture had been dominant since the time of Alexander, and this culture had spread to the other "Roman" territories (pp. 57-61).

NOTES ON THE ILLUSTRATIONS FOR GREEK AND GRECO-ROMAN SCULPTURE.

(80-137, inclusive.)

Nos. 80, 85 (pp. 141, 142) represent the archaic period of Greek art down to a time closing about 500 B.C. No. 87 represents the transition to the perfected art after 470 B.C.

Nos. 87-94 represent original Greek sculpture for architectural decoration.

Nos. 95-97 represent original Greek statues by distinguished sculptors of recent discovery.

Nos. 98-103 (pp. 157-160) are typical pieces for the style and conceptions of Greek sculpture in the 5th century B.C. All of them are individually later copies by individually unknown artists.

Nos. 104-113 (pp. 163-168) are typical pieces for the style and conceptions of Greek sculpture in the 4th century B.C., before the time of Alexander the Great. All of them are individually later copies and, excepting 106, by individually unknown artists.

Nos. 114-124 (pp. 171-179) are typical pieces for the style and conceptions of the Alexandrine and Greco-Roman art.

Nos. 127, 134, 137 illustrate the class of Roman historical reliefs—a class of subjects not treated by Greek sculpture. The Arch of Titus is shown in text-cut at p. 122. Nos. 126, 128-133, and 136 represent the Roman portrait art. A certain number of Greek portrait statues or busts are known, but they are exceptional cases.

126. Onyx Cameo, Vienna. Emperor Claudius and his wife, Agrippina the Younger. His uncle Tiberius and his mother Livia.

127. Relief from the Arch of Titus.

ROMAN PORTRAIT BUSTS.

128. Tiberius, Vatican. 129. Caligula, Vatican. 130. Scipio Africanus, bronze, Naples.
131. Nero, Vatican. 132. Hadrian, Vatican.

133. STATUE OF AUGUSTUS, VATICAN.

134. MARBLE RELIEF, ROMAN FORUM. Lictors bringing tablets of taxes, remitted by the Emperor Trajan, to be burned.

135. Head of Bacchus. So-called Ariadne. Capitol Museum.

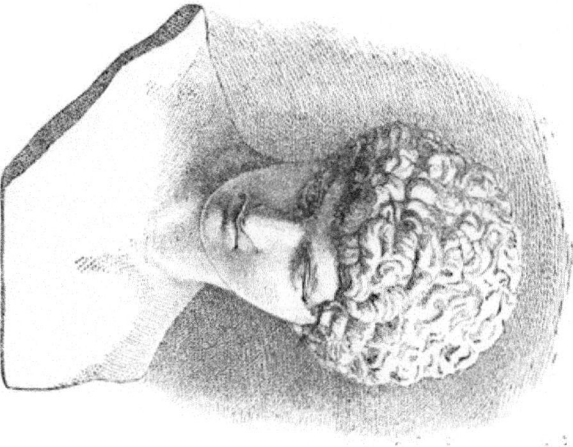

136. Head of Antinoüs, Vatican.

137. FROM THE DESTROYED TRIUMPHAL ARCH OF THE EMPEROR MARCUS AURELI Iᵃ
The Emperor grants terms of peace to conquered Germans.

THE MIDDLE AGE.

BYZANTINE AND MEDIEVAL SCULPTURE.

The **Connecting Link** between Antique and early Christian sculpture is found in the stone sarcophagi just mentioned. Some of the ancient myths commonly represented on sarcophagi were susceptible of Christian interpretation; for instance, those relating to Psyche (the Soul), and the decoration of the stone coffins with Scriptural subjects was, of course, an admissible branch of Christian art.

Christian Antagonism to Pagan Art.—Although Christianity first developed within the limits of the Roman Empire, and had existed in it since the time of the first Emperors, its antagonism to ancient art was almost absolute. This antagonism is explained by the subjects which ancient art affected. As these were representations of Pagan beliefs, the early Christians found themselves in bitter opposition both to these beliefs and to their external representations in art. The main field of Greco-Roman sculpture was the Greco-Roman Mythology, and thus the art of sculpture was destroyed in the downfall of Paganism. The statues of Pagan divinities were melted when they were of metal, broken up when of stone, or burned in the lime-kilns if they were of marble. It was impossible to accomplish this wholesale destruction without detriment to the art of design, and this did not recover itself entirely until the Italian Renaissance. The sarcophagus represented at 138 (with reliefs of the Story of the Passion) is a fair type of the short-comings of early Christian art during many centuries. As noted under the history of architecture (p. 81), Christianity became the favored religion of the Roman State soon after the opening of the 4th century A.D., and Pagan worship was made illegal at the close of the same century. It was, therefore, in the 4th century that the Christian destruction of Pagan art was mainly accomplished. The ravages of the German invasions in the 5th century (p. 81) completed this destruction.

Christian Art Affected by Decline of the Antique.—Before this active destruction, which was so detrimental to the arts of design, the Antique sculpture and art in general, had entered its period of decay. This decline of ancient sculpture was one result of the waning moral and physical forces of Antiquity in its dotage and old age. But above all, the decline of the Empire and of its art is explained by the expansion of its civilization. Such immense numbers of foreign tribes were brought under its influence, both within and without the geographical boundaries, that they ultimately reduced this civilization almost to the level of their own barbarism. This, at least, was the condition of Western Europe for some time after the 5th century A.D.

In the Byzantine Countries (pp. 81, 82), this barbaric influence is not in question, and we must look to the spirit of early Christianity for the essential explanation of the nature of their art. Antiquity, especially in its later days, had found its ideals of happiness in the well-being and beauty of the bodily form. Christianity was inspired by the consciousness of a conflict between the flesh and the spirit. It could not exalt the former without detriment to the latter, as long as the physical and unspiritual stand-point of Pagan antiquity continued to have influence in the world.

Influence of Mosaic Decoration on Design.—The history of medieval sculpture is, therefore, for many centuries, rather a blank than even an account of deficiencies. As will appear in the history of painting, the art of mosaic decoration in glass, which was used for the inner surfaces of the churches (see also p. 91), influenced the minor and less practiced arts of design, including sculpture. The set, stiff formulas of mosaic design repeat themselves in the elongated forms and lifeless execution of the scanty sculptural works. Sculpture sank mainly to the level of decorative carving, but in this field produced many beautiful works.

The Period of Absolute Decadence, as characterized by Nos. 138 and 140, lasted from the 4th to the 13th century. In its earlier time it is relieved by a survival of Antique beauty in some of the ivory carvings (No. 139), book-covers and writing tablets especially. At a later period of this decadence, Byzantine art experienced a partial revival, which has only in the last few years attracted the attention of students. In spite of this partial revival, the bronze doors of certain cathedrals, which were monuments of the best effort

138. EARLY CHRISTIAN SARCOPHAGUS IN THE LATERAN MUSEUM. FROM THE ROMAN CATACOMBS. Fourth Century
Subjects from the Story of the Passion.

139. IVORY DIPTYCH AT MONZA.
Galla Placidia and her son, Valentinian III. Fifth Century.

140. IVORY TABLET IN THE HOTEL CLUNY, PARIS.
Emperor Otto II. and wife, Theophano, blessed by Christ. Tenth Century.

141. From the "Beautiful Well," Nuremberg.   142. From south side portal, main front, Strassburg   143. From the Frauen Kirche, Nuremberg.
Fourteenth Century.   Cathedral. Fourteenth Century.   Late Fourteenth Century.

of the 11th and 12th centuries, are characterized by absolute barbarism of design.

The Revival of Sculpture in the 13th century finds its earliest monuments in France and Germany, in the cathedral sculptures; especially those of Rheims and of Chartres in France, and of Freiberg (Saxony) in Germany. Throughout the Gothic period in Northern Europe (Wells Cathedral in England, and elsewhere), there are many monuments of sculpture interesting for their fresh and innocent character and for spiritual beauty. These are almost universally of an architectural and decorative character. The immense amount of sculptured decorations usual in the later Gothic cathedrals, was often detrimental to the perfection of individual pieces. In many localities, the earlier medieval ignorance of design and indifference to the study of the human form continued through the Gothic period, and were not overcome till the time of the influence of the Italian Revival (pp. 13, 117) over Northern Europe.

REVIVAL OF SCULPTURE IN ITALY.

Importance of the Italian Revival.—Although dating also in Italy from the 13th century, the revival here was later than in France or Germany, but it has always attracted more attention because its subsequent development in the works of Ghiberti and Michael Angelo far surpassed any thing produced by Northern Europe.

Nicolo of Pisa.—The revival in Italy is connected with the name and work of a single artist, Nicolo of Pisa. His most famous work is the marble pulpit of the Baptistery in Pisa (Ne 144), dating from the third quarter of the 13th century (1260). A less quoted but also beautiful work by the same artist, is the pulpit of the Siena Cathedral. These pulpits are unique monuments. Aside from a pulpit in Pistoja (pes tō' yä) by Nicolo's son, Giovanni (jō vän' ō), and a now destroyed pulpit of the Pisa Cathedral, nothing of the same character or quality was subsequently accomplished. Details of the Pisa Baptistery pulpit at 145, 146.

Influence of the Antique.—The citizens of Pisa were among the earliest to cultivate that interest in antiquity which afterward grew into the Renaissance. Their enthusiasm led them to collect the sculptured coffins of the Greco-Roman art, and the art of Nicolo was inspired by antique reliefs still shown in Pisa.

Italian Sculpture in the 14th Century.—Nicolo's son, Giovanni, did not reach the distinction of his father, but was a superior artist for his time. Other Pisan sculptors produced interesting works during the 14th century. Andrea Pisano (pee sah'no) is a leading name (bronze door of the Florence Baptistery). The reliefs of the Florence Campanile (p. 116), from designs by the painter Giotto (jŏt'ō, are of classic reputation. In general, however, the art of sculpture subsided into comparative quiescence or neglect during the 14th century in Italy. This was the period of the first development of Italian painting, and this art more especially absorbed the interest of the time.

The Renaissance in Sculpture.—Notwithstanding the quiescence of Italian sculpture in the 14th century, it attained the full perfection of modern art in the century following. The later modern sculpture has never subsequently rivaled the Italian works of the 15th and 16th centuries. From the point of view which considers all modern civilization as a development of the Italian Renaissance, and which unites the 15th, 16th, 17th, 18th, and 19th centuries in one single period, having its starting-point in Italy, there is nothing surprising in this early perfection of modern sculpture. For a definition of the "Renaissance," and for the inspiration and tendencies of its historical movement, see pp. 117-126, where the history of modern architecture is shown to have been dependent on it (see, also, p. 13). The Antique influences apparent in Renaissance architecture were no less prominent in the art of sculpture, and were equally connected with that Italian interest in the ancient classic languages and history, which was the most remarkable feature of Italian culture in the 15th century.

Distinction between the Renaissance and the Greek Revival.—It is important to understand that the remains of ancient art in Italy were not the less enthusiastically studied because there was a mistaken theory as to their origin (p. 117). The virtues of the ancient art were credited to the Romans rather than to the Greeks, but they were not on that account the less admired. No attention was paid, it is true, to those aspects of the Antique Greek art which were first insisted on by Winckelmann. The Italian interest of the Renaissance was centered rather on the technical perfection of execution and natural appearance. By contrast with the barbarism of medieval design still general in Northern Europe (p. 197), all ancient statues were revelations of an interest in beauty and nature which the Italians were struggling to revive. It was especially this interest in nature and in the beauty of the human form which was the bond of sympathy between the art of the Renaissance and that of the ancients.

144. PULPIT IN THE PISA BAPTISTERY. NICOLO PISANO. Thirteenth Century.

145. Niccolo Pisano. The Nativity. Detail of 144.

146 Niccolo Pisano. Adoration of the Magi. Detail of 144.

199. EQUESTRIAN STATUE OF GUATAMALATA. BY DONATELLO. PADUA.

ITALIAN RENAISSANCE.

15TH CENTURY SCULPTURE.

The Bronze Doors of the Florence Baptistery, by Lorenzo Ghiberti (gē bĕr' tē), are the epoch-making works of modern sculpture (No. 148). Not begun till after 1400, not finished till after 1450, the gap between them and the work of Nicolo covers nearly two centuries. The door by Andrea Pisano has been mentioned; there are two by Ghiberti. The one most quoted is that illustrated. The illustrations of these designs are more eloquent than description could be. A curious feature is the absence of related works of even approximate perfection. Similar bronze doors were not again attempted in Italy till the Italian decadence (p. 121) had set in. Of this later time are the doors of the Pisa Cathedral, by John of Bologna.

Luca della Robbia.—During the 15th century, the Florentine sculptors were by far the most noted of all Europe. Most of them were assistants of Ghiberti in the work on the doors in question. Luca della Robbia (look' ä dĕl' lä rôb' e ä) is famed for his reliefs of a marble choir railing for the Florence Cathedral, which was never placed in position, but which is still preserved in Florence. This artist devoted himself especially to the designing of reliefs in enameled terra-cotta, and this art was continued after his death by other members of his family. The secrets of the family manufacture perished with its last member. The works of "Robbia" ware are spread all over Tuscany. They are mainly altar-pieces and lunettes* for architectural decoration (147). There is a fine Robbia altar-piece in the Art Museum of New York.

Donatello was another famous 15th century Florentine. Lacking the tendencies of Ghiberti and of Luca della Robbia toward

---

* Lunettes are the curved spaces arranged above the top straight beam of a door.

ideal beauty, he is distinguished by nervous vigor and by honest veracity of design. His most noted work is shown at 149.

The Florentine Verocchio (vä rŏk'yō) had a related character, tending sometimes to an appearance of quaintness by the rigor and sincerity of his effort. A noted work at 150. Pollajuolo (pŏl ah-you ō'lō) was a Florentine of similar tendencies.

Mino da Fiesole (mee'no dä fe a'sō lā) and Desiderio da Settignano (set in yah'no), of the later 15th century, are known for reliefs of Madonnas, etc., of peculiar purity of sentiment.

Leonardo da Vinci (lä o när'dō dä vin'chē.—The connecting link between the studies of these sculptors and those of Michael Angelo, in sequence of time, was furnished by Leonardo da Vinci, but there are no preserved works of sculpture by this artist. A colossal equestrian statue of his patron, the Duke of Milan, was twice completed in model, but these models were destroyed before casting in bronze. One of them was probably destroyed by accident, the other by the French invaders of Milan in 1499.

16TH CENTURY ITALIAN RENAISSANCE.

MICHAEL ANGELO (1475-1564.)

Early Works.—Michael Angelo was born near Florence, in 1475, and grew up as a native of that city and Republic. Although distinguished as architect (p. 118) and painter, his original and peculiar profession was that of sculpture. Ghiberti and Donatello were his models. The earliest work of the artist's youth, a Faun's mask, is still preserved in Florence. The much quoted Cupid, his next effort, which was buried and then sold as an Antique, has disappeared. (Other Cupids by Michael Angelo—one in the South Kensington Museum of London and one in Turin—are of later date.) He next executed, 1494, an Angel for the tomb of St. Domenic, in Bologna, still to be seen in that city. The "Bacchus" of the Florence Uffizi dates from the year 1494.

The Pietá.—In 1499 was finished the group of the Virgin holding the dead Saviour, now in St. Peter's, at Rome (156). The technical Italian name for this subject is Pietá (pee ä tah').

The Colossal Statue of "David," in Florence (151), was set up in 1504. A year later, Michael Angelo went to Rome to undertake the future tomb of the then reigning Pope Julius II.

150. EQUESTRIAN STATUE OF COLLEONI, BY VEROCCHIO. VENICE.

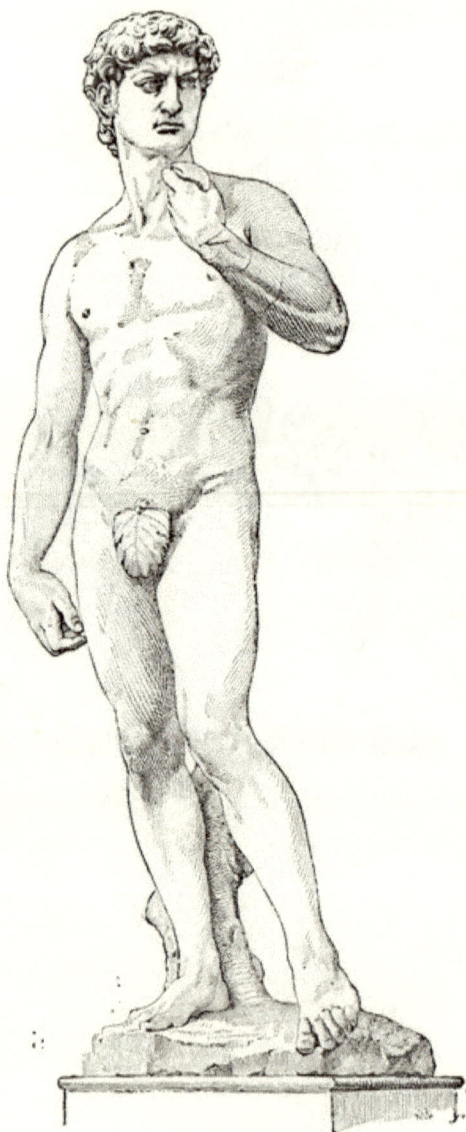

151. MICHAEL ANGELO. DAVID. FLORENCE.

152. Michael Angelo. "The Day." Florence.

153. Michael Angelo. "The Night." Florence.

154 MICHAEL ANGELO. MOSES. ROME.

The "Moses."—He began, as part of this monument, the statue of "Moses" (154), which was not finished till forty years later.

In 1507 he finished a bronze statue of Julius II, for the town of Bologna, which was destroyed during a revolt in this town a few years later.

After this time, from 1508 to 1512, he was engaged on the ceiling frescoes of the Sistine Chapel, to be subsequently noticed.

The Two "Captives," now in the Louvre, were finished before or about 1513 (illustrations 155 and 157). They belong to a design for the tomb of Julius II., which was abandoned after the Pope's death. The statues were originally intended for an allegorical series, representing the arts and sciences as held captive by the Pope, and expiring with him. The date of the "Madonna" in Bruges is uncertain—the same holds of the "Adonis," in Florence.

Tombs of the Medici.—No important sculpture commission was undertaken after this time until 1519, when the "Tombs of the Medici" (may' dtchy), in Florence, were undertaken (details at 152, 153), but the work on these was so deferred that the completion of the groups was not undertaken till 1530, and not finished till 1534.* These tombs are in a chapel of the Church of San Lorenzo, in Florence.

The commission for the picture of the "Last Judgment," in the Sistine Chapel, was undertaken in 1534, and finished in 1542, as mentioned later. In 1546 Michael Angelo was made architect of St Peter's. The building had been begun in 1506 (p. 118).

In 1545 he finished the colossal "Moses" (154), the greatest of his works—which forms the most important portion of the tomb of Julius II., in the Church of San Pietro in Vinculi (pee ay'trō in. vin'qu ly), at Rome.

Contrast between the Art of Michael Angelo and the Antique.—The foregoing list includes the more important statues by Michael Angelo, excepting the statue of the Saviour in Santa Maria sopra Minerva, in Rome (1521). They are at once monuments of his individual genius and of the greatness of his period (see matter for the "Renaissance," p. 196). The influence of the ancient statues, which began at this time to be excavated from the ancient ruins, was an important element in Michael Angelo's studies, but he was most attracted by those Antiques which coincided with the realistic tastes of his own time, especially the "Belvedere Torso," the "Laocoön," and the "Dying Gladiator" (pp. 170-178). The realism of

* They were never quite finished.

Renaissance Italian sculpture is in strong contrast with the idealizing tendencies of the Greek Antique. Each method was best for the time which chose it. The Greek statues which represented personifications rather than persons, could not imitate literally an individual form without losing their ideal meaning. The statues of the Renaissance Italians were vigorous studies of individual models, and did not pretend to be more. Statues were a natural expression of Greek religious beliefs and Greek ideals of culture, and hence their ideal form corresponded to an ideal meaning, but with the Italians they were one phase of the re-awakened interest in nature and in natural form which succeeded to the medieval civilization. And this realism is the spirit which makes them interesting as works of modern art, and as foils and contrasts to the Antique.

The Influence of Italian Renaissance Sculpture spread over Northern Europe, together with its style of architecture and its literary taste. It followed the same course as regards the decadence of the 17th and 18th centuries, and for similar reasons (pp. 121-125). It was antagonized by the Winckelmann Revival (p. 130), at the close of the 18th century, just as the Greek Temple style sought to overthrow the Renaissance in architecture (p. 15), but with much greater success.

Without attempting to enumerate many names and works of the Renaissance, or of its Northern development, which would lead to confusion as to the simple fundamental facts, the following are worthy of special distinction.

Sansovino (sän sō vē' nō), contemporary of Michael Angelo. The bronze doors of the sacristy of St. Mark's, at Venice, are a much quoted and characteristic work.

Benvenuto Cellini (běn vā noo'tō chěl lee' nō), the famous Florentine goldsmith and sculptor, was born twenty-five years later than Michael Angelo. His great work, the "Perseus," in Florence, is characteristic for the middle portion of the 16th century (158).

John of Bologna, a Fleming of Italian education, is the leading name in Italy for the later portion of the 16th century. His "Rape of the Sabines," in Florence, is an important work. His "Flying Mercury," in Florence, has been made familiar by many modern repetitions (160.)

16th Century Renaissance in Northern Europe.—Germany slightly preceded France, in time, in the development of a national Renaissance style. Peter Vischer, in Germany (Tomb of St. Sebald, in Nüremberg, 163), and Jean Goujon, in France ("Diana," in the Louvre), are leading names. A characteristic work, by Germain Pilon (159),

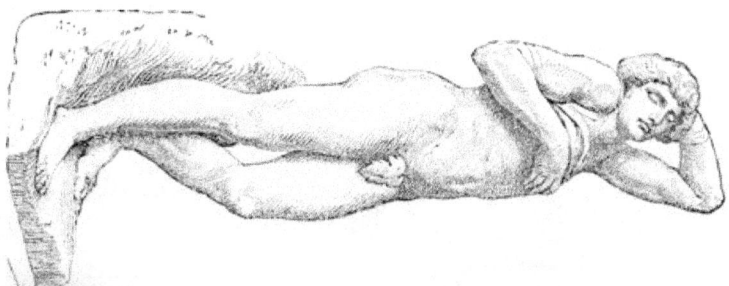

155. Michael Angelo. Captive. Louvre.

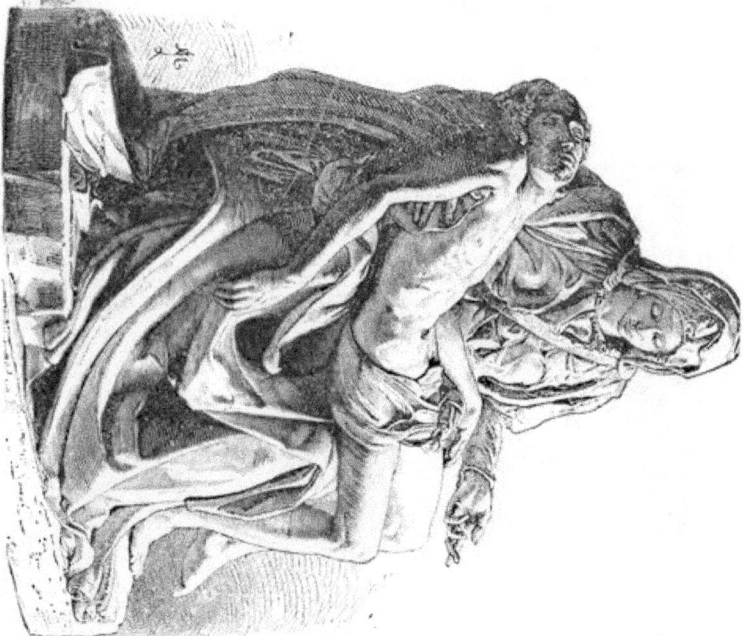

156. Michael Angelo. "Pietà." Rome.

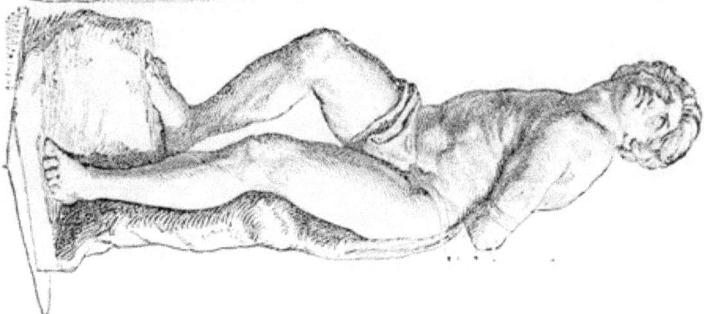

157. Michael Angelo. Captive. Louvre.

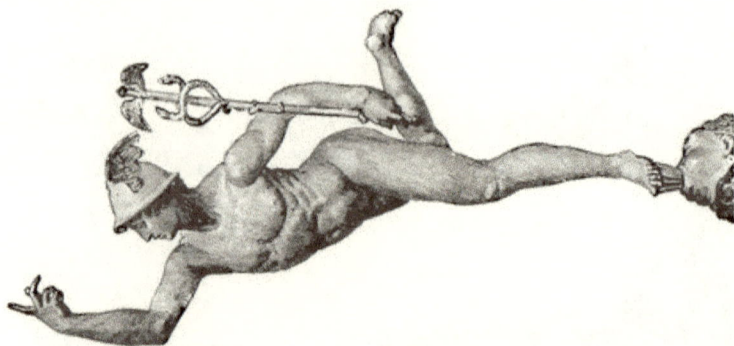

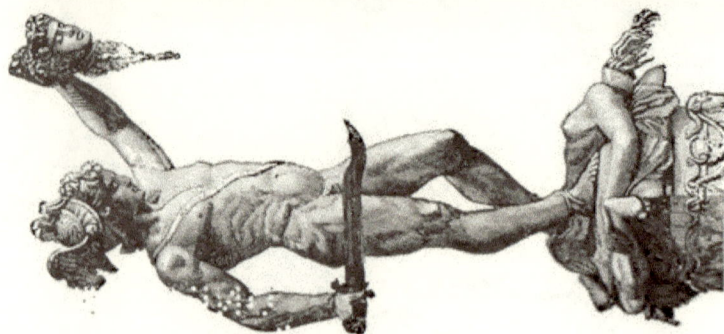

158. Benvenuto Cellini. Perseus. Florence. 159. Germain Pilon. The Graces. Louvre. 160. John of Bologna. "Flying Mercury." Florence.

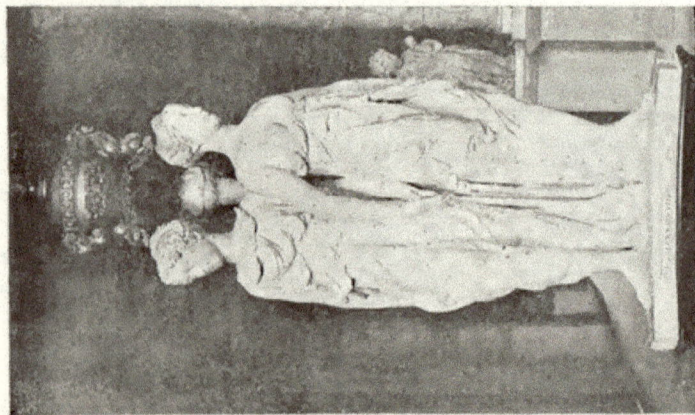

161. Bernini. Apollo and Daphne. Borghese Villa, Rome.

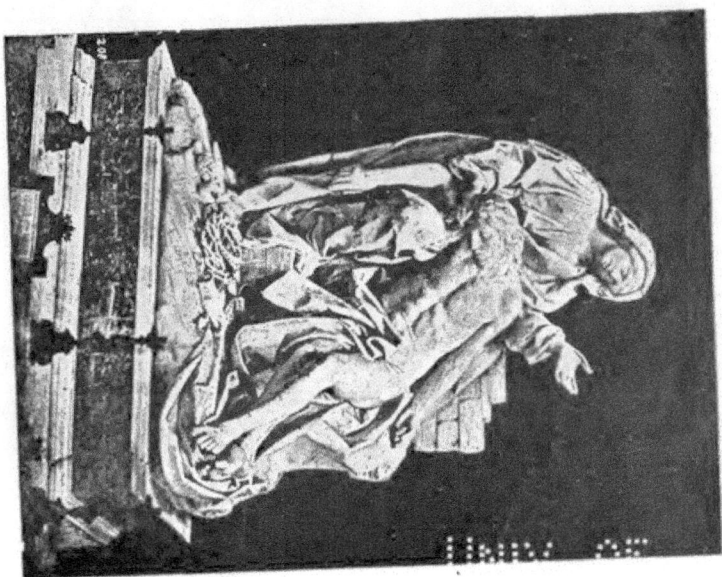

162. Bernini. "Pieta." St. John Lateran, Rome.

163. PETER FISHER. TOMB OF ST. SEBALD. NUREMBERG.

has been chosen as illustration for this French art developed from the Italian Renaissance. The Italian influences in England are attested and illustrated by the tomb of Henry VIII., in Westminster Abbey, by the Florentine Torrigiano (tŏr ē jä' nŏ).

17TH CENTURY RENAISSANCE SCULPTURE.

Bernini.—The name of the Italian Bernini (bĕr nē' nē) is the most important for this period, but his style is that of countless contemporaries. This style had lost the masculine character of the 16th century. It is theatrical, affected, overstrained, and sentimental. Compare his Pietá (162) with that of Michael Angelo (156), observing that the cherubs over the latter, in photographs, are a later addition. Bernini's style is also realistic to that extreme which contradicts reality of effect by unnatural imitations in one material of the texture and surface of another. Bernini, like many other artists of his time, was a man of great genius, but from the statuesque stand-point his works have met general condemnation since the time of Winckelmann. His group of "Apollo and Daphne" (161), in the Borghese Villa, at Rome, is another characteristic work. (Daphne, to escape the pursuit of Apollo, transforms herself into a laurel tree.)

In Germany, the name of Andreas Schlüter (schlew' ter) marks an exceptional artist for such a period. His statue of the "Great Elector," in Berlin, is universally quoted as a successful and serious work.

18TH CENTURY SCULPTURE.

Before Winckelmann. — Before the Winckelmann revival this century continued in the lines of the preceding time, but with still inferior force. The straining and overstraining for effect is a constant trait of the period. Some of its most remarkable works, as regards technical execution, are wanting in every quality of good taste.

After Winckelmann.—In external repose and simplicity, the art of the Italian Canova (cä nō' vä) and of the Dane Thorwaldsen (tor' väl zen), offers a refreshing contrast to the style which preceded (Nos. 164-168). The relation of this latter art to the studies and influence of Winckelmann has been described at p. 130.*

* See also p. 14, for matter concerning the Greek revival, of which this sculpture was one phase.

Canova (1757-1822).—In many cases the works of Canova border on the extravagance of the ante-Winckelmann time, and the change of style in these cases is mainly apparent in a method of execution supposed to be that of the Greek Antique, but which was really more allied to that of the Roman copies. It can not be said, however, that Canova's execution of details ever reached the vigor even of these. An illustration of his departure from Antique conceptions of repose in the subject of Hercules is found in his group of "Hercules and Lichas," in Venice. He was most successful in subjects where a tender or delicate sentiment harmonized with his refinement of execution and his native predispositions in art. The illustrations (164, 166) are examples of this character.

Thorwaldsen (1770-1844).—As far as a later time could go in reviving the style of Greek sculpture, Thorwaldsen probably went. But this revival was wanting in the spontaneous and popular elements which inspired the early Italian Renaissance. A comparison of Thorwaldsen with Ghiberti will show that the latter, with less appearance of external imitation, much more nearly approached the ingenuous simplicity of the Greek art. Thorwaldsen was born at Copenhagen, but was enabled to study in Rome, and subsequently resided there. Many of his works are in Copenhagen, and others are scattered through Europe (illustrations 167, 168).

During the Early 19th Century, sculpture followed, in general, the Antique style, represented by the two leading names just recorded. Next to these, the German, Dannecker ("Ariadne," in Frankfort, at 167), and the Englishman, John Gibson ("Cupid Disguised as a Shepherd," now a loan in the Metropolitan Museum of Art, in New York), are the most prominent. The name of Hiram Powers has been much quoted for American sculpture, but there are many living American sculptors whose work is vastly superior to his. Powers also reflects in weaker execution the imitative "Grecianizing" sculpture of the moderns above named.

A fine example of the more independent tendencies of the later 19th century is offered by the recently deceased French sculptor, Carpeaux (car po´) ("Group of Dancers" of the Paris Opera House, etc.). There is no affectation of Antique resemblances in the work of this artist, and yet his execution has related merits of vigor, and his conceptions have a similar power of honesty and directness. The names of Daniel C. French, E. C. Potter, Augustus St. Gaudens, Olin

164. CANOVA. HEBE. BERLIN.

166. Canova. Cupid and Psyche. Louvre.

165. Dannecker. Ariadne. Frankfort-on-Main.

Warner, and Edwin Elwell are among those which represent the best tendencies of contemporary American sculpture. Hamo Thornycroft is one of the leading names in England.

Notes on the History of Sculpture.—It appears from the foregoing sketch that the history of sculpture is mainly a history of the influence of Greek art on later times. In the late 18th and early 19th century, it was a model of external style; in the 15th and 16th centuries, it was a model for the study of nature; in the centuries of the Roman Empire, it was a universally dominant model as regards its mythological subjects. It is clear that these phases of the history of statuary are only special phases of the general history of culture and civilization, which has shown at the times specified a corresponding Greek influence, either consciously or unconsciously, in many other ways.

As the unanimous verdict of artists and critics has given the preference to Greek art, over modern, in point of style and execution, and as the Greco-Roman art is also admitted to have been generally superior to that of later periods, some matter-of-fact explanation of this perfection is desirable. This is to be found, especially as regards mechanical excellence, in the enormous numbers of statues which were made in Antiquity. The number of artisans and artists employed in this branch was infinitely more numerous than at any later time, and there was a corresponding facility in the manual dexterity of production. The habits of Greek life corresponded to those in which the sculptor's art would most successfully flourish. Gymnastic exercise was a matter of compulsory State education, on which the military system of the Greek Republics depended. Hence, the study and knowledge of the human form were a matter of unconscious and natural education. The religious system was a polytheism of divinities, which were really personifications of human virtues and human perfectibility, and admirably adapted for representation through bodily forms.

Aside from these conditions, which made sculpture the natural art expression of Greek life, it is undeniable that the general refinement and nobility of Greek taste were also important factors in its excellence. Notwithstanding the difficulties which beset the modern sculptor in rivaling the perfection of the Greek art, it must be remembered that an unpretentious modesty is its greatest charm. Wherever a similar refinement of nature and taste favor a similar unpretentious expression in art, the Greek style will be fairly rivaled and achieved without the toil of ineffectual imitation.

The peculiar interest of the Greek sculpture, from a historical stand-point, lies in the meaning of its mythological subjects (p. 151) as formal personifications of human emotional and intellectual activities; as ideals of human perfectibility in bodily beauty and in spiritual excellence. As regards its dignity of pose and expression, it must also always be a source of enjoyment and admiration, and a model of all the virtues of good-breeding in deportment.

The revolution in literary taste which closed the 18th century, and subsequently inspired the poets and authors of all modern nationalities, had for its starting-point the study of the Greek statues (pp. 14-16). This fact gives them an interest for modern times which may fairly remove the last vestige of any prejudice considering the subject of Greek art as foreign to the interests of the 19th century.

NOTES ON THE ILLUSTRATIONS FOR MEDIEVAL, RENAISSANCE, AND MODERN SCULPTURE.

(Nos. 138 168, inclusive.)

No. 138 represents the early Christian art as reflecting the decadence of the last period of the ancient. No. 139 illustrates the isolated survivals, which occasionally appear in the ivory carvings, of a style more nearly approaching the ancient classic art. No. 140 shows the elongated figures, and stiff, formal character of the Byzantine style, as copied by a contemporary artist of Western Europe.

Nos. 141, 142, 143, are typical illustrations for the better class of Northern Gothic sculptures, dating between the 13th century and the Northern Renaissance. Compare with 159, for the North European style after 1500. This developed under Italian Renaissance influence, whose rise and culmination are represented by the series of reliefs and statues 144-157.

Nos. 161, 162, represent the sentimental, theatrical style of the 17th century, common to the whole of Europe, but inspired by the ruling Italian taste of the time.

Nos. 164-168 show by contrast the works affecting the simpler Greek style and dating after the Greek revival of the 18th century.

167. THORWALDSEN. VENUS. COPENHAGEN.

60. THORWALDSEN. MERCURY. COPENHAGEN.

PAINTING.

INTRODUCTION.

Modern Painting has asserted far greater independence of historical art than either modern architecture or modern sculpture. In these latter arts, even the latest modern efforts at free modern expression have developed from historical influences which were still dominant within the life-time of the present generation. But modern painting has developed many schools which may claim almost entire independence of historic influences, and which show absolute novelty of standpoint, methods, and aims, as compared with older painters.

The "Old Masters."—On the other hand, the general modern interest in historical painting is much greater than that in historical architecture or in historical sculpture. Most of the difficulties in the study of historic paintings are connected with this fact, that modern interest in them is so general, while modern pictures are so different. The Old Masters can not be viewed or criticised from the standpoint which applies to 19th century pictures, and when this stand-point is taken, the result is disappointment to the student.

Scarcity of Originals in America.—The peculiar impediment for an American book to even a brief essay on the subject of historic painting, is found in the scarcity of well-known and generally quoted good originals in this country.* Casts and photographs may go far to supply the absence of original works of sculpture, but copies or photographs of paintings have relatively inferior value. Although acquaintance with the originals is, of course, the main object of the study in question, some matter of fact concerning them is also a department of general education. For students contemplating European travel, it is an essential thing to have in mind a scheme of the subject, a knowledge of the places and objects to be seen. Moreover, the literary outline of the subject is an interesting aspect of history, and a matter of necessary education for many persons.

The Closing Period of Historic Art.—Broadly speaking, the great periods of historic painting ended in the 17th century, and the 18th century is almost a blank in this field. This gap is closed by the 18th century painters of England, their still later outgrowth

---

* The best accessible examples of the Old Masters in America are in the collections of the Historical Society, New York, Metropolitan Museum, New York, and Boston Museum of Fine Arts. In all these collections there are some fine examples.

in artists like Rembrandt Peale, Copley, and Charles Gilbert Stuart in America, during the later 18th and early 19th centuries.

The Last Historic Italian School is that of the 17th century. Of the same time are the leading Spanish artists like Velasquez and Murillo (moo rel' yo), the best known Flemings, like Rubens and Van Dyck (vän dīke'), and the Dutch school, headed by Rembrandt.

The First Quarter of the 16th Century is the greatest period of Italian painting—the time of Leonardo da Vinci (vin' chē), Michael Angelo, Raphael Correggio (cŏr rĕd' jō), and Titian (tĭsh' ăn). The German artists, Albert Dürer (dew' rer) and Holbein (hŏl' bīne), flourished at the same time. The period of these artists is that of the early Renaissance (pp. 117, 118, 204, 209).

15th and 14th Centuries.—The painters above named were all born in the 15th century, and had for teachers men of its distinct and earlier style. This, again, is quite different from the art of the 14th century, the earliest in the development of modern painting.

The Four Centuries of Historic Painting.—Thus the scheme of this subject comprises four centuries, in each of which a different style prevailed, and these centuries were (aside from the history of English painting) the 14th, 15th, 16th, and 17th centuries. The English school produced its leading painters in the 18th century, as above mentioned. Lely (lee' lī) and Kneller, generally quoted for English portrait art in the 17th century, were Germans.

The Art which Preceded the development of painting in the 14th century needs some preliminary mention, and this may include, also, a brief notice of painting in Antiquity, although the remains of Greek and Roman art in this field are scanty. The ancient Oriental painting was mainly limited to the decoration of mural surfaces in tombs, palaces, and temples.

ANTIQUITY.

ASSYRIA, EGYPT, GREECE, AND ROME.

Assyrian Painting.—Our knowledge of Assyrian design is bounded by the reliefs already described, such as 72, 73 (p. 134), and by remains of decorated objects largely of Phœnician manufacture, but supposed to be based on Assyrian models. The reliefs mentioned were colored, and belong as much to the domain of painting as of sculpture. The decorated objects are mainly of metal (with embossed or *repoussé* * designs) or of pottery (Phœnician or Greek manufacture) decorated with Assyrian emblems and patterns.† From the stand-point of decorative art, these Assyrian emblems and patterns are extremely interesting, because they exhibit such fine decorative qualities, and because they have not unfrequently been adopted as models by the Greeks and moderns.

ASSYRIAN LION HUNT (FROM THE SCULPTURES).

Egyptian Painting of Architectural Reliefs.—Much of the Egyptian painting was also the coloring of architectural carved reliefs (169). These were associated with the carved hieroglyphic inscriptions of the temple walls, and, in a sense, formed a portion of them. They are characterized by the same schematic and conventional character. These carved relief designs were stuccoed and then colored. Very slight attention to the external forms of Egyptian hieroglyphic writing will show that the signs for the syllables,

---

* *Repoussé* is a word used to indicate embossed designs in metal which are hammered out, or "pushed out," from the inside.

† Recent investigations show that much that has been called Assyrian style in early Greek and Italian art is Egypto-Phœnician and Greco-Egyptian.

letters, and ideas, which are variously conveyed by them, are pictures, or have a pictorial origin. The reasons why these pictures should have been abbreviated and simplified for the convenience of carving or writing are apparent; hence, a schematic style which reacted on the pictorial art connected with them.

Characteristics of Egyptian Painting.—The wall paintings of the Egyptian tombs, among which those of Beni Hassan (p. 41) are especially famed, exhibit in some of the earliest known examples a

freedom and natural verity parallel with that of the early statues already mentioned (p. 132). They are always, however, in outline, without perspective effects or elaborated details. This simple and typical method of Egyptian painting had great value

EGYPTIAN WAR CHARIOT (THEBES).

as a system of surface decoration. Some of its peculiarities are manifestly national and characteristic expressions of the tendencies otherwise apparent in the Egyptian architecture and sculpture. The rigid outlines of the pictorial figures, the fixed pose of the statues, and the solemn massiveness of the temple constructions, are related facts. The peculiar Egyptian method of drawing face, legs, and feet of the human figure in profile, combined with a front view of the body and shoulders (169), shows an unwillingness to break the appearance of surface solidity by the slightest appearance of recession or projection.

Egyptian Use of Color.—From a decorative stand-point, the Egyptian use and combinations of color were extremely harmonious and effective.* The durability of their paints, plastering, and stuccoes has been such as to leave abundant remains for modern study. The scheme and tones of the Egyptian colors can be noted

---

* See Owen Jones' "Grammar of Ornament," and Prisse d'Avenne's "Histoire de l'Art Égyptien."

169. TYPE OF EGYPTIAN PROFILE DESIGN, KING SETI I. ABYDOS.

170. BATTLE OF ISSUS. MOSAIC. POMPEII.

in the mummy cases and in the minor objects of Egyptian decorative art commonly exhibited in Museums.[*]

Origin of Greek Art.—Historically speaking, the Greeks developed their art of surface design, as well as their sculpture, from Egyptian and Oriental sources (pp. 139, 140).

The Greek Vases, found in tomb excavations, have been preserved in such numbers as to furnish a record of the development of the independent Greek style from these influences. The paintings of the great periods of Greek art have all perished, but there is no doubt that they rivaled in excellence the statuary art, which has been more fortunate as regards preservation. Large mural decorative pictures were the most important works; as in the case of the later Italian art.

The Greco-Roman Art.—The general dependence of the art of the Roman Empire on earlier Greek sources, has been already indicated (pp. 128-130). The copies of the Roman period, which have been preserved in painting, were made by ordinary house decorators, and are the only remains (aside from some mosaics) which give an idea of an otherwise lost Greek art. These works, notwithstanding the relatively humble character of the artisan designers, are wonderfully beautiful in color, and often vigorous in drawing.

Pompeian Frescoes.—The most abundant remains are on the plastered walls of the Pompeian houses (p. 79). Many of these frescoes have been removed from Pompeii to the Naples Museum. In many cases the colors are still vivid and fresh. Some similar works of great beauty have also been found in Rome. The photographs of these Greco-Roman frescoes are peculiarly unfavorable copies of the originals, and much allowance must be made—as always in photographs of originals in color—for their necessary short-comings.

The "Aldobrandini Wedding."—A small fresco in the Vatican, known as the "Aldobrandini Wedding," is thus named from the villa near which it was found. It is supposed to be a copy of a Greek work of reputation, representing an antique marriage scene.

The "Battle of Issus."—The mosaic in the Naples Museum, known as the "Battle of Issus," is also supposed to be a copy of a Greek original. This mosaic was a floor decoration in Pompeii. These are the two most generally quoted Antique pictures, but there are hun-

[*] Abbott Collection of the New York Historical Society, Collections of the Metropolitan Museum, N. Y., Boston Museum of Fine Arts, etc.

dreds of others of almost equal interest. Both the designs mentioned
show that method of foreground composition, and of decorative
effects based on the outlines of the human figure, which re-appears
in the best period of Italian art. This was, partly at least, inspired
by Antique originals.

Panel Pictures of the Greeks and Romans.—In other cases, the
realistic and illusive effects so highly prized by the taste of the
19th century, were successfully attained. Paintings of the latter
class were generally on panels, like the pictures of our own time,
and have consequently perished, but some Antique mosaics show
that this realistic art was extremely successful. The mosaic of the
"Drinking Doves," in the Capitol Museum at Rome, is a well-known
example of this class.

Greek Vase, Munich.

ITALIAN PAINTING.

EARLY CHRISTIAN ART.

Pictures of the Catacombs. — The art of mosaic decoration forms the connecting link between ancient and modern painting. The wall paintings of the Catacombs of Rome (the underground cemeteries of the early Christians) are of the greatest interest from the stand-point of Christian archæology, but they did not develop into any later school of painting. They exhibit, in Christian subjects, a continuation and late survival of the ancient Greco-Roman wall pictures, as regards method and design. When Christianity was relieved from persecution, and the consequent necessity of using these underground cemeteries as places of refuge and places of worship, this method of wall decoration was generally abandoned for the more sumptuous and more lasting art of mosaic.

Mosaic Pictures were made in Antiquity both from cubes or colored glass and from cubes of colored stone. The Antique remains are generally of the latter material, and they are generally found in use for floorings, although they were also occasionally employed for wall decorations. In early Christian art, on the other hand, the mosaics were used preferably for wall decoration, and were constructed from small cubes of colored glass. The upper interior wall surfaces of all important Christian churches were decorated with mosaics during many centuries. The art was practiced mainly by Byzantine artists (pp. 81, 82), as well in Western Europe as in the Byzantine countries (North Africa, Egypt, Syria, Asia Minor, and territories of later European Turkey).

Remains. — In many of the early Roman Basilicas remains of these mosaics, dating from the 5th, 6th, and later centuries, may still be seen. St. Mark's, at Venice, offers the best existing example of the original effects of many other churches. As far as the Basilicas are concerned, only one of them has retained its side-wall mo-

saics down to the 19th century, the Church of San Apollinare
Nuovo (ä pō lē nä' rä noo ō' vō), at Ravenna (44, p. 83). This
church has lost the mosaic of its apse. The designs date from the
6th century.

Mosaic Style and Methods.—The mosaic pictures (examples 171,
174. 175, 176) were constructed from an architectural and decorative stand-point. Gorgeous effects of color were the main object.
The backgrounds were of gold—that is, cubes of glass in this color.
The figures were of stiff and formal outline, but in brilliant colors,
relieved and set off by the gold background. The influence of early
Christian feeling and surroundings on the arts of design has been
explained under the section for sculpture (p. 189).

The Technical Construction of the mosaics necessitated the
employment of a multitude of artisans, working from patterns
which could not be accurately copied in the coarse material (as
illustrated by details of No. 175). This intractability of the material
used, as regards refinement of expression or delicacy of outlines,
tended to create a schematic, formal style. Much of the stiffness
and formalism of Byzantine art in general is doubtless owing to
the reaction of mosaic art on other branches of design.

The Byzantine Panel Pictures were painted in similar set and
formal outlines, and the style thus formed has continued in the territories of the Greek Church, and in Russia, down to a recent time.

The Influence of Religious Tradition, and the conservative
spirit of Byzantine history, which was in many ways a sort of
petrified survival of ancient civilization, were also influential in
Byzantine style. It may be finally observed that Oriental influences
are very apparent in Byzantine art and history, and that Oriental
art has generally shown a tendency to the decorative in color, with
comparatively little feeling for beauty of outline in form.

NOTES ON THE ILLUSTRATIONS FOR THE BYZANTINE MOSAICS AND EARLY CHRISTIAN ART.

(171-176, inclusive.)

No. 172 shows a typical fresco from the Roman catacombs.

The mosaic represented at 171 dates from the 5th century; subject—Christ with
His flock conceived as the Shepherd guarding his sheep. It is one of the interior
decorations of the tomb of Galla Placidia, in Ravenna. Galla Placidia was the
sister of the Roman Emperor Honorius and wife of the Visigothic Chieftain
Athaulf. The period is that of the overthrow of the Roman Empire of the West.

171. THE GOOD SHEPHERD. MOSAIC. TOMB OF GALLA PLACIDIA.

172. The Last Supper. Fresco. Catacombs of San Calisto. Rome. Third Century.

173. Miniature Painting. The Apostle Matthew. From the Evangelasium of the Emperor Charlemagne. Vienna.

174. Emperor Justinian and Courtiers. Mosaic. San Vitale. Ravenna.

175. Christ before Pilate. Mosaic. San Vitale. Ravenna.

176. THE SAVIOUR. MOSAIC. CHURCH OF SANTI COSMA E DAMIANO. ROMAN FORUM.

The mosaics from San Vitale (see tä´lä), represented at 174, 175, date from the 6th century. The interior of the Church of San Vitale is shown at No. 48, p. 88. The mosaic 174 is in the choir seen at the left of this picture. The church was built by the East Roman Emperor Justinian, whose territories included Italy, after his armies had expelled the German Ostro-Goths from the country. As specified in the title of the illustration, it represents the Emperor and his courtiers. The original of 176 is the grandest and most imposing work of early Christian art. The figures are of colossal dimensions.

The above illustrations are typical in a broad way for the Byzantine mosaic art during the entire period of its continuance in Italy, viz., from the 4th to the 14th century. It was not till the 14th century and the time of Giotto, that there was any substantial change in the pictorial art of Italy. These illustrations are therefore intended to contrast broadly with those which follow for the 14th century. (133-136, inclusive.)

The brilliant colors and gold backgrounds of the originals compensate for the coarseness of the work and for the stiff attitudes and formal expressions.

The manuscripts of the period were written on vellum, and frequently decorated with carefully executed paintings in miniature (173).

REVIVAL OF ITALIAN PAINTING IN THE 14TH CENTURY.

Earlier Wall Paintings.—Byzantine mosaic decoration was still habitually employed in Italy during the 13th century. There are some remains of wall paintings preceding the 14th century, but they are of barbarous character. In Northern Europe, the Romanesque period (pp. 92, 99) had produced a school of decorative wall painting, whose scanty remains bespeak great power and simplicity of composition and fine effects in color. But this school of art had been swept away by the rise of the Gothic style. The large stained glass windows of the Gothic (p. 106) were as detrimental to design outside of decoration as the Byzantine mosaics had been, and for similar reasons.

Precedence of Italy in Modern Art.—The indisposition of the Italians to adopt the Gothic style of architecture has been already noticed (pp. 109, 110). The precedence of Italy in the history of modern painting is especially explained by this fact. Italian painting first developed in the decoration of the wall surfaces which were left intact by the non-adoption of the Gothic style, and its large surfaces of stained glass. After two centuries of practice, Italy so far surpassed Northern Europe in design that when the Gothic style was overthrown, at the opening of the 16th century, the expansion of Italian style and influence over Europe was inevitable. This expansion was assisted by the general causes already explained (p. 118). Thus Italian painting precedes and influences that of the rest of Europe, as far as its modern development is concerned. The exceptions to this general law, found in early German and in early Flemish art, will be subsequently noticed.

Influence of Nicolo of Pisa.—As usual in the history of art, so at this time in Italy, the study of concrete form preceded that of surface design and color. Nicolo of Pisa (p. 195) is recognized as the predecessor, and in some sense, as the inspirer of the Florentine painter Giotto (jŏt′ō).

School of Giotto.—The 14th century style of painting in Italy is headed by the name of the Florentine Giotto (1276–1336), in the sense that his works were the first to create a wide-spread movement, and to produce a new school of art, and the first to show thorough independence of the Byzantine style.

Cimabue (chee mäh boo′ā) was the teacher and earlier contemporary of Giotto, and is usually quoted as the first who overthrew the Byzantine style. It is true that his few remaining works show some deviations from Byzantine models; also true that they continue to resemble them in general aspect. The contrasts and similarities will speak for themselves in illustration (Soule photographs). There is a mosaic of Byzantine style by Cimabue in the apse of the Pisa Cathedral. His best remaining paintings are Madonnas in the Church of Santa Maria Novella, and in the Academy at Florence, and frescoes in St. Francis, Assisi.

The **Lives of the Italian Painters** have been written by Vasari (vä sä′ rē), an Italian who lived in the 16th century. There is an excellent English translation in "Bohn's Library." All that is known of these lives, in the way of anecdote and detail, may be found in Vasari's work, which is extremely readable. As regards criticism, his book is not now rated as of great worth, but this does not affect its value as regards the biographies themselves. Although the book reaches the extent of six volumes, the choice of the reader may select the more important names, and it may in this way be abridged at discretion.

Giotto's Epoch-making Work was the decoration in fresco of a small building, in Padua—the Chapel of Santa Maria dell'Arena * (ä rä′ nä). The subjects of the side-walls are from New Testament

---

* Fresco is the Italian word applied to paintings on plaster, that is, on wall surfaces. The word itself relates to the method generally employed, which colored the plaster while it was wet or "fresh." In this method, an amount of plastering sufficient for one day's work was laid on the wall each day. The surface in question naturally did not favor deep shadows or dark colors, nor was it adapted to minute finish of minor details. The dictates of decorative feeling relating to the use of color on large surfaces, therefore, coincided with the methods naturally employed on a plaster surface. Thus the old Italian frescoes are distinguished by a gay, light tone, and also by the decided outlines most favorable in figure compositions to decorative effects. The painter was obliged to work with a certain rapidity. Colors or outlines once laid on, could only be changed by removing the plaster surface affected, and renewing the work. Thus the art tended to broad methods in coloring, and to vigorous and correct off-hand design. For the first two centuries of Italian painting, nearly all the leading works were wall-paintings. The same holds of many of the greatest Italian pictures of the 16th century. The wall decoration of churches and public buildings demanded subjects and conceptions corresponding to the importance and significance of the structures themselves. The external conditions were thus highly favorable to

177. Giotto. The Birth. Fresco. Padua.
178. Giotto. Presentation of the Virgin. Fresco. Padua.

179. Giotto. Flight into Egypt. Fresco, Padua.
180. Giotto. The Flagellation. Fresco, Padua.

history, arranged in four lines, one set above the other. (Nos. 177-183 are examples.) At the ends of the building are larger compositions. These are less successful and less quoted.

Frescoes of Santa Maria dell'Arena.—In the illustrations 177-183, may be noticed the features which distinguish the style of Giotto from that of the Byzantine mosaics, and the abandonment of their stiff attitudes and rigid pose. When compared bluntly with 19th century pictures, much that is curious and quaint will appear, but it was impossible that one artist, or one generation, should entirely conquer the Byzantine formalism which had been dominant in Italy for ten centuries. Moreover, some departures from the style of our own time are related to the decorative necessities of wall-painting. An elaborate execution of landscape background would have broken the effects of the color scheme employed, and would have interfered with the outlines of the figure compositions. In the original colors these pictures are still very effective architectural decorations.

Characteristics of 14th Century Style. — The most important aspect of the 14th century art is the sincerity and depth of its religious feeling. No other period, except that of the Christian paintings of the Catacombs, has shown more reverence for the worth of the subjects themselves, as distinct from the effort to impress the spectator with a display of technical skill, or to interest him in the mere reproduction of natural forms and appearance.

Subjects.—The art of the time was confined to the traditions of Christianity, and to the illustration of the Bible events and stories. An attitude which considers the gravity of the subject first, and then fairly weighs the difficulties to be overcome, and the actual success achieved, will have no difficulties in respecting and admiring the art of Giotto and his school. There are many other wall pictures by Giotto, especially in Florence and at Assisi (as see'zy), but those in Padua are the most famous and the most characteristic.

The Scholars of Giotto.—A peculiar feature of the 14th century Italian art, is the general correspondence in the appearance and quality of pictures by many distinct individuals. So marked are the resemblances that much confusion has crept into the records connecting individual names with individual works. There is no period of art in which the name of the artist is so unimportant. The leading scholars of Giotto, and all Italian artists of the century were his scholars in one sense or another, often rival his

the development and the support of artistic genius. Public sympathy and popular approval were the sure reward of every success. The work of the artist in fresco was not concealed in a private studio, or sold to a private individual.

greatness, and rarely fall below it. None of them introduced any manifest departure from the style which he had created.

Frescoes of the Capella Spagnuoli.—Among many interesting works, there are two groups of wall-paintings, which require especial mention beside those of the Paduan Chapel. One of these is the series of the Capella dei Spagnuoli (day ee span you o'le), in Florence. This "Chapel of the Spaniards" adjoins the famous Church of Santa Maria Novella. The chapel dome and walls are decorated with frescoes, by artist whose names are not certainly known.

Combinations of Subject in One Field.—The four triangular sections of the dome are best adapted for complete photographic reproduction. The compositions of the side walls are too extensive for reproduction in a single photographic picture. In one of these dome frescoes, that representing the Resurrection, a feature appears, which is a constant occurrence in Italian art, viz., the union of various related subjects in a single field. For instance, in this case, the women coming from Jerusalem to visit the Tomb, are in one angle, the Resurrection is in the center; in the other angle we see the meeting of Christ and Mary Magdalen after the Resurrection. This association of related subjects without indications of local separation, is partly a result of the large spaces to be decorated, which could not artistically be subdivided into minor separate panels, but it also belongs to the ideal spirit of an art whose mission was rather Biblical instruction, or illustration, than realistic illusion. Such instances are of constant occurrence in the best periods of Italian art. They assist to comprehension of the absence of local details in the individual scenes, which has a similar explanation.

Frescoes of the Pisan Campo Santo.—A third series of 14th century frescoes, in Pisa, claims equal rank with the works of the Chapel in Padua, and with those just mentioned in the Capella dei Spagnuoli. Although there are many other wall-paintings of the same school and period, there are none quite equaling the quality and reputation of those mentioned. Near the Cathedral and Baptistery of Pisa, stands the Cemetery, or Campo Santo. The interior is an oblong quadrangular open space, surrounded by open arcades, and a cloistered gallery. The inner walls of the gallery are covered with frescoes of 14th and 15th century art. Among the former are two of special note—the "Triumph of Death," and the "Last Judgment"—both of uncertain authorship.

The "Triumph of Death" combines a series of episodes in one moral. At the lower left of the painting we see a group of coffins, which suddenly block the path of a hunting party. Beyond them a group of cripples, so miserable that

181. Giotto. The Judas Kiss, Fresco, Padua.
182. Giotto. The Deposition. Fresco, Padua.

183. Giotto. The Resurrection. Fresco, Padua.
184. Giotto. St. Francis of Assisi preaching before Pope Honorius III. Fresco, Assisi

they can not endure life, hold out their arms in appeal to the Angel of Death to release them. The latter, without regarding this appeal, hovers over a pleasure party seated in a garden.

In the upper part of the picture angels and demons contend for the souls of the dead, which are represented by small, nude bodies. In the upper left section of the painting we see a monk's cell, and its tenants near at hand,—a representation of the life which is spent in contemplating the moral which is the subject of the rest of the picture.

The "Last Judgment."—Immediately adjacent to this composition is one of nearly equal size—the "Last Judgment." Christ and the Virgin enthroned are surrounded by apostles and prophets. On the left of these the lost souls bewail their fate; on their right, those who are saved look upward toward the Redeemer. In the center, yawning tombs give up their dead, and the angels of the Judgment separate and assign to either side those who are rising from them.

Fra Angelico (1387-1455).—The style of the 14th century is so distinct from that of the 15th, that it is best to include with the former one particular artist of the 15th century who adhered to the earlier style. Fra Angelico da Fiesoli (ahn jay' lee ko dah fē ay'sō lē), whose last name indicates his birthplace—a mountain village near Florence—was a monk of the Dominican Convent of St. Mark's, of this latter town. His most important works were a series of frescoes in the cells of this convent.

Frescoes of St. Mark's Convent, Florence.—This series shows the spirit of the time of Giotto and similar methods of art. These methods are especially interesting here, since a new and naturalistic style was already current, of which the monk could have easily availed himself if it had belonged to the spirit of his work to do so. Fra Angelico is otherwise best known by the copies in color of the Angel Musicians which surround one of his Madonnas in Florence. In this and other oil-paintings his coloring is remarkably delicate and vivid. The expressions of his faces are pure and soulful to a degree scarcely otherwise known to art. (A picture of the Madonna at 191.)

NOTES ON THE ILLUSTRATIONS FOR ITALIAN PAINTING OF THE 14TH CENTURY.

(Nos. 177-184, inclusive.)

As compared with Byzantine mosaics (171-176), we observe some elementary efforts at depicting backgrounds and natural scenery. These are, however, kept in strict subordination to the figure compositions, i.e., to the essential facts of the Scripture stories. In the figure compositions there is a dramatic element of action and expression wholly wanting in the Byzantine period. The grouping of the figures ("composition" of the picture) is frequently carried to a high pitch of perfection. 182 has been almost universally selected by compendiums of art history as an example of this quality. The faces have frequently a typical resemblance

(179, 182). Individual portraiture was not generally attempted. Facial expressions are more or less rigid or contorted if emotion is depicted (180, 182).

For the use and contrasts of color during this period, the reproductions of the Arundel Society, " Arundel Chromos," may be consulted. Owen Jones' "Grammar of Ornament " gives examples in color of the decorative borders in common use at the time. The compositions can be fairly judged only in the original colors and architectural location, and the short-comings of photographic reproduction must be kept in view.

ITALIAN PAINTING OF THE 15TH CENTURY RENAISSANCE.

The Revolution in Italian Art which distinguishes this century did not begin till its first quarter had passed away. The 14th century style lasted a full century and a quarter, without reference to the still later isolated case of Fra Angelico.

Influence of Ghiberti.—The changes effected in the 15th century are nearly all summed up in the designs of the bronze doors by Ghiberti, which have been illustrated (148, pp. 200, 201), and which are equally important monuments for the history of painting and of sculpture. They are an astounding monument of genius when we observe their pictorial character, and then compare them with the pictorial art of the 14th century style just illustrated. The designs of the Baptistery doors first made by Ghiberti (not illustrated) are a connecting link and transition from the one style to the other, but otherwise the step taken by Italian art under the direction of this one genius is as sudden and complete as the illustrations would make it appear. We pass, almost without warning, from a style which is in many ways awkward and quaint for modern feeling, to another thoroughly allied to our own. The doors by Ghiberti are thus a monument of history, as well as a monument of art. They show where, when, and how "modern" feeling first developed—in the Italian Renaissance.

A Similar Suddenness of Development has already appeared in the contrast between the style of Giotto and that of the Byzantine mosaics. Another parallel between 14th and 15th century art lies in the similar rapidity with which both new styles mastered the whole of Italy as soon as they came into existence. Among the artists employed to assist Ghiberti was one named Masaccio (ma-sät'cho), and in the field of painting proper the new revolution first took shape in his works. The Giottesque style was definitely and decisively displaced by it.

186   MASOLINO. Fresco from Scenes in the Life of the Virgin. Castiglione d'Olona.

Masaccio (1402–1429). —The only well-authenticated pictures attributed to this artist are the famous ones in the Brancacci (brän kät'chē) Chapel, in Florence. This chapel is a portion of the Church of Santa Carmine (sän'tän kär mē'nō. Among these pictures, that of the "Tribute Money," painted about 1426, is especially distinguished (185).

The "Tribute Money."—Comparison with the works of Giotto and of his century will show a new facility in the disposition, action, and grouping of the figures, and an ability to portray faces and facial expressions, quite lacking in the earlier period. The introduction of landscape backgrounds, and of other naturalistic accessories, is in remarkable contrast to earlier works, but photographs are too feeble to portray faithfully these distinctions. The colors, already well-combined and contrasted by Giotto's period, are still more successfully harmonized by Masaccio and his followers.

Characteristics of Masaccio.—In addition to these points of contrast with 14th century art, we may observe a quiet reticence and dignity of feeling, and an elevation of conception which grow on the observer (of the originals at least), until Masaccio's distinction in the history of art becomes quite comprehensible. Many later contemporaries, scholars, or rivals, of the same century, equaled him in naturalistic details, but none of them attained his composure and his reserve. In all the compositions, so far in question, of either period, the lifesize scale of the individual figures, and large dimensions of the entire works, are very important elements of the effect.

Other Frescoes of the Brancacci Chapel.—Two of the frescoes, in the Brancacci Chapel, are by Filippino Lippi (fē lē pē'nō lēp'ē). Others are ascribed traditionally, but without exact certainty, to an artist named Masolino (mä sō lē'nō).

Masolino.—Certain pictures by Masolino, little known to art students, and rarely quoted (at Castiglione d'Olona [käs tēēl yō'nä dō lō'nä], near Milan), show him to be a predecessor of Masaccio in many of the innovations ascribed to the latter, and furnish a connecting link in the curious gap between the styles of the 14th and 15th centuries (186).

Benozzo Gozzoli (1424–1496?). —We may now return to the Campo Santo, in Pisa, to notice other works of the 15th century style. Among these, and among the most famous in Italy, are the frescoes by Benozzo Gozzoli (bān ŏt'sō got'sō tē), a Florentine. The much quoted "Story of Noah," is a fine illustration of the art of the period. Although many years later than the "Tribute Money," it shows no advance as to methods, and in some ways is a retrogression, as compared with the work of Masaccio's superior person-

ality.   The same remark applies to the illustration 187, a fair type
in photograph of 15th century Italian style.

Characteristics of 15th Century Style.—It is a general characteristic of 15th century frescoes, aside from Masaccio's works, to
overload the foreground with figures, and to overload the background with details.   The delight in the newly discovered arts of
naturalistic detail, is an apparent cause of this excess, and atones
for it.   The vigorous design of some figures contrasts with a quaint
awkwardness in other cases.

Bible Scenes in Local Costumes.—Bible scenes are represented
with the costumes and local surroundings of the contemporary
Italian period.   This habit, although foreign to our own conceptions, illustrates an interesting phase of Italian Biblical art.   The
subjects were so much a part of the every-day life and learning of
the people, that they did not care to give them foreign costumes and
foreign local surroundings.   It appears also that the artists found
in the traditional subjects an excuse for painting the life around
them; and certainly one great interest of the Italian pictures of
this time is the knowledge they afford of the period itself.

The Frescoes by Ghirlandajo (gheer län da′yö (1449–1494), in
Santa Maria Novella, in Florence, are another important series of
this period.   Aside from many other works of importance, may be
mentioned the series of frescoes by 15th century artists, which
decorate the lower walls of the Sistine Chapel, in the Vatican.
At 206, the location of these pictures in the Sistine Chapel may
be seen just above the painted tapestries.

The Following Additional Names of the Florentine School are too important to
be passed without mention: Filippo Lippi (1412–1469); Verocchio (1432–1488), also a
sculptor (p. 205, and No. 150); Lucca Signorelli (lŏŏ′ kah seen yō rĕl′ lē) (1441–1524);
Perugino (per ōō jee′ no) (1446–1524); Sandro Botticelli (bŏt ē chĕl′ lē) (1449–1510);
Filippino Lippi (fē lē p′ nō) (1459–1504).   Verocchio was the master of Leonardo
da Vinci.   A painting is shown at the Academy in Florence in which an angel's
head is said to be the work of the pupil.   Perugino, the master of Raphael, is
represented by 188.   The view is especially important as reminder of the architectural place and significance of all Italian frescoes.   Ghirlandajo, above mentioned, was the master, in painting, of Michael Angelo.   One of his frescoes is
shown at 189.   190 is a Madonna by Filippo Lippi.

It is a general law of art development that the study and knowledge of concrete form have preceded that of surface design as regards modeling and shading
Should any one be disposed to doubt the science in design of the 15th century
Italians, let the equestrian statues by Donatello and Verocchio be considered

187. BENOZZO GOZZOLI. ST. AUGUSTINE TAKEN TO SCHOOL. FRESCO. SAN GEMIGNANO.

188. FRESCOES BY PERUGINO, MERCHANTS' EXCHANGE (Cambio), PERUGIA.

(Nos. 149, 150). Let it also be remembered, aside from photographic short-comings, that any reproductions, in small size and without color, must be unfair to the original paintings. The illustrations of oil-paintings are, however, superior in effect to the views of larger pictures, whose details are more diminished by the reproductions. A picture of small dimensions appears to better advantage in a small printed illustration than a life-size composition.

Oil-paintings began at this time to be more generally made. The art of oil-painting found its way to Italy by way of Naples from the Flemish School of the Van Eycks (ikes. Oil had been used as a medium for color before this time, and the invention of the Van Eycks apparently related to a mixture with elements which made the art more practical by causing the colors to dry more rapidly.

This Increased Use of oil-painting is especially related to a larger demand for panel pictures—that is, for portable paintings, as distinct from wall decorations. This again may find its explanation in an increased production for private ownership. Panel pictures were, however, painted for altar-pieces in all periods. Wood was more generally employed than canvas for the panel pictures of this time, but both surfaces were used.

Comparative Merits of Oil-paintings and Frescoes. — The oil-paintings of the 15th century (examples at Nos. 190, 191) are generally religious in subject. Their smaller dimensions, and the inexperience in the technical methods involved, render these paintings relatively inferior to the wall-paintings of the same period.

School of Padua.—During the later 15th century the town of Padua produced a remarkable school of art, headed by Andrea Mantegna (män tän′ yä) (1431-1506). His greatest work is the series of nine canvases representing "The Triumph of Cæsar," now at Hampton Court Palace, in England. Mantegna's art is somewhat hard in its outlines, but is otherwise a wonderful revelation of the science and study of the 15th century.

School of Venice.—During this same period, and largely under Paduan influence, the beginnings of the later Venetian School were made, but these so immediately preceded the higher development of Venetian art, that brief mention of them may be connected with it subsequently.

The Venetian, Giovanni Bellini (jō vän′ ē bel lē′ nē), was a scholar of Mantegna, and the illustration at 211 will indicate some qualities of the work of that master, as well as those of his pupil.

Importance of Florence.—Aside from the schools just named, Italian art in general converged toward Florence in the 15th century, and also radiated thence. Siena had rivaled the precedence of Giotto for a moment with the name of Duccio (dew'chi yo), but did not subsequently equal the promise given by this isolated genius. Perugia, where Raphael's teacher was long resident, became in art a dependency or connection of Florence. At this time there were no artists of great distinction in Rome, in Southern Italy, or in Northern Italy, aside from the Schools of Padua and Venice.[*] Rome, at all times in the history of Italian art, has owed her great artists to the surrounding Italian States.

It was from the Florentine School of the 15th century that the great artists developed who made the glory of Roman art at the beginning of the 16th century. As there was no later important development from the Paduan School of the 15th century, except influences on Venice, and as the Venetian painters only begin to assume importance toward the opening of the 16th century, it is clear that the Florentine art is that to which a summary view of the 15th century should especially attach itself. To appreciate its virtues and beauties, the student should especially consider the reliefs of the Robbias and of Ghiberti (147, 148). Engravings of these are free from the unfair impressions which engravings of colored paintings must necessarily convey. Of course, the word "Florentine" covers the Tuscan district of which this city was the capital and center, and the works of artists of the school wherever they were summoned in Italy.

NOTES ON THE ILLUSTRATIONS FOR ITALIAN PAINTING OF THE 15TH CENTURY.

(185 191, inclusive.)

In contrasting 185-191 with types for the 14th century, 177-184, the essential distinction lies in the effort of the 15th century to realize a naturalistic effect. In facial expressions, posing of the figure, and accessories of all kinds, this one distinction is the important one, however quaint the imitation of nature may appear in certain cases. Compare the backgrounds of 187, 189 with those of 177, 179.

In oil-paintings (Nos. 190, 191) the hard outlines, absence of shading, etc., are to be understood as characteristics of a school of art developed from the practice of wall decoration.

Considering that the school of art in question directly preceded the perfection of the 16th century (types 192-221, pp. 225-263), the illustrations may also serve, by contrast with these, to explain its merits, and the inventive genius of its great artists. Much of the science of this greater period was, however, laboriously developed in the 15th century, and lies hidden under the frequently quaint and sometimes awkward appearance of its paintings. For this science the works of

[*] The word "school" is used by common consent to indicate a group of artists centering about some one locality, to which a distinct style can be attributed. The "style" is, of course, a general resemblance resulting from local methods and tastes, which influenced all the artists of the locality, and so produced some traits of general resemblance distinct from the individual character of each particular artist. Sometimes such a style or school was produced by the individual genius of some one artist of such influence and popularity that others attached themselves to his studio, became his assistants, and reflected his peculiarities. In such cases the word "school" explains itself, and from these cases it has extended and expanded to the broader and more important sense, often covering an entire century or an entire district.

159. GHIRLANDAJO. THE VISITATION. From the Frescoes in Santa Maria Novella, Florence.

190. Filippo Lippi. Madonna, Florence.

191. Fra Angelico da Fiesole. Madonna, St. Mark's Convent, Florence

the sculptors are especially significant. The real founders of the painting art of the 16th century were Ghiberti, Donatello, Verocchio, and Luca della Robbia (pp. 203, 204). Leonardo da Vinci, Michael Angelo, and Raphael were all expert sculptors.

The most satisfactory representations of the Italian art of the 15th century are the reliefs of the Ghiberti Gates. This is not only on account of their individual perfection, but also because engravings of reliefs are more satisfactory illustrations than engravings of paintings.

ITALIAN PAINTING OF THE 16TH CENTURY RENAISSANCE.

LEONARDO DA VINCI (1452-1519).

The Transition.—It has been observed that the 15th century style did not develop till the close of the first quarter of the century. The development of the 16th century style slightly anticipates, in its earliest examples, the beginnings of the 16th century. Some artists of the older generation continued to work in the older style after the new one had developed. Others of the older generation, who survived, were more accessible to the new influences. In this case, the transition epoch has the complex and manifold aspects which the individual details of a transition naturally exhibit, and which are so strikingly absent in the rise of the 14th century and 15th century styles. Still, on the whole, the art of Leonardo da Vinci may be considered as an abrupt and rapid development of all that subsequently distinguished the art of the 16th century from its predecessor.

Leonardo da Vinci was a Florentine, whose birth-year falls just after the middle of the 15th century, 1452. His studies were not confined to painting alone, and in this art also he was given to exercises and problems distinct from the creation of works for the public, which occupied him for many years of his life. His greatest and epoch-making picture, the "Last Supper" (192), was not finished till 1498. This date, which so closely approaches the opening of the 16th century, allows us to consider the picture as the first great work of the 16th century style.

The "Last Supper."—For the interesting details of Leonardo's life, reference should be made to the "Lives of the Painters," by Vasari (p. 238). Leonardo had been for some time in the service of the Duke of Milan, Ludovico Sforza (loo dō' vee ko sfort' sä), when this picture was undertaken. It is in the refectory (dining-room) of the Convent of Santa Maria delle Grazie (del lay grät zē'ä), in Milan. In Italian frescoes, the individual figures are usually life-size. Here they are double life-size, and the composition has corresponding dimensions. The picture has suffered to such an extent from subsequent restorations, that none of the faces can now be considered as original work. Notwithstanding this damage, the general scheme of coloring and of the composition, is well preserved and of astounding effect. The original designs for most of the heads of the Apostles are at Weimar, in Germany; the original design for the head of the Saviour is in the Gallery of Milan.

Characteristics of the "Last Supper."—Both photographs and engravings of the "Last Supper" will show its marked distinctions from the 15th century style, for instance, by contrast with 187, 188. The overcrowding of figures usual in the preceding period, is replaced by a clear and dignified composition. The quaint and awkward aspects which it sometimes exhibited, are supplanted by a uniform ease of natural position and action. As far as Masaccio himself was concerned, his dignity and repose could hardly be surpassed (185, p. 249), but no one had attempted to represent the dramatic agitation and excitement of such a moment as the one chosen in the "Last Supper," before da Vinci.

The Battle of the Standard.—The "Last Supper" is the only wall-painting which Leonardo completed. A commission which was undertaken for the Florentine Republic in 1503, remained unexecuted, but part of the design of the cartoon which was made for it has been preserved by a later copy (193).* The decoration of the Council-room, in the Palazzo Vecchio (pä läts'sō věk'ě ō) (City-Hall) of Florence, was proposed at this time, and both Leonardo and Michael Angelo were commissioned with designs for it. Political troubles intervened which prevented the execution of the paintings.

The "Bathing Soldiers."—The design of Michael Angelo's cartoon has also been partially preserved by a subsequent copy known as the "Bathing Soldiers." These cartoons were publicly exhibited, and gave a powerful impulse to the studies of the Florentine artists. The final perfection of the Italian painting may be dated from them, as the "Last Supper" was remote in locality from the most active center of Italian art. A comparison of the illustration for Leonardo's cartoon with that for the fresco of Benozzo Gozzoli (187), will show its epoch-making character. The latter had been executed not many years before.

Rivalry with Michael Angelo.—As Michael Angelo was twenty-three years the junior of Leonardo, it occasioned the latter great chagrin after this contest, that

---

* Wall-paintings were previously sketched out in crayon design on cartoons; that is, on paper surface of corresponding size.

193. LEONARDO DA VINCI. BATTLE OF THE STANDARD.

his own art should have been approached or equaled. He was doubtless conscious that the progress made by the Florentine artists in general, during the preceding twenty-five years, was directly or indirectly largely owing to his own studies; in other words, that he himself had made the weapons for his rivals.

Subsequent Career.—A visit soon after made to Rome, found Michael Angelo also engaged here in important commissions, which were lacking at the time in his own case. It was only a few years later that Raphael's light also began to shine at Rome (1508), and Leonardo ultimately left Italy for France, probably because he felt slighted by the preference accorded the younger men, who had profited by his epoch-making studies.

Life and Pursuits.—This great artist was distinguished by proficiency in almost all the branches of science cultivated by the 16th century. Much of his time was also devoted to literary labor. His work on the theory of painting and of colors is still considered, in our own times, the masterpiece of related literature. He was especially distinguished as a civil and military engineer. It is probable that Leonardo's wonderful versatility explains the deficiency of important commissions in painting after the time of the "Last Supper." As he was actively engaged in many studies and pursuits besides that of painting, those who were more constantly devoted to the one pursuit were probably more quoted at the moment in connection with it. The Duke of Milan, who had been his patron, was expelled by a French invasion, in the year after the "Last Supper" was finished; and this personal misfortune which obliged Leonardo, as a man of mature age, to seek new connections and employment, is also an explanation in this connection. He went to France by royal invitation, and lived there till death in the king's service, but no important works are quoted for these last years of his life.

Portrait of "Mona Lisa."

—The most famous panel-painting by Leonardo, is the portrait of "Mona Lisa," in the Louvre. This picture was purchased by the French King Francis I. during the artist's life-time. The portrait represents the wife of one of Leonardo's friends. Her family name, Gioconda (jō cŏn' dä), has given a second name to the picture which is thus known as "La Joconde," "the joyous one," a French mistranslation, based on the family name. The colors in this painting have darkened to an extent peculiarly disadvantageous to photography. There are other famous Leonardos in the Louvre, but the whole number in Europe is small.

Technical Improvements.—These are apparent in all ways when Leonardo's pictures are contrasted with those of earlier date. The hard outlines and unshaded designs of the earlier Italian oil-paintings are supplanted by the arts of modeling, shading, and fusion of coloring which through him became the common property of later art, our own included. (Compare 187 with 194.) Even the photographs of his oil-paintings exhibit these distinctions from earlier works. A picture by his pupil Luini (lōō' nē) (194) shows the improvements of Leonardo's works in oil.

The year 1508, ten years after the date of the "Last Supper," and four years after the date of the celebrated cartoons just mentioned, was the time when Pope Julius II. caused to be undertaken the wall-paintings executed by Raphael and by Michael Angelo in the Papal Palace of the Vatican at Rome. The Sistine Chapel is the Pope's chapel in this palace, and here are found the celebrated frescoes by Michael Angelo—on the ceiling the "Story of Genesis," and at the chancel end of the chapel the "Last Judgment," which was painted under a later Pontificate. Raphael's work was the decoration in fresco of the Papal office and adjoining rooms on the third story of the Vatican. He subsequently decorated one of the galleries opening on the court about which the palace is built. Both series of frescoes were completed under the Pontificate of the following Pope, Leo X. Although generally quoted as the greatest patron of Italian art, Julius II. deserves this distinction.

Raphael's Period.—The time of these pictures corresponds, in English history, to the period of Henry VIII.; in Spanish history, to the period of Ferdinand the Catholic; in French history, to the period of Louis XII. and of Francis I.; in German history, to the period of the Emperor Maximilian. It is the time just after the first maritime discoveries in America and India, and just preceding the Spanish colonial conquests in Mexico and Peru. The period corresponds in its vitality and productive spirit to the somewhat later time of Shakespeare in England, which was largely influenced and inspired by it.[*]

Raphael was Born in 1483, at Urbino (ōōr bē′ nō), a city heading a small civic principality in central Italy, but his early instruction at Perugia (pā rōō′ jä) was under an artist of Florentine connections and tendencies (Perugino, see p. 250, and No. 188), and he lived himself at Florence some years, completing there his artistic development. His authenticated wall-pictures, aside from one fresco in Perugia, all date after the beginning of this Roman residence, and are all in Rome.

Raphael's Three "Manners."—His oil-paintings (panel pictures) are divided into three classes, corresponding respectively to his success-

* The matter relating to the general history of the Italian Renaissance, and to its influence on Europe, is especially in point here (pp. 13, 117, 118, 190).

194. LUINI. TOBIT AND THE ANGEL. MILAN.

196. Raphael. 'Granduca" Madonna. Pitti Gallery, Florence.

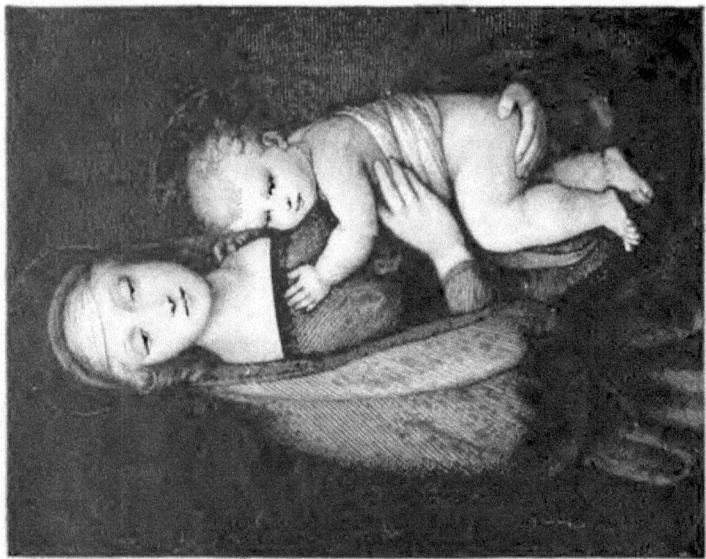

195. Raphael. Madonna della Sedia. Uffizi Gallery, Florence.

sive residences in Perugia, Florence, and Rome, and designated as belonging to the "Peruginesque," "Florentine," and "Roman" manners. On account of the great number of Raphael Madonnas, these styles are most easily noted and distinguished in this class of works.

The Peruginesque Manner exhibits in some cases somewhat childish or youthful expressions in the faces, and in its later works (196) has a peculiarly solemn and serious religious character, which reflects the tendency of the period in central Italy, remote from the more worldly interests and stirring life of Florence. Here established in 1500,* Raphael executed a large number of pictures during the two years preceding the beginning of the Roman period.

The Florentine and Roman Manners.—The Florentine manner is more vivacious and less serious than the Peruginesque. The large architectural commissions of the Roman period show their influence in the somewhat more staid and mature character of the Madonnas in the "Roman" manner. The differences are not always marked, but pictures like the Sistine Madonna and the Foligno (fō len′ yo) Madonna were not painted before the Roman period, and in these the distinction is quite clear.

Notes on the Raphael Madonnas.—The only Raphael Madonna in Rome is the "Foligno," or Madonna del Donatore (dōn ä tō′ rä) of the Vatican Gallery of oil-paintings. Its names are derived from the town for which it was originally painted, and from the donor (donatore), whose portrait appears in the picture. The introduction of such figures in paintings of the Madonna corresponds to the ideal stand-point of the Christian Italian art. The "Sistine" Madonna—in the Dresden Gallery since the middle of the 18th century—was originally painted for the Convent of San Sisto, in Piacenza (pē ä chěn′ zä), whence its name. The picture represents an apparition, or dream, in which the Virgin, attended by Saint Barbara, was said to have revealed herself to Pope Saint Sixtus IV. The most important Madonnas in Florence are those known as the "Granduca" (grän dōō′ kä) and "Seggiola" (sěj ō ō′ lä), in the Pitti Palace, and the "Cardellino" (cär děl lē′ nō), in the Uffizi. The "Granduca" (196) is thus named after a Grand Duke of Tuscany, who carried this painting with him on his journeys as his altarpicture. The word "seggiola" means chair. The same Madonna (195) is indifferently called the Madonna della Sedia (sā′ dē ä), or "of the Chair." The "Cardellino" Madonna is thus named from the goldfinch held by the Infant Saviour. A picture similar to the last is the "Belle Jardinière" (zhär din yār′) of the Louvre. The Madonna "with the diadem" is another famous Raphael of the Louvre. There are several fine Raphael Madonnas in England; that of the Bridgewater Collection is the most quoted. In the gallery at Madrid is the "Pearl"; in St. Petersburg is the "House of Alba." Several Madonnas are named like this one, from the house or family which formerly owned them; thus, the "Colonna" (cō lō′ nä) and the "Solly" in Berlin, the "Tempi" (těm′ pē) in Munich, etc. The Madonnas quoted are among the more celebrated, but in the entire number painted by Raphael there is not one which does not claim distinction for nobility of conception and exquisite workmanship. The "Solly" Madonna in Berlin dis-

* His first visit to Florence was in 1504.

pates with a similar picture in Perugia the distinction of being the earliest known work by Raphael. It was painted when he was about fifteen years old. The youth of the artist, and his dependence at this time on the earlier style of the 15th century, are apparent in it, and make this picture interesting by contrast with his more perfected works.

Of the Madonna Subject it may be said that it represented in Italian art not only the Virgin Mary in particular, but also the sanctity and ideal of maternity in general. Its constant repetition, so far from being wearisome, is an expression of all that made the Italian art beautiful and great, and of its thoroughly popular character and origin. In the Greek statues and in the Italian paintings, the recurrence of typical subjects demonstrates a constant popular demand in all localities, and through many generations, to which the artists responded. To express and meet this demand they existed. The great technical perfection in Greek and Italian art, the ultimate freedom and rapidity of execution, the indifference to the petty, trivial, and accidental aspects of nature, are all results of a training which was developed in connection with a limited range of subjects. The men of subordinate genius could at least copy their betters; for the subject itself, rather than individual originality, was the thing mainly sought. The men of greatest genius were not obliged to create their subjects. These were ready at hand, and it was only a question how to improve and supplement methods already practiced, how to add some few new elements to a conception already existing.

Criticism of the Raphael Madonnas.

The Raphael Madonnas are distinguished among all Italian pictures of their class; as against earlier ones, by perfection of design and color; as against later ones, by purity and dignity of feeling; and as against contemporary ones, by a peculiar grace and balance of figures and outlines. Symmetry of arrangement is a uniform feature in Raphael's art, and is the distinguishing feature of the great wall compositions which were the most important works of his life.

Frescoes of the Vatican.

The Papal office already mentioned (p. 262) was known as the Camera della Segnatura (käm′ä rä dĕl′lä sän yä tōō′rä), i.e., the "Room of Signature." Here are the four wall-paintings representing "Theology," "Philosophy," "Poetry," and "Jurisprudence"—to which round medallions with allegorical female figures (Sibyls) on the ceiling respectively correspond.

Traits of the Vatican Frescoes.—The great charm of these pictures is their freedom from tedious allegory, the spirit of beauty which tempered the abstract nature of the subjects, and the freedom of conception which refused to be bound by the more obvious mechanical expedients offering themselves. For instance, there is no effort to represent the entire body of distinguished theologians, philosophers, poets, and jurists. Only as many figures are introduced in each painting as will accommodate themselves to large proportions in the figures themselves, and to an easy and uncrowded spacing of these figures in or near the

197. RAPHAEL. "POETRY." VATICAN FRESCO.

298.   RAPHAEL. "OVERTHROW OF HELIODORUS."   VATICAN FRESCO.

foreground. The architectural symmetry of arrangement is varied by natural poses and well-studied diversity of action.

The "Poetry," chosen for illustration (197), is also known as the "Parnassus" (the Mountain of the Muses). Apollo, in the center, is playing the violin. This shows that he is introduced as a symbol of musical inspiration and culture for modern times, whereas the classic lyre would associate him with the extinct beliefs of Paganism. Around him are grouped the Muses. These also are designed without reference to external imitations of Antique conceptions. On the left, Homer is recognized by his evident blindness, and Dante by his profile and cowl. Some other names are indicated for certain figures, but it is evident, from the small number introduced, that a pictorial catalogue is not intended.

The Two Rooms Adjoining the Camera della Segnatura are also decorated with frescoes by Raphael. In the "second" room we find the subjects known as the "Overthrow of Heliodorus" (198), the "Miracle of Bolsena," the "Meeting of Pope Leo I. and Attila," and the "Liberation of Peter." The most important fresco of the "third" room is the "Incendio del Borgo" (199). The last three mentioned were executed during the pontificate of Leo X., who succeeded Julius II. in 1513.

The Story of Heliodorus (198) is found in the Second Book of the Maccabees, in the Apocrypha. It relates to the attempt of the Greek ruler of Syria to introduce the Pagan Greek worship into the Hebrew Temple. Heliodorus was the agent employed to accomplish this profanation. The attempt was foiled, and led to a revolt of the Jews, by which the independence of their State was established under the rule of the Maccabees, as High-priests. On one side we see the apparition described in the Apocrypha, and the overthrow of Heliodorus; on the other, Pope Julius II. is borne in a sedan-chair and, with his attendants, beholds the miracle. The picture is an allegory relating to the efforts of the Pope to protect Italy from the invasions of the French.

The "Incendio del Borgo," or Fire of the Borgo (199).—The Borgo was a district of the city of Rome. Tradition related that a conflagration had been extinguished here by Pope Leo IV. in a miraculous manner. The choice of subject had reference, as had also the fresco "Leo I. and Attila," to the name of the reigning Pope, whose predecessors of the same name were thus commemorated. The literary enthusiasms of the Italians of the Renaissance are curiously illustrated by this picture, which contains a group on the left representing Aeneas bearing off his father, Anchises, from the burning ruins of Troy.

The Stanze. — The above list relates to the noted works by Raphael, which are generally known as the Vatican "Stanze" (stän´zây).* The "Battle of the Milvian Bridge," representing the triumph of the Emperor Constantine over his rival Licinius, is an

* The Italian word stanza (stän´zä) means room. Stanze is the plural.

important composition of this series, in an adjacent department. It
was designed but not colored by Raphael.

"**Raphael's Bible.**"— On the same story of the Vatican, near to
the apartments just described, are the fresco decorations known as
the "Loggie" (lōd´jā). The Italian word "loggia" (plural, loggie) is
frequently applied in the plural use to a gallery of which one side
is open to the air. Such galleries surround the court of the Vatican
Palace on all its stories, but only the gallery of the second story,
facing one side of the court, has the decorations in question. The
wall opposite to the open arcades, which were subsequently glassed
in, is decorated with world-renowned arabesques which were inspired by Antique designs, still to be seen at that time in the ruins
of the Baths of Titus, and since destroyed. The walls are faced by
pilasters at distances corresponding to the width of the gallery,
thus dividing it into a series of square compartments, which are
vaulted with small domes. In each of these domes are four pictures—making in all a series of fifty-two—treating subjects mainly
from Old Testament history. The execution of the arabesques and
of these pictures was done by Raphael's assistants, from his drawings. The pictures of the domes are known as the "Loggie" pictures; also as "Raphael's Bible." They are famed for their graphic
simplicity and unpretentious, explicit design (illustrations 200,
201).

The Cartoons.—Another important commission executed under
Leo X. was a series of Cartoons for tapestries; ten subjects from
the New Testament. (One of these is illustrated at 202.) The tapestries were executed in Flanders, and were hung on the lower portion
of the wall of the Sistine Chapel, where the painted tapestry decoration is now seen (No. 206). The set was removed to Paris during
the French Revolution, and is now placed in another portion of the
Vatican. The tapestries show those deviations from the original
Cartoons which artisan copies made in a coarse material must
necessarily exhibit. The Cartoons themselves, being Raphael's own
work, have consequently a much higher value. Seven of the original
ten have been preserved, and are now exhibited in the South Kensington Museum, in London. They were formerly in Hampton
Court Palace, and were purchased by the English King Charles I.,
through the mediation of the painter Rubens. They had meantime
been for a century in Brussels, where the original tapestries were

109. RAPHAEL. "INCENDIO DEL BORGO," VATICAN FRESCO.

200. Raphael. Abraham and the Angels, Vatican Loggie.

201. Raphael. Jacob and Laban, Vatican Loggie.

202. RAPHAEL. CHARGE TO PETER. SOUTH KENSINGTON.

205. RAPHAEL. POPE LEO X. WITH CARDINALS, PITTI GALLERY, FLORENCE.

204. RAPHAEL. ST. CECILIA, BOLOGNA.

205. RAPHAEL. TRANSFIGURATION, VATICAN.

made, and where some subsequent reproductions were also executed, which are now scattered between Berlin, Dresden, and Madrid.

In the Church of Santa Maria della Pace (pah'chä), in Rome, is a single fresco by Raphael, the "Four Sibyls," a picture of great beauty.

The Farnesina Villa.—The list of Raphael's mural paintings is closed by mention of the series in the Villa Farnesina (fär nä sē'nä), at Rome. One apartment of the Villa Farnesina contains the famous fresco of "The Triumph of Galatea." This work is by Raphael's own hand. In the adjacent gallery is the series of frescoes from the "Story of Cupid and Psyche," executed by scholars from his designs.

Of Portraits by Raphael there are several fine examples. One of the most noted is that of the "Violin-player," in the Sciarra-Colonna (shä' rä-cō lō' nä) Palace at Rome. See also 203.

The "Transfiguration."—Beside the Madonnas and portraits, there are many oil-paintings by Raphael of great celebrity. His latest work, not entirely finished at his death, was the "Transfiguration," now in the Vatican Gallery of oil-paintings. The coloring of the lower portion is by a scholar (205).

Criticism of the "Transfiguration."—The composition has been criticised as having a divided interest, because the story of the possessed boy attracts more attention than the "Transfiguration" itself. This is doubtless because Raphael felt the latter subject to be beyond the powers of art. He, therefore, chose rather to present in a single picture, the two events described by the Bible narrative as having occurred at the same time—the "Transfiguration" and the episode of the possessed boy from whom the disciples could not cast out the devil while the Saviour was on Mount Tabor. The dependence of the Apostles on Christ's bodily presence thus symbolizes the dependence of His disciples on His spiritual aid.

The Picture of St. Cecilia, in Bologna (bō lōn' yä), is another fine illustration of the nobility of Raphael's conceptions (204). The musical saint is not playing on her instrument. It is the music of the angelic choir which absorbs her attention, and that of her companions, St. Paul, St. John, St. Augustine, and Mary Magdalen. Musical instruments which lie disregarded under the feet of this group, emphasize the moral conveyed—the music of Heaven excels that of earth.

Other Noted Oil-paintings.—"Christ Bearing the Cross," is a notable Raphael, in Madrid. Other specially notable works are the

"Entombment" (Borghese Gallery, in Rome); "Coronation of the Virgin" (Vatican Gallery); "Vision of Ezechiel" (Pitti Palace, Florence); "Betrothal of Mary and Joseph" (Milan), also generally known as the "Sposalizio" (spō sä leets' yō).

MICHAEL ANGELO (1475-1564).

The Frescoes of the Sistine Chapel by Michael Angelo are, broadly speaking, his only work in painting (206, 207).[*] He had no predilection for painting in oil, and his few efforts in this direction are regarded rather as interesting curiosities than as characteristic works of art. There is, moreover, only one finished panel picture in existence by his hand—the "Holy Family," of the Uffizi Gallery, in Florence.

Cartoon of "The Bathing Soldiers."—A memorable work which did not attain completion, was foreshadowed by the Cartoon of "The Bathing Soldiers." This was designed under the conditions noted at p. 258. The Cartoon itself was destroyed, but survived through a copy, subsequently lost, which was engraved in the 17th century.

Description of the Cartoon.—The choice of the episode is significant for the tastes and studies of the artist. In the wars between Florence and Pisa, a troop of Florentine soldiers had been surprised, while bathing, by a Pisan force. Michael Angelo's proficiency in the design of the nude form, and his interest in anatomic study, led him to select this incident for his subject, and the same proficiency and interest are equally apparent in his works of sculpture, and in the frescoes of the Sistine Chapel. The contorted and twisted attitudes which characterize this Cartoon, are also found in his sculptures, and in the frescoes named. This tendency to twisted attitudes is partly explained by the desire to exercise the knowledge of foreshortening, and develop the science of anatomy which he possessed to such a wonderful degree, but also resulted from an uneasy and misanthropic nature which found vent in these unrestful and violent explosions of creative power.

Character of Michael Angelo.—Michael Angelo is famed for an imperious and noble spirit, for an impatient hatred of the base and petty failings of human nature, for devout, religious character, and for a tendency toward the colossal and the grandiose in his artistic conceptions. These characteristics are as apparent in the details of his life as in the works of his brush and chisel. The passionate individuality of nature which his statues exhibit (pp. 204-211), is at once their greatest charm, and the feature which separates them

[*] The Sistine Chapel is the Papal Chapel in the Palace of the Vatican.

206. SISTINE CHAPEL, PALACE OF THE VATICAN.

from the simple and reposeful conceptions of the Antique. The reliefs of Greek sculpture frequently exhibit violent attitudes and subjects, and in this sense are remarkably different from the majority of Antique statues, but the general result of these Antique figure compositions in relief is always one of architectural balance and repose.

The "Story of Genesis."—In the frescoes of the Sistine Chapel, Michael Angelo's tendencies toward the sublime and the grandiose in art coincided with the dimensions of the work and with the subject chosen. The subjects of the "Story of Genesis," which decorate the ceiling, were peculiarly allied to his own individual sympathies and character (detail 207).

Subjects of the Ceiling Frescoes.—Panels of alternating sizes are ranged along the center of the ceiling with the following subjects:

The Creation of Light.
The Creation of the Sun and Moon.
The Separation of the Waters of the Firmament.
The Creation of Adam.
The Creation of Eve.
The Temptation and Expulsion.
The Sacrifice of Cain and Abel.
The Deluge.
The Drunkenness of Noah.

The male figures at the angles of the panels (207) are supposed to symbolize the architectural forces of the vault, or may be purely decorative adjuncts. They are in general remarkable examples of the tendency to twisted attitudes which has been noted.

The vault of the Sistine Chapel is constructed with a series of triangular recessions corresponding in position to the round arches of the side-windows. In these recessions are groups representing the "Forefathers of Christ," i. e., symbolical forms through which the Old Dispensation is represented as the preparation for the New. In the angular spaces of the vaulting which separate these recessions are represented, in alternate arrangement, "Prophets" and "Sibyls." The "Sibyl" type had been adopted by the Italians from the ancient historical mythology, as a personification of prophecy. At the four corners of the vaulting, where it descends into the angles of the walls, are represented the "Four Salvations of the Children of Israel"—the stories of the Brazen Serpent, of David and Goliath, of Judith and Holofernes, and of the punishment of Haman.

The Year 1508 has been already indicated (p. 262) as the time of the beginning of these ceiling frescoes. They were completed about 1512. No assistants whatever were employed.

The "Last Judgment."—Of much later date, and materially different character, is the picture of the "Last Judgment," at the chancel end of the Sistine Chapel. This was begun in 1534 and finished in 1542, under the pontificate of Pope Paul III.

Personal History.—As a patriot, Michael Angelo had meantime lived to see the overthrow of his native Republic of Florence (in 1530), and to witness the social revolutions and the decline of Italian civilization, which internal dissensions, commercial causes, and the invasions of foreign powers had combined to produce (p. 125). He himself had been the engineer of the fortifications and chief conductor of the defense of his native city during the devastating siege which prepared and preceded its overthrow (1529–1530). The tombs of the Medici (Nos. 152, 153) were conceived by Michael Angelo and by his time as the tombs of the Florentine Republic.

In the gloom which these disasters had produced, Michael Angelo undertook the "Last Judgment" in a spirit which conceived his country's doom as having befallen it in recompense of its sins and in judgment of its iniquities. With access of trouble and disappointment in life, the contortion of the human figure had become an almost constant phase of his art. With access of years, the exercise and exhibition of anatomic science had become a species of mania.

Criticism of the "Last Judgment."—Thus we observe peculiarities in the "Last Judgment," which are explained by earlier tendencies, and by subsequent personal and national trials. In studying this picture, some allowance must be made for the Italian habit of using bodily forms for the expression of spiritual ideas. It must also be remembered that where pictorial art was so constantly devoted to Biblical illustration, the necessary inconsistencies between spiritual conceptions and physical representations were more easily overlooked than they could be in our own time. There is not, however, any more of this incongruous character in the "Last Judgment" than there is in the "Paradise Lost" of Milton.

The Arrangement of the Painting conceives the Saviour as the Judge, and places the Virgin by His side. In the upper angles are groups of Angels with the instruments of the Passion, the Cross, and the Pillar of Scourging. A group of Martyrs surrounds the Saviour and the Virgin. To the left and right are groups of the Saints. At the base of the picture we see the Resurrection and the Ferry of Charon, the Angels blowing the trumpets of doom and a group of lost souls bewailing their fate.

Place of the "Last Judgment" in Italian Art.—The "Last Judgment" is the last great monumental work in fresco of 16th century Italian art, and closes the period which opened with the "Last Supper." The Venetian colorists alone offer a striking exception to the general law as to the dates of works of art of the great period. Venice alone continued to develop a great school of art after 1530, and it was the only important Italian State which preserved its independence after this date. Venetian painters, however, confined themselves to canvas painting in oil. In the case of architectural decorations, canvases were painted and subsequently fastened directly to the walls which were to be decorated. The

Venetians did not affect, or succeed in, the great monumental style of the Florentines. Harmonious and beautiful coloring was their special gift, and in this they were and have been unrivaled.

Before naming the artists of the Venetian School, it will be advisable to mention artists of other portions of Italy, who did not outlive the limit fixed by the "Last Judgment," and by the national misfortunes which immediately preceded its creation.

The Later Years of Michael Angelo were especially devoted to the construction of St. Peter's Church (p. 118), and to the completion of the statue of "Moses" (p. 181 and No. 154).

CORREGGIO (1404-1534).

The Most Important Contemporaries of the three great Florentine artists already mentioned [*] are, by common consent, Correggio (cor rĕd' jō) of Parma, and the Venetian Titian (tĭsh' ăn). Titian, as a member of the Venetian School, will be subsequently mentioned. Correggio died in 1534, and the limit of his life corresponds in time to the general rule outside of Venice.

The Baptismal Name of this artist was Antonio Allegri (äl lā' grē). Correggio, a small town in the civic Principality of Parma, was his birthplace.

Frescoes in Parma.—There are frescoes by Correggio in Parma, which have furnished subjects for attractive engravings (by Toschi), but his style of design and methods in color were more especially adapted to oil-paintings, and these are his most important works.

Oil-paintings.—Being portable, these paintings have been dispersed through all the Galleries of Europe. Thus Correggio may be known without visiting Italy. This holds as well of the Venetian art, which also affected the portable canvases. For obvious reasons the same rule does not hold of the Florentines, whose greatest works can only be seen in the buildings for which they were designed.

Correggio's Method in oil-painting was based on a use of lights and shadows ("chiar-oscuro") (chē är'-os cy' ro), of which Leonardo da Vinci was the originator, and which spread through North Italy from his scholars and his Academy in Milan. Correggio developed this method as a means to the representation of sudden expressions and rapid movements of face and gesture. In his conceptions of

* Raphael was a Florentine as regards his School.

religious subjects, he is not as serious or as thoughtful as the Florentines. In realistic representation of details, he went much farther than the Florentine art. His composition and arrangement of figures are not as symmetrical. His pictures are not distinguished by the varied yet balanced arrangement of Raphael, and the types of his figures and faces have not the same elevation and nobility. On the other hand, Correggio's paintings have a beauty and grace peculiarly their own, and in mythologic subjects especially, he is only rivaled by Titian. His pictures appeal readily to the modern eye, and there is no artist of the 16th century who will more easily find and hold modern admiration (208, 209).

Important Works.—Among many notable paintings by Correggio may be mentioned "The Holy Night," and "The Penitent Magdalen,"* in Dresden; the "Madonna della Scodella,"† in Florence; the "Mystical Marriage of Saint Catharine," in the Louvre at Paris; the "Education of Cupid," in the National Gallery of London; "Leda and the Swan," in the Museum of Berlin, and the "Danäe" (da nä´ē), in Rome.

OTHER 16TH CENTURY ITALIAN ARTISTS, NOT VENETIANS.

The Catalogue of Names and works belonging to the first quarter of the 16th century might be extended indefinitely. There is scarcely an Italian artist of the period who did not occasionally rival the greatest masters in certain individual works. There are many artists who are only placed in the second rank because of the supreme genius of their great rivals. Of these, Sodoma (sō dō´mä) (1480–1549), a resident of Siena; Andrea del Sarto (sar´tō, of Florence (1487–1531), and Sebastian del Piombo (pē om´bō) are especially noteworthy (aside from the Venetians).

Sodoma's works are rare, but he is distinguished by a most peculiar beauty of outlines and of color. **Del Sarto's** best work is the series of frescoes in the court of the Church of the Annunziata in Florence. No. 210 shows one of his "Holy Families." **Sebastian del Piombo** is especially famed for the "Resurrection of Lazarus," in the National Gallery of London.

---

* Engravings are frequently seen in pairs, one of which is from the Magdalen by Correggio. The other is from a picture, also in the Dresden Gallery, a little larger and a much more coarsely painted picture of the 16th century, by an artist named Battoni (but to us, of no great distinction.

† Thus named from the plate held by the Virgin, the subject is the repose of the Holy Family during the Flight into Egypt.

208. CORREGGIO. "THE HOLY NIGHT," DRESDEN.

710. ANDREA DEL SARTO. HOLY FAMILY, MUNICH

211. Giovanni Bellini. The Dead Christ, Milan.

212. Carpaccio. Presentation of the Infant Christ to Simeon, Venice.

The Beginnings of the Venetian School were connected with the School of Padua (p. 253), but diverged from it rapidly. As distinct from works whose mention belongs to the local history of Venice, the first important Venetian names are those of the brothers Bellini (bel lee′ nē)—Giovanni (jō vä′ nē) and Gentile (jĕn tee′ lē). These artists flourished in the later 15th and early 16th centuries.

Giovanni Bellini (1426-1516) is the more important of the two. Among the works of this one artist may be found some which have the harsher qualities and stiffness of the older style (211), and others which are abreast with the perfected style of the 16th century (213). His works are especially to be studied in Venice. Another artist of special note, belonging both to the 15th and 16th centuries, was Vittore Carpaccio (vit tō′ rā cär pätch′ yo) (212).

Venetian Color.—The Venetians had long been familiar with the gorgeous colors of Oriental decorative art, and their main occupation was the trade in Oriental fabrics and luxuries. Hence, doubtless, the development of that taste in color for which they have a supreme distinction. The climate and atmosphere of Venice also led its artists to observe objects rather in masses of color than in distinct outlines. Hence the preference for oil-painting in opposition to the more rigid outlines of fresco.

Giorgione (jôr jō′ nä) (1477-1511).—The first artist, in point of time, who reached the whole perfection of all the later Venetian art was Giorgione. His works are extremely rare. An important picture is represented by the illustration 214.

Titian (1477-1576), the great head of the Venetian School, was the scholar of Giorgione. His greatest picture is probably the " Assumption of the Virgin," in Venice. His leading picture in Dresden is the " Christ and the Tribute Money." In Berlin, the " Daughter of Titian"; in Florence, the " Bella"; in Rome, the " Venus Blinding Cupid," of the Borghese Gallery, are noted works. Individual mention is, however, at the expense of the pictures excluded from the list. Characteristic works are shown by the illustrations 215-217.

Palma Vecchio (vĕk′ yo) and Paris Bordone (bor dō′ nä) were contemporaries and, occasionally, equals of Titian in quality, though not in productiveness. Palma's most quoted picture is the "St.

Barbara," in Venice (218). Another illustration (219) is a fine example of the noble qualities of the Venetian School.

Tintoretto[*] **(1512–1594)** is an artist especially exalted by Ruskin, and with justice. The dates show that, as regards time, he is somewhat later than the artists so far mentioned. Tintoretto is distinguished among Venetian painters for his intellectual qualities. His execution was occasionally hasty, and occasionally lacking in the finish of his great contemporaries. Important works by Tintoretto are among the decorations of the Doge's Palace in Venice (220), where all the painters named are also represented.

Paul Veronese[†] **(1528–1588)** was the last, in point of time, of the great Venetians. His favorite pictures were immense canvases, in which, under the guise of Scripture subjects, the Venetian life of his own time was portrayed. Such are the "Marriage of Cana," in the Louvre, and the "Feast of the Levite," in the Academy at Venice. Among other important works in this latter gallery is the one shown by illustration 221.

During the 17th Century, the School of Venice did not flourish. The decay of the State and of art went hand in hand. Meantime a revival took place elsewhere, especially in Bologna and in Naples. Venice produced, in the 18th century, some exceptions to the general dearth of illustrious artists at that time (p. 223). In religious art, two painters of the same family and name, Tiepolo (see āy' pō lō), produced fine works, which do not, however, rival those of earlier date. Canaletto and Guardi (gwär' dē) were successful portrayers of views of the city of Venice.

NOTES ON THE ILLUSTRATIONS FOR ITALIAN PAINTING OF THE 16TH CENTURY.

(102-221, inclusive, pp. 257-207.)

The "Last Supper," by Leonardo da Vinci, has been included in these illustrations for reasons mentioned in text, although its date of completion preceded by two years the opening of the 16th century. In the arrangement of matter and of illustration, the precedence given Leonardo indicates his relation to the period in general, as regards precedence in time and general influence. Otherwise the order of arrangement has no reference to order of time (the painters being contemporaries), with exception that the Venetian school is placed last because it continued in a flourishing condition after the decline had begun elsewhere. Tintoretto and Paul

---

[*] The baptismal name of this artist was Jacopo Robusti (ro bōō' tē).

[†] The baptismal name of this artist was Paolo Caliari (cal yäh rē).

213. Giovanni Bellini. Madonna and Saints, Venice.

214 Giorgione. Head of the Madonna, at Castelfranco, near Venice.

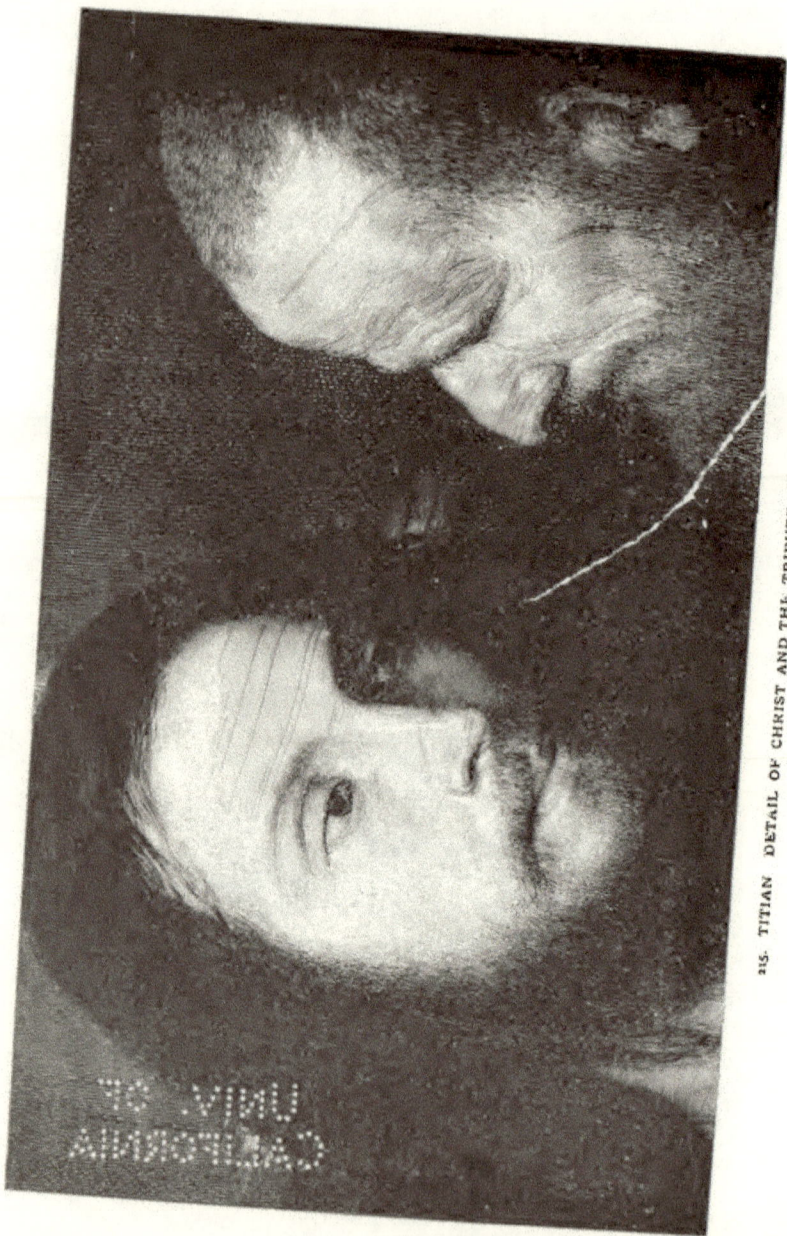

215. TITIAN   DETAIL OF CHRIST AND THE TRIBUTE MONEY, DRESDEN

216. Titian. "Earthly and Heavenly Love," Rome.

217. Titian. Venus and Bacchante, Munich.

218. PALMA VECCHIO, SAINT BARBARA, VENICE.

219. Palma Vecchio. Christ and the Widow of Nain, Venice.
220. Tintoretto. Mercury and the Graces, Ducal Palace, Venice

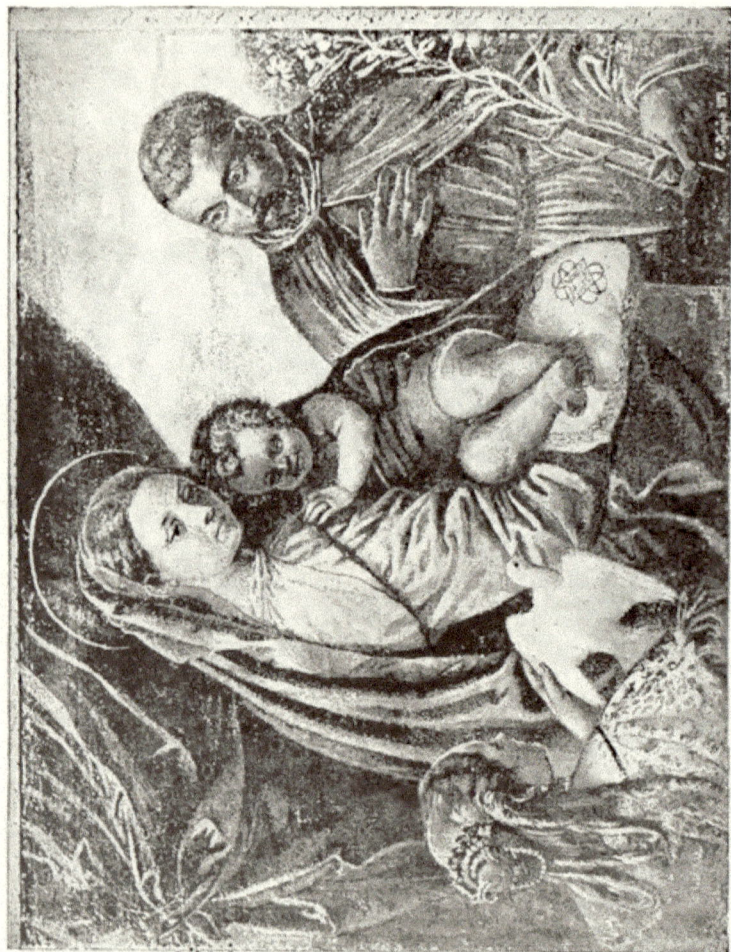

221. PAUL VERONESE. THE MADONNA AND ST. ANTHONY. VENICE.

Veronese are also placed last among the Venetians, because they especially represent the best work of the Venetian School in the later part of the 16th century.

Raphael and Michael Angelo are associated in arrangement with one another,
because they were the two artists by whom the great monumental works in Rome
were executed, and they are associated in arrangement with Leonardo, because all
were of the Florentine School.

A fair idea of the general distinctions between the style of Italian painting in
the 16th century and that of the 15th century may be obtained by comparing in
bulk the entire illustration 192-221 (pp. 257-297), with the Nos. 185-191 (pp. 246-
257). A fair comparison of the two centuries can not, however, be made without
including the pictorial relief compositions of the Ghiberti Gates in the contrast
(p. 200).

A summary review of the typical illustrations for the 16th century may serve
to show that its distinction is by no means founded on purely mechanical and
technical perfection, in which, however, its productions have been rarely rivaled
and never excelled—but more especially on a thoroughly honest, worthy, and dignified treatment of the most exalted subjects which have ever been represented
by pictorial art.

For the contemporary art of Northern Europe, see Nos. 245-249 (pp. 321-327).

ITALIAN PAINTING OF THE 17TH CENTURY RENAISSANCE.

SCHOOL OF BOLOGNA.

A General Decline of the Italian art, aside from the School of
Venice, had begun directly after the death of Raphael in 1520,
with the opening of the wars, in 1521, which were fought on Italian soil between Charles V. of Spain and Germany, and Francis I.
of France. The fourteen years which intervened between 1520 and
1534 (the time of Michael Angelo's "Last Judgment") witnessed
the death of nearly all contemporary artists who were not themselves affected by the decline of style which began for the new
generation. A most important episode and cause of this decline
was the sack of Rome, in 1527, by the troops of Charles V. The
Papal city has never recovered the loss of material splendor which
it suffered at this time, and the artists congregated there who were
dispersed and ruined by this disaster, never found a parallel center
of encouragement and support. The fate of individuals, as influenced by this event, may easily be followed in the "Lives" by
Vasari (p. 238).

The Siege and Capture of Florence (1529-1530) by the same
army (p. 282), consummated the misfortunes which had been
caused by the sack of Rome. The relations of Italy with the rest
of Europe were much promoted by these wars and foreign con-

quests, especially as the Italian States were by no means united against their foreign foes, and because each one of the rival foreign antagonists had allies and supporters among them. The decline of Italian culture is thus contemporaneous with its spread over Northern Europe (p. 125). Although the cupidity of the Northern Powers had first been roused by the more material aspects of Italian wealth and civilization, they could not resist the insensible influences of the Renaissance culture, which rapidly mastered the whole of Europe. We have seen that the history of modern architecture offers a curious illustration of this influence.

Nearly Three Quarters of a Century had succeeded the great period of Italian painting, which were an almost absolute blank as regards the production of meritorious works, aside from the School of Venice. Some of the portraits of this time, especially those of the Florentine Bronzino (brŏn zee′ nō, make an exception to this rule. The most characteristic name for this later 16th century period, is that of Baroccio (bä rŏt′ chō). His pictures are extravagant as regards pose and expression, and weak as religious conceptions—they are characteristic of the general style of a large number of pictures belonging to this period which are scattered through Italian churches, and which have never received attention, even from the worst subsequent taste.

The Caracci.—Toward the beginning of the 17th century, a revival of taste and of art made itself felt in Italy, which found its centers of activity especially in Naples and in Bologna. The School of the latter town deserves, as a whole, the pre-eminent mention. Three artists of one family, an uncle, Agostino (ä gŏ stä′ nō), and two nephews, Ludovico (lōō dō vā′ kō) and Annibale (än nē bä′ lä), of the same family name, Caracci (cä rät′ chē), were its leaders.

Their Scholars.—They were themselves more especially Academic instructors, and their own paintings are not numerous. Their scholars were more prolific and, as painters, are more generally celebrated. Three of them are especially prominent in the history of art, Guido Reni (gwee′ dō rāy′ nō), Domenichino (dō mĕn ē kē′ nō), and Guercino (gwĕr chē′ nō.

The School of Bologna.—The School is indifferently known as the School of Bologna, or School of the Caracci. It is also called sometimes the School of the Eclectics, or Imitators. These latter names indicate the self-confessed dependence of its artists on the

212. GUIDO RENI. AURORA, ROSPIGLIOSI VILLA, ROME.

225. Guido Reni. Sibyl, Florence.

226. Guido Reni. Magdalen, Rome.

227. DOMENICHINO. LAST COMMUNION OF ST. JEROME, VATICAN.

models of the early 16th century, and their effort to be universal
or eclectic in this dependence or imitation, and to combine the
virtues of the various great artists of the former period.

Guido Reni (1575-1642).—Of the three scholars of the Caracci
just named, Guido Reni was much the most prolific, and in some
ways the most gifted.

His Famous "Aurora" is a fresco on the ceiling of an apartment
in the Rospigliosi (rō spēl yō' sē) Villa, at Rome, of very effective
coloring, especially resplendent in the yellow hue (indicating the
dawn) which forms the background on the left, and spreads over
the painting from that point in gradually lessening intensity. The
composition is an effective decoration, although the details of the
execution will scarcely compare to advantage with the great works
of the 16th century. This remark applies to the original. As far
as engravings are concerned, the distinctions are not apparent.
Guido is otherwise well known for a large number of pictures,
several of which are used as illustrations in the subsequent notes
on the 17th century types (Nos. 222-226). His most universally
illustrated picture, aside from the "Aurora," is the fine portrait of
Beatrice Cenci (chēn' chē, in the Barberini (bär bā ı ē' nē) Palace,
at Rome.

Domenichino (1581-1641) was a more conscientious artist than
Guido in his nature and in his pictures. As usual in this period, his
more attractive works are rather from the field of mythology than
of religion.

His Noted Works.—A fine example of this class of painting is
his "Diana and Nymphs," of the Borghese (bor gā' sā) Gallery, in
Rome, one of the best works of the century. His pictures of a
"Sibyl" are known in several examples. His "St. Cecilia," in the
Louvre, is also a quoted work. The "Last Communion of St.
Jerome," in the Vatican Gallery of oil-paintings, is noted for its
conscientious and able execution (227).

Its choice of subject illustrates a general tendency of the time
to views of imaginary episodes in the lives of the Saints, whereas
the earlier tendency was, by preference, rather to Biblical history,
at least in the greatest masterpieces. The subject and moment
chosen in this picture also illustrate a general tendency to realistic
and tragic effects. These contrast again with the more sedate and
serene aspects of earlier paintings. Compare, for instance, the

motives and subjects of Ghiberti's doors. The pictorial character
of the work justifies this reference. It may be noted here that
paintings of martyrdoms, in their more revolting aspects, were not
congenial to the earlier classic period of Italian art. The illustration
chosen for Ribera (236) has this bearing for the new period.*

Guercino (1590-1666)† was the least important of the three
painters named, but is also distinguished for exceedingly fine paintings. His "Abraham and Hagar," in the Milan Gallery, is a well-
known example. As is the case with Domenichino, his most attractive subjects are mythological (228-230).

The Name of Carlo Dolce (dōl' chä) (1616-1686) is not attached
to any particular school, but it is one of the best known and most
characteristic of the time. He was a native of Florence.

Noted Works.—His well-known "St. Cecilia," in the Dresden
Gallery (repetitions elsewhere), may be contrasted with the picture
by Raphael (p. 277, and No. 204) as significant for the general
distinction between the 16th and 17th century art. The latter
rarely reaches the nobility of conception which is found in the
16th century, but it can not be denied that its pictures are beautiful and attractive. A Madonna by Carlo Dolce is illustrated as
232. The "Annunciation," or "Angel Gabriel," in Florence, by the
same artist, is also a typical example (233). The "Annunciation"
is treated in earlier art as an historical event. Here the subject
is indicated by a picture which is more satisfactory as a painting
than as a definite reminder of the Biblical account.

THE SCHOOL OF NAPLES.

The School of Naples is headed by artists who are more distinguished for their great mastery and power of technique than by
elevated art.

Caravaggio (kä rä väd' jō) (1569-1609) was one of its leaders. His
pictures are fine works of brush painting, but frequently ignoble in
choice of subject or in conception.

His Works.—Pictures of Martyrdoms are much affected by him,
and they are characteristic for his time, as previously observed.

* The real name of this artist was Domenico Zampieri (dō mē′ nē kō dzäm pē ā′ rē). The
nickname used is that by which he is generally quoted.
† The real name of this artist was Francesco Barbieri (frän chēs′ kō bär bē ā′ rē). Guercino
was the name of his birthplace.

228. GUERCINO. "FAMA." FRESCO, LUDOVISI VILLA, ROME.

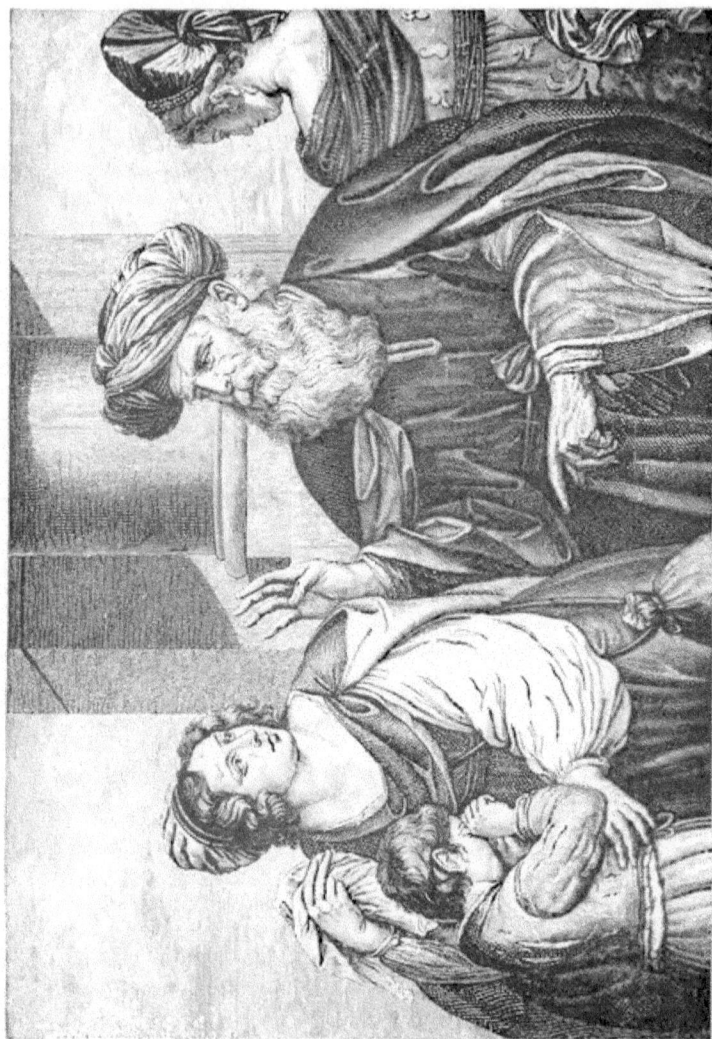

320. GUERCINO. ABRAHAM AND HAGAR. MILAN.

Martyrdoms are rarely represented in the earlier Italian art, because its good taste disliked the repulsive details which attend such subjects. Caravaggio's "Entombment" (237), in the Vatican Gallery, is an illustration of his fine technical ability, and also of the vulgarity of the types which are common in his pictures. His "Gamblers," in the Sciarra (shä' rä) Palace at Rome (repetitions elsewhere), illustrates the rise of a new class of subjects, distinct from the ideal tendencies of both Italian Mythologic and Scriptural art.

Ribera (rē bä' rä), also called **Spagnoletto** (spä nyō lĕt' ō) (1588-1656), was a scholar of the foregoing. One of his finest paintings is the "St. Mary of Egypt," in the Dresden Gallery. See also illustrations (235, 236). Ribera was a Spaniard, and may with equal justice be classified with the Spanish School.

Salvator Rosa (1615-1673) is one of the greatest artists of his time in landscapes and battle scenes. These are scattered through various European galleries. Two of his best landscapes are in the Pitti Palace at Florence. The sketch illustrated (238) is also in Florence.

CHARACTERISTICS OF 17TH CENTURY RELIGIOUS ART.

Typical Subjects.—More important than a catalogue of names is some knowledge of the general conditions by which the 17th century art differed from the preceding periods, and of the peculiar types which it produced. To the hints on this matter already offered some additional points may now be added.

Changed Political Conditions.—The Italian Civic States, whose rivalry and active political life had stimulated the earlier Italian art, had been supplanted by petty despotic governments of foreign blood or connection, ruling in the interest of the trading class. Art was therefore dependent on the patronage of rich and influential individuals, rather than on commissions of general public interest, as in earlier times. Architectural decorations were occasionally undertaken, but with one exception—the well-known "Aurora," by Guido Reni—few works of this kind achieved distinction.

Frescoes Replaced by Panels.—The period is mainly one of portable panel pictures on wood or canvas, as far as characteristic and important works are concerned. This portability explains the fact that the picture galleries of Northern Europe are so largely filled with

17th century pictures. The history of Italian art should preferably be studied first in Italy, as this preponderance of the later works in Northern Europe is apt otherwise to give erroneous views.

Preference for Heads, Busts, and Half-figure Compositions.—This appears to result from a wish to preserve a large scale of proportions, notwithstanding an average diminution in the size of the paintings. In the 16th century, half-figure compositions are confined to the Venetian painters.

The Madonna Type tends to heads or busts of somewhat sentimental character. The eyes are frequently turned upward, somewhat in the manner of theatrical photographs. Raphael's Madonnas have at once a more dignified and more unconscious expression, and this is the general rule for his time and for earlier Madonnas. Heads or busts of the Madonna (see 231), as distinct from the "Holy Family," or from the "Virgin and Child," are not known before the 17th century. The preference for the new type indicates a general tendency toward the realistic in details, and the sentimental or ecstatic in expression, which is almost universal in the religious pictures of the period.

Comparison of Madonnas.—Subjects of the "Holy Family," or of the "Virgin and Infant Saviour," are also treated in the realistic and sentimental spirit (232). The Madonnas of this period tend to portrait-like representations of actual models, rather than to idealized conceptions of maternity, or of the Mother of God. If the Madonnas of Carlo Dolce are compared with Raphael's (195, 196), it appears that the expression of the former is more on the surface—the motherly tenderness is exhibited by the outward action. With Raphael it lies in the nobility of nature and character, which is made apparent by dignity of pose and expression. Held in reserve, the effect is more permanent.

The "Ecce Homos."—In the representations of the Saviour, the now familiar "Ecce Homo" type, that is, of the head of the Saviour crowned with thorns, is a characteristic one for the 17th century (223). The subject is rarely seen before this time, and in such rare cases, is mainly depicted as the "Handkerchief of St. Veronica," on which the print of the Saviour's face appears. The earlier periods of Christian art conceived the Saviour preferably in His entire physical form and in relation to the historic events of His career. The sentimental tendency of the later period is again apparent here.

230. Guercino. "Sleeping Endymion," Florence.

231. Carlo Dolce. "Mater Dolorosa," Florence.

233. Carlo Dolce. The Annunciation, Florence

232. Carlo Dolce. Holy Family, Rome.

234. Carlo Dolce. Magdalen, Florence.
235. Ribera. St. Bartholomew, Madrid
236. Ribera. Martyrdom of St. Bartholomew, Madrid

238. Salvator Rosa. John the Baptist, Florence.

237. Caravaggio. Entombment, Vatican.

"Assumptions" of the Madonna and "Immaculate Conception" are also characteristic. Aside from Titian's famous "Assumption," they were rarely attempted in earlier art. The ecstatic character of these subjects explains their frequency at this time (265).

The Subject of the "Penitent Magdalen" is again characteristic for the new period, and for its sentimental tendencies (226). The single pictures by Correggio and by Titian treating this subject, are rare exceptions to its earlier absence.

Half-figures of Saints, or Apostles, are also typical subjects (235). Here again the point applies, that in earlier art the separation of a character from the Scriptural historical incidents through which it is known, was uncommon except in altar-pieces. In altar-pieces of earlier art full figures were the rule.

Half-figure Pictures of Scriptural Events and stories, are common in the 17th century, and were not previously affected, except by the Venetians, as above noted.

The Sibyl Type.—It has been observed (p. 281) that the Sibyl subject in earlier Italian art was one adopted from the ancient mythology as a personification of inspiration and of prophecy. The "Sibyl" of the 17th century is rather the portrait of an interesting model beautifully painted, as, for instance, in the picture by Guido Reni (225), than an attempt to realize this earlier ideal. The Sibyls of Michael Angelo, on the ceiling of the Sistine Chapel, or by Raphael, in Santa Maria della Pace (p. 277), are interesting contrasts.

Mythological Subjects. — In other mythological subjects (220, 222, 228, 230), the Italians had never been intent on classical or critical accuracy. These subjects were suggested by Italian interest in ancient literature, but were, notwithstanding, treated without reference to archæological considerations, and were rather excuses for beautiful paintings or decorative compositions than efforts to be consistent with Antique representations of similar subjects.

Italian Influence on Europe.—It was in the 17th century that Italian painting (both of this and of the earlier time) began to exercise a decisive influence on other European Schools. Thus painters like Murillo, Van Dyck, and Rubens exhibit many parallels, in choice and treatment of subject, to the points above indicated. For artists of distinction outside of Italy, study in this country had now become a matter of course.

NOTES ON THE ILLUSTRATIONS FOR ITALIAN PAINTING OF THE 17TH CENTURY.

(222-238, inclusive, pp. 297-313.)

To obtain a fair general idea of the art of the 17th century as a whole, the above numbers should be immediately associated with Nos. 250-268, inclusive, observing that the intervening illustrations necessarily make a break in the order of time. As regards Nos. 222-238, it must be observed that they have been chosen especially to represent certain broad contrasts with 16th century Italian art, and that they can not be considered fairly representative, as regards number and variety of choice. They have been more especially designed to represent the sentimental and realistic traits considered in the text. Comparison with Nos. 192-221 (pp. 257-297) will probably make clear the difference of taste in the 16th century. As regards conceptions of the Saviour, compare 219 (p. 295) with 223 (p. 300). For the Madonna type, compare 195, 196, with 231, 232. For the general attitude in religious art, compare 200-202 with 227, 236.

Carlo Dolce.   St. Cecilia, Dresden.

HISTORIC PAINTING IN NORTHERN EUROPE.

NETHERLANDS AND GERMANY.

Schools in Question.—The influence of Gothic architecture on painting in Northern Europe has been noticed (p. 237). Although the local studies of specialists reveal the existence of painters in all parts of Europe during the 15th and 16th centuries, those of Germany and the Netherlands are the only ones whose Schools, for these two centuries, are now generally known by large collections in modern galleries. In the 17th century the Spanish art, whose earlier work is mainly of local interest only, is the only notable addition to the Schools of the Netherlands, that of Germany having meanwhile almost disappeared. England first makes her appearance as the home of native painters of great reputation in the 18th century.[*] As for France, there are some few notable names scattered through these various periods, but her distinction begins more especially at, and after, the time of the French Revolution, at the close of the 18th century.

Distribution of Paintings.—In the double order of time and importance, attention must therefore be first paid to the Netherlands and to Germany. The galleries of Munich, Berlin, and Cologne offer, in the order named, the best large collections extant of early German and Netherland art. Pictures of the 17th century Dutch and Flemish Schools have been so widely distributed through the various galleries of Europe, that all of them offer many good examples. Dresden is the richest in works of these Schools, next to the collections which are in Belgium and Holland.

Relation of Netherland Art to German.—In the most comprehensive historical point of view, all Netherland art is a branch of the Germanic, and the modern Netherland territories of Belgium and Holland were actually portions of the Germanic "Empire" until 1648.

[*] Lely and Kneller, of the 17th century, were German foreigners.

In the Early German Art there was no question, as in Italy, of large fresco decorations and monumental paintings. Pictures were confined to altar-pieces and small panels of religious subjects, for Church decoration. The rivalry of the stained glass art (p. 196) was one element contributing to this relative backwardness, but there were other causes. Italy far surpassed Germany in the 15th century in wealth and culture, in the physical beauty of its population, and therefore of the types and models at disposal of the painter—and above all in the sense for beauty of form, which in Italy at this time closely approached that of the ancient Greeks

15th Century.—The Van Eycks.—In the 15th century the Dukes of the French Duchy of Burgundy had, by purchase and conquest, extended their territorial rule over nearly all the Netherland provinces. For these territories, which were in no way connected with France, they owed feudal allegiance to the German Emperor, but this allegiance was nominal. The "Burgundian" Dukes were really independent princes of vast wealth and possessions. Corresponding to this importance of the Burgundian Dukedom is the development in painting of the School of the two brothers Van Eyck (the), centering about the towns of Bruges and Ghent (in modern Belgium).[*] Quantities of the works of this School have been dispersed and destroyed, especially during the religious troubles and wars of the Reformation, and in the wars of the Netherlands with Spain, which inherited these territories in the 16th century, but enough remains to demonstrate a rare science and perfection in the paintings of the Van Eycks themselves. Their leading work is an altar-painting, "The Adoration of the Lamb," of which the center piece remains in the Church of St. Bavo at Ghent (finished in 1432). Smaller panels, which closed on hinges over the central picture, were decorated with paintings on both sides, so that, whether the panels were open or shut, pictures were visible. These smaller panels are an important possession of the Museum of Berlin (239, 240, 241). These and other paintings of the brothers Van Eyck are characterized by a wonderfully conscientious execution of minute details, by great warmth of color, and by a serious and noble conception of the subjects themselves. The precedence of these artists in the successful use of oil-colors has been noted at p. 253.

The School of Cologne was contemporary with that of the Van

[*] Hubert Van Eyck, 1366-1426; Jan Van Eyck, 1390-1440.

239, 240, 241. Hubert and Jan Van Eyck. Details from the "Adoration of the Lamb." Berlin.

242. MASTER STEPHAN. ADORATION OF THE MAGI. Central portion of the Altar Painting in Cologne Cathedral.

241. ROGER VAN DER WEYDEN. DESCENT FROM THE CROSS, MADRID.

144 HOLBEIN THE ELDER. THE PRESENTATION. MUNICH.

Eycks, and represents the wealth and importance of this city at
the time. Its greatest picture is the altar-piece of the Cologne
Cathedral, known to Germans as the "Kölner Dom-bild" (kel'ner
dome-bildt), i.e., the "Cologne Cathedral picture" (242).

The Kölner Dom-bild.—The subject of the central panel is the "Adoration of
the Wise Men." Panels which close over this, relate to the patron Saints of the
city, St. Ursula and St. Gereon. This painting (dating about 1426) has a truly
wonderful perfection of execution and purity of feeling which no reproductions can
approach. It is the work of a Master Stephan. A contemporary Master William
was also distinguished. Many works of the School are preserved in Cologne.

Roger Van Der Weiden (1400-1464).—The later art of the 15th
century does not rival the perfection of these masterpieces. Roger
Van Der Weiden (vīde'en) is a noted Fleming of the middle period
of the century. Characteristic works in the Berlin Gallery show
the small dimensions and stiff design usual in Germanic art of this
time, but they have the deep warm colors and devout spirit which
are also its characteristics. A painting in Madrid (243) is an excellent illustration of Van Der Weiden's art.

Hans Memling [*] is the most important name in Flemish art for
the later 15th century. His pictures are generally of small size
and remarkable for delicacy of spirit and perfection of color. As
compared with contemporary Italian pictures, they illustrate, however, the backwardness of Germanic art. The same may be said
of the South German artists of this time. Of these, Martin Schön-
gauer (shern'gow er) and Michael Wohlgemuth (vole'gã mõõt) are
among the most noted.

Hans Holbein the Elder (1460-1524) is a less quoted name, but an illustration
from his work (244) has been chosen as a good typical picture.

GERMAN PAINTING OF THE 16TH CENTURY.

Albert Dürer (dew'rer) **(1471-1528).**—The greatest of German
artists, Albert Dürer, was a native of Nüremberg, in South Germany. He was a scholar of the art and period just named, and
must be judged by the progress which he made beyond it, as well
as by actual worth. This actual worth is, however, very great. A
certain quaint and fantastic quality, which inspires much of his art,
belonged to his individual nature, and not to any inadequacy or
ignorance of methods. Dürer's works in oil-painting are not numer-

---

[*] Died about 1495.

ous, and among these his portraits are most renowned. His own portrait (246) is especially famed. He was especially devoted to the art of engraving, and in this field his productions are still ranked among the very greatest ever produced (245).

Hans Holbein the Younger (1495-1543), of Augsburg, in South Germany, stands next to, and beside, Dürer as the greatest of German painters. He was more successful in obtaining commissions, and has left a much larger number of works. His most renowned picture is the large Madonna of the Dresden Gallery, known as the "Meyer Madonna." It was painted for a Burgomaster Meyer, in Basle, whose family appears at devotion in the painting. The gallery in Darmstadt possesses a duplicate of this work. Holbein's life as a painter was spent mainly at Basle, in Switzerland, and in England, where he died, as court painter of Henry VIII. The gallery in Basle is thus an important center for the study of his works. Many others, mainly portraits, are in England, and represent leading English persons of the time. The "Meyer Madonna" is illustrated at 247.

Lucas Cranach (1472-1553) was a German artist (Saxon) of importance, subordinate to the above named, but known to history as a friend of Luther, and of Frederick the Wise of Saxony (248).

Limits of the Period.—Dürer died in 1528; Holbein left Germany permanently soon after 1530. Thus it appears that the dates which limit the productivity in Germany of her greatest artists correspond very nearly to those which close the great period in Italy (p. 282). The religious wars and social revolutions which attended the Reformation are an explanation of the sudden decline of German art in painting after 1520. It must also be remembered that the Protestant movement was long antagonistic to the pictorial embellishment of churches. This involved an antagonism to religious subjects, and these were almost the only paintings at this time.

In the Netherlands the productivity was not quenched so suddenly, but it experienced influences which prejudiced its value and interest. The style of the Italians was long imitated before it could be absorbed and digested. Meantime, an unhappy combination of unassimilated Italian traits with national characteristics was so detrimental to Netherland art that most of its paintings in the later 16th century are only valuable as historic memoranda, and for contrast with the later successes of Rembrandt and Rubens.

CHRISTO · SACRVM ·

·ILLE DEI VERBO · MAGNA PIETATE · FAVEBAT ·
·PERPETVA · DIGNVS · POSTERITATE · COLI ·

·D · FRIDR · DVCI · SAXON · S · R · IMP ·
·ARCHIM · ELECTORI ·
·ALBERTVS · DVRER · NVR · FACIEBAT ·
· B · M · F · V · V ·
· M · D · XXIIII ·

245. ALBERT DÜRER. ELECTOR FREDERICK THE WISE OF SAXONY.
Engraving on Copper.

248. ALBERT DÜRER. HIS OWN PORTRAIT, MUNICH.

247. HANS HOLBEIN. THE "MEYER MADONNA," DRESDEN.

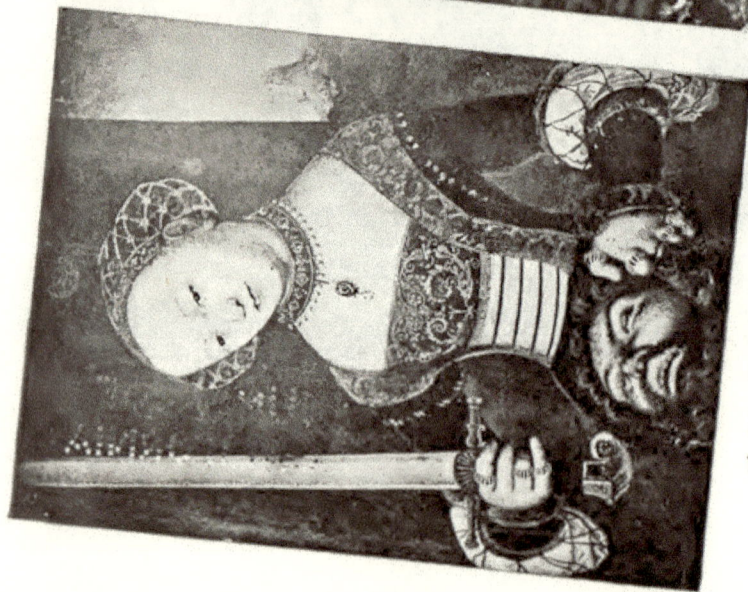

248. Lucas Cranach. Judith, Cassel.

249. Quentin Matsys. "Pieta," Munich.

Netherland Artists of the 16th Century frequently exhibit in earlier works the independent Netherland style developed from that of the 15'h century, and subsequently illustrate the inharmonious mixture with Italian traits. Their two styles are thus absolutely unresemblant. Among artists showing this transition may be named Jan Mabuse (1499–1562).

Quentin Matsys (1466–1530) was the most distinguished Flemish artist of the 16th century (249). Antwerp was his home.

17TH CENTURY DUTCH PAINTERS.

Political and Religious History.—At the beginning of the 17th century the Netherland artists had succeeded in acquiring all that could be learned from technical studies in Italian art without sacrificing, as in the 16th century, their own native tastes in conception and in choice of subjects. Meantime, the divisions of religion and of politics had separated the Protestant Dutch Republic (Holland) from the Southern Belgic Netherlands. (The latter remained a territory of Spain until they were returned to Austrian rule in 1713 by the treaty of Utrecht.) Hence the division between the "Dutch School," headed by Rembrandt, and the "Flemish School," headed by Rubens and Van Dyck. This division is not always distinct, and it sometimes disappears. The Dutch painters were, however, foremost in the choice of a class of subjects especially affected by the 19th century, viz., landscapes, cattle-pieces, and domestic scenes.

The Dutch Republic.—After separation from Spain during the later 16th century, the Dutch Provinces became the commercial carriers and sea-traders of the world. They were especially active in the trade with India and the East. A period of almost fabulous prosperity ensued, in which the common people became the patrons of a domestic art which contrasts in every possible way with the styles and school of the Italians. Technically, however, it had drawn much from these.

Rembrandt Van Ryn (1606–1669), generally known as Rembrandt, was resident at Amsterdam. He is distinguished from the Dutch artists in general by the larger size of his paintings, and by a less trivial class of subjects, and is noted, like them, for the realism of his methods and the absence of ideality in his conceptions. His subjects, when religious, have none of the traditional character, and are frequently lacking in the dignity which a traditional religious type is apt to possess. His "Christ," in the Louvre, and his "Samson," in the Berlin Museum, are instances of this class.

In Technical Methods Rembrandt continued, and elaborated the "chiar-oscuro" of Correggio (p. 283), but in thoroughly independent and masterly execution. His preference for contrasts of deep gloom and dark background, with some few salient points of bright light, was such that photographs of most of his pictures are almost useless as illustrations.

Rembrandt's Portraits are world-renowned examples of masterly execution, as well as of perception of character. Only three other artists of the 17th century—viz., Rubens, Van Dyck, and Velasquez—can claim to be his equals in portraiture.

Compared with the Earlier Italians, for instance, with Raphael, Rembrandt must yield the distinction which belongs to the superior nobility of their subjects and conceptions; although standing on equal ground as regards execution and science of design.

His Most Noted Painting is the "Street Patrol," at Amsterdam. The popular title of this painting, which is generally known as the "Night Watch," is an illustration of his preference for strong effects of light and shadow, as this title is attached to the picture of a scene by day-light. An important work in the Dresden Gallery is the "Portrait of the Artist with his Wife." All the leading galleries of Northern Europe contain important works of the artist. Among these is the one chosen for illustration (250).

Other Painters of the Dutch School.—The multitude of Dutch painters is great, and familiarity with their works is the best means to memorizing their names. Each artist was mainly distinguished for some special class of subjects, so that the mention of the list is a means also to the specification of important types of paintings.

In Landscapes, the leading names are: **Meindert Hobbema, Jacob Ruysdael,** and **Aldert Van Everdingen.** Ruysdael is especially distinguished for the mysterious gloom and tragic wildness of his storm-tossed skies and mountain scenery and for somber mood (251).

In Cattle-pieces, Albert Cuyp and **Paul Potter** (252) are the representative names.

In Marines, William Van de Velde and **Ludolf Backhuysen** are most quoted.

Genre Paintings.—Domestic, anecdotal, and other trivial subjects are generally classified under the French word "Genre." Many Dutch artists were distinguished in different specialties of this field. The most noted are **Franz Hals, Adrian Van Ostade** (254, 255), **Franz Von Mieris, William Von Mieris, Gerard Terburg** (253), **Gabriel Metzu, Adrian Brouwer, Caspar Netscher,** and **Jan Steen.**

The illustrations chosen for some of these artists will give an idea of the subjects affected by them. The pictures of the Dutch

250. REMBRANDT. PORTRAIT OF AN UNKNOWN MAN, ST. PETERSBURG.

251. JACOB RUYSDAEL. THE SWAMP, ST. PETERSBURG.

35. PAUL POTTER. YOUNG BULL, THE HAGUE.

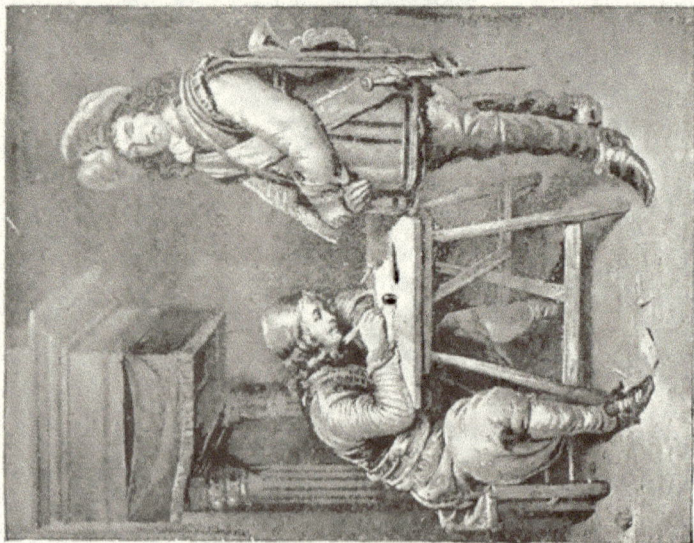

253. Terburg. The Trumpeter, Dresden.

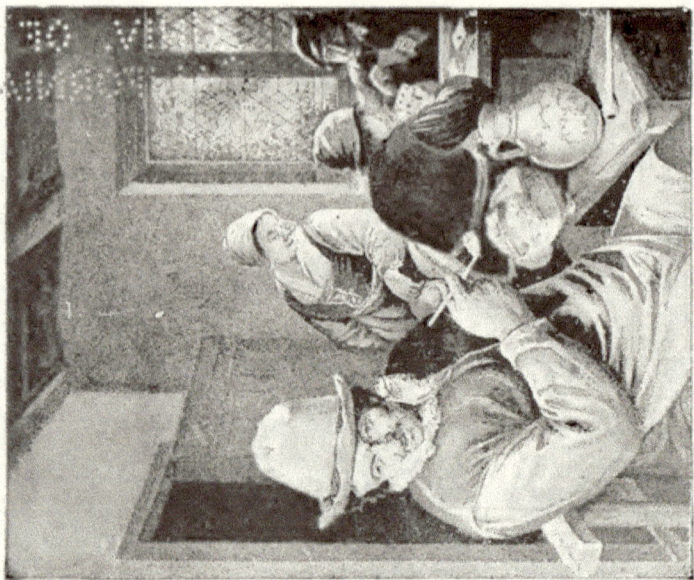

254. Adrian Van Ostade. The Smoker, Dresden.

255. ADRIAN VAN OSTADE. LANDSCAPE, ST. PETERSBURG.

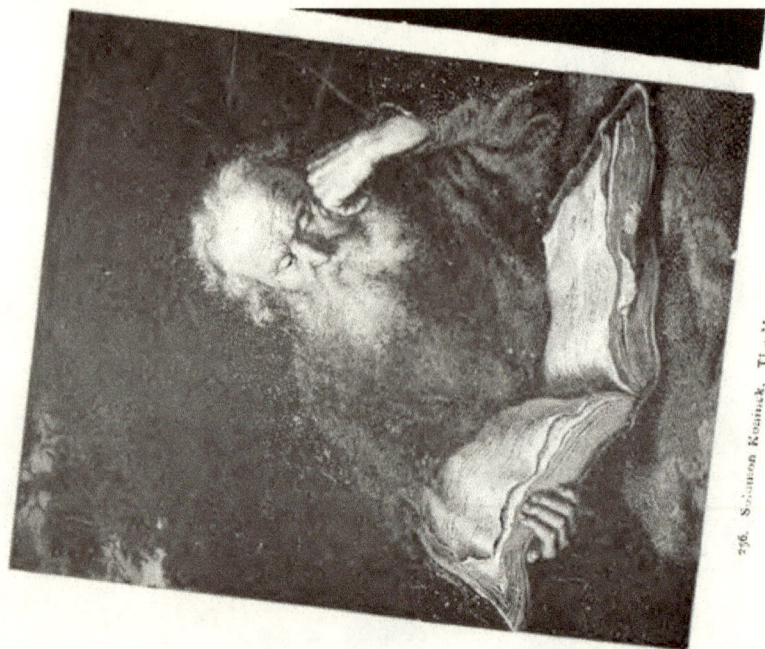

296. Salomon Koninck. The Hermit, Dresden.

School are generally characterized by small size, carefully elaborate execution, and apt preceptions of character. On the other hand, none of its painters rival or approach the great Italians, as regards elevation of subject and conception, unless it be the artists in landscape.

In Paintings of Flowers and Still Life, which are also characteristic works of the Dutch art, Jan David De Heem and Jan Van Huysum are most quoted. The latter belongs to the 18th century.

Adrian Van der Werff was almost the only Dutch artist who affected Biblical and mythological subjects. The peculiar finish of his pictures makes them available subjects for photograph copy, but this finish is cold and over-refined.

Battle-pieces and equestrian scenes have a noted illustrator in Philip Wouvermans.

Tavern Scenes are a favorite subject of the Dutch School. Adrian Van Ostade, already mentioned, an artist of German birth, belongs to the Dutch School by residence and studies, and is one of the distinguished names in this field (254).

Solomon Koninck (256) and Godfrey Schalken (257) are less distinguished names.

17TH CENTURY FLEMISH ARTISTS.

Flemish Painters achieved distinction in all the classes of subjects just enumerated, but, as rated by relative importance, only the following need be mentioned in a brief summary:

David Teniers (the Younger) was a noted painter of tavern scenes and peasant life (258).

Jan Fyt and Franz Snyders were noted painters of animals, hunting scenes, game, and still life (260).

All other Flemish names are, however, thrown into shade by those of Jordaens, Van Dyck, and Rubens.

Peter Paul Rubens (1577-1640) was an artist of remarkable fertility, surrounded by many pupils, and exercising wide-spread influence. His greatest picture is conceded, by universal consent, to be the "Descent from the Cross," in Antwerp, where he was resident. All the important galleries of Europe contain notable examples of his work, in religious art, in mythological subjects, and in portraits. Examples at 261 and 262.

Characteristics of Rubens.—In both Dutch and Flemish art there was an element of coarseness in the models who served as types for the artist. This coarseness was the result of life in a climate where much eating and drinking are essential to existence. Rubens' spirit was vivacious and exuberant, and his colors are ruddy and warm. Under these conditions, the Flemish models lost none of their own abundance of flesh and hearty life. Thus the pictures of this artist constantly find themselves subject to criticism by delicate natures who have not learned to condone this element of coarseness, or who have not seen the greatest works of the master. The authoritative criticism of experts is agreed, however, in placing Rubens beside Rembrandt and Velasquez, as one of the greatest artists of the century, when judged by his best works. The points which give him this standing, aside from his fine technical qualities as a painter, lie in his vigorous and powerful spirit, and in a serious nature which rarely deserts him in religious subjects. This serious element is otherwise very generally lacking in the religious pictures of the century, aside from those of the Spanish School.

Anthony Van Dyck (1599-1641) was a pupil of Rubens, and as a technical expert may be placed beside him. In the matter of conception he was by no means his equal. This appears in his religious subjects, which are weaker in sentiment. As paintings, these works are also remarkably fine, and as a portrait-painter Van Dyck is among the greatest of all time. The portrait of Charles I., in the Louvre, is a well-known work. The "Children of Charles I.," in the Dresden Gallery, is also one of his best. A good example at 263.

Jacob Jordaens (1593-1678) also belonged to the School of Rubens. The Flemish coarseness, which has been noted, appears to excess in his works, and they are only relished by those who can excuse this quality on account of the exuberant vigor and vitality of the artist. Jordaens was an excellent colorist and painter, but not distinguished for elevation of conception or serious qualities. A very fine Jordaens, "The Triumph of Bacchus," is owned by the Museum of New York. A characteristic picture at 259.

SPANISH SCHOOL OF THE 17TH CENTURY.

Political Connections with Italy.—Flanders, Naples, and Milan were all Spanish provinces at this time. Italian influences in Spain are easily understood through this political connection, which also reached in indirect ways over other Italian States. As with Rubens and Rembrandt, so with Velasquez and Murillo (mōō rēl′yō), the art was technically drawn from Italian sources, modified by the national and individual genius and surroundings. There are other

258. DAVID TENIERS THE YOUNGER. VILLAGE TAVERN, SCHWERIN.

259. JACOB JORDAENS. FAMILY CONCERT, BERLIN.

260. SNYDERS. LIONESS AND WILD BOAR. FLORENCE.

261. RUBENS. CHRIST AND THE MAGDALEN, MUNICH.

262. RUBENS. PORTRAIT OF MARIA MEDICI, MADRID.

263. VAN DYCK. PORTRAIT OF GUSTAVUS ADOLPHUS

264. VELASQUEZ. THE INFANTA MARGUERITA, LOUVRE.

265. MURILLO. DETAIL OF THE "IMMACULATE CONCEPTION," LOUVRE.

266. MURILLO. VISION OF ST. FRANCIS, MUSEUM, SEVILLE.

267. Poussin. "The Seasons Dancing before Time.

263. Claude Lorraine. Evening. Acis and Galatea.

Spanish painters of distinction beside the two just named, but none who are as generally quoted, or who are as well known in foreign galleries.

Velasquez (1599–1660), a resident of Madrid, is especially well known for his portraits (264). These rank among the greatest pictures in existence, but the Gallery of Madrid contains a number of fine pictures in other fields of art. His masterpiece is the "Surrender of Breda," in this gallery.

Murillo (1618–1682) was resident at Seville. His talent was first perceived and encouraged by Velasquez. His most generally quoted painting is the "Immaculate Conception," in the Louvre. The Gallery of Madrid is rich in his best pictures, and all the European collections contain good examples. Religious subjects were his preference, and they have no equals, for warmth of feeling, during the same period. The illustrations (265, 266) are indications of his style. Next to, or beside, Rubens he was the greatest religious artist of his day.

FRENCH PAINTERS.

Early Period.—Aside from names known to local and specialist investigations, French painting has not left much of renown dating from the 15th and 16th centuries.

The 17th Century is especially distinguished by the name of Nicholas Poussin (1594–1665).—With this artist, classical tendencies in composition and subjects are very apparent (267). His genius was of superior order. Jaques Callot (zhäk cä lō´) was a contemporary, famed for his sketches and caricatures.

Claude Lorraine (1600–1682), whose specialty was landscape painting, occupies an exceptional position in the art history of the 17th century. The province from which he is named was then, as regards government, a Germanic territory, although French tendencies and culture were already dominant in it. Claude is generally numbered with French artists. His residence was, however, mainly in Italy, and his influence was most apparent on scholars of the Netherlands. As an artist, Claude also occupies an exceptional position.

Claude's Landscapes (267) reflect the classical atmosphere of Italy in details and surroundings, and are distinguished for their effects of hazy golden sunlight. There is no other landscape artist who is so generally quoted by the history of art, and by popular reputation, and in his peculiar field he is unrivaled. There are important works by this painter in nearly all the European galleries.

Other Landscape Artists.—Ruysdael and Hobbema (p. 328) may probably be considered his equals in their own peculiar and different sphere. The whole century is, however, especially distinguished by its landscapes, and independent landscapes as distinct from the backgrounds of other subjects had rarely been painted before this time. In this field, many Italians of the period were very successful; for instance, Domenichino, in the landscapes of his mythological pictures. The name of Salvator Rosa has already been mentioned in this connection (p. 307). Rubens and Rembrandt were also very great landscape painters, although their works of this class are rare. The landscapes of Nicholas Poussin are also of great excellence.

THE 18TH CENTURY.

Historical Review.—The middle of the 17th century is, generally speaking, the limit of its best works in Italian painting. Not many of the greater artists mentioned, either of the Italian, Dutch, or Flemish schools, lived beyond the third quarter of the century. Important dates, nearly contemporary with the decline in painting, may be noted to advantage. This decline begins about the time of the opening of the reign of Louis XIV., of France, during the period of the English Charles II., and after the Peace of Westphalia in German history. This peace (in 1648) established the petty despotic sovereignties of Germany as independent States, and in all European countries this was the time when the courts of the despotic sovereigns became the centers of national life. It is true that these despotisms had been established in the interest of the trading and commercial classes, but they produced or reflected an artificial condition of society which continued during the 18th century until the Greek Revival (p. 130) and the French Revolution. Probably the deficiency of vital art during the 18th century has a related explanation.

Germany.—Some few names, aside from the greater ones of English art, may be quoted for this period. In Germany, Denner represents a minutely realistic art, in which the microscopic imitation of details is carried to the extreme pitch. Angelica Kauffmann and Raphael Mengs, Germans long resident in Rome, were superior artists; both representatives of the purer and nobler tendencies which were beginning to be manifest.

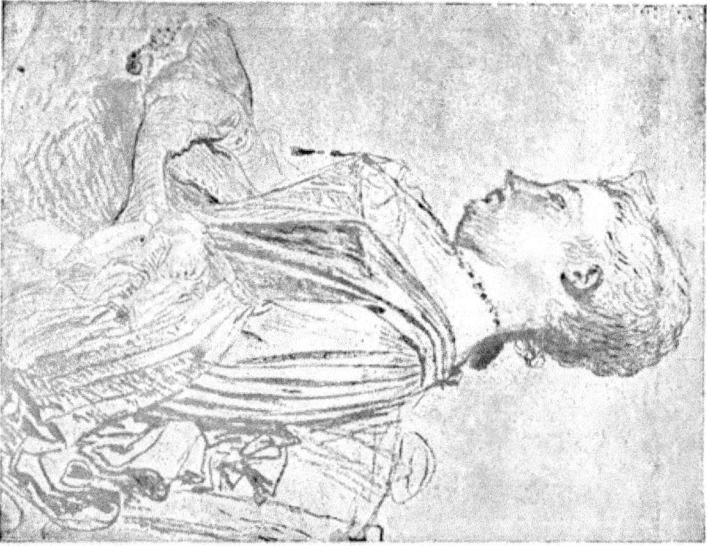

269. Watteau. Bust of a Girl (Drawing), Louvre.

270. Greuze. Head of a Girl, National Gallery.

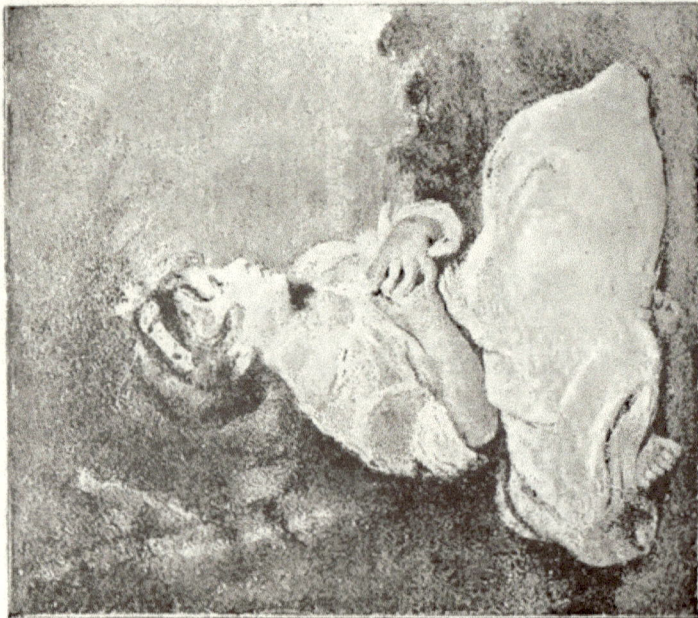

271. Sir Joshua Reynolds. Age of Innocence, National Gallery.

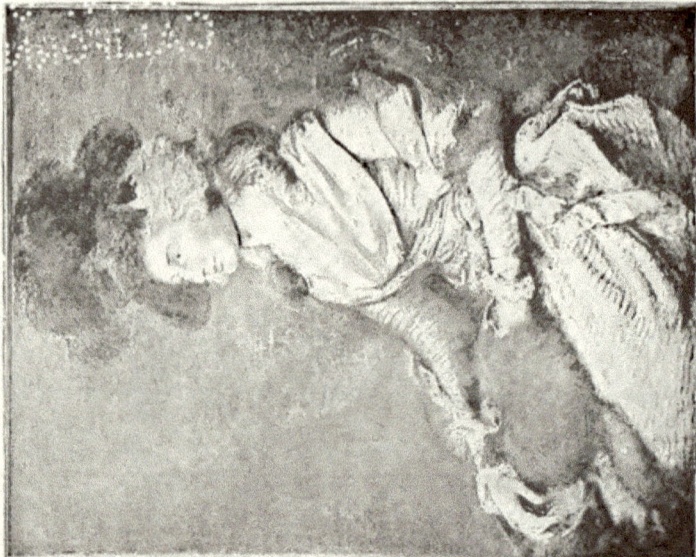

272. Thomas Gainsborough. Portrait of Mrs. Siddons, National Gallery.

France.—In the French art of the 18th century, Antony Watteau is especially celebrated (269). Most of his pictures represent the court life and court amusements of the time. Besides this historic interest, they are by no means destitute of fine qualities. The name of Greuze holds the next place in popularity (270).

Italy.—The Tiepoli,* of Venice, have already been mentioned (p. 290), with the names of Guardi and Canaletto.

ENGLAND.

Reynolds and Gainsborough.—England was the most important center of the art of painting in the 18th century. Sir Joshua Reynolds (1723-1792) and Thomas Gainsborough (1727-1788) revived or kept alive the great traditions of earlier masters with independent spirit and individual genius. It is for their portraits especially that these artists are renowned (271, 272).†

CONCLUSION.

The study of historic painting is a branch of polite culture which may, and must, be followed up without close reference to technical criticism. We may, with equal justice, occasionally criticise the grammar of Shakespeare, or the drawing of Michael Angelo, but the quality of the art is not affected thereby. With modern paintings, also, it is desirable that we should be able to rise above the elementary principles of technical instruction, that we should understand how to look for ideas, how to weigh the spirit of the work. In order to aim at, or reach, this standpoint in a spirit of modesty, of catholicity, of forbearance, and of appreciation, the preliminary study of historic art is an almost essential or highly desirable preparation.

NOTES ON THE ILLUSTRATIONS FOR HISTORIC PAINTING IN NORTHERN EUROPE.

(239-272, inclusive; pp. 315-351.)

For the 15th century, see Nos. 239-244. For the 16th century, see Nos. 245-249. For the 17th century, see Nos. 252-268. For the 18th century, see Nos. 269-272.

* Plural of Tiepolo.
† One of the very finest works of Sir Joshua is in the Metropolitan Museum, N. Y.

NINETEENTH CENTURY PAINTING.

In all summaries of important subjects where space is restricted and the details are numerous, the first thing to consider is the perspective of the subject as a whole. We need to maintain such a balance in the presentation of the facts that the most important do not escape us in the multitude of details. In condensed summaries regarding modern art, our task is especially difficult, and the arrangement of facts must be carefully considered. The names of many painters claim equal attention, if strict justice is to be done. American art deserves special attention from Americans. In addition, each European country must have some special mention. We shall, therefore, adopt the following plan of treatment.

First, the broadest and most important facts in the history of modern painting will be sketched. The claims of American art will next receive attention. Then, a brief summary regarding important artists, not previously mentioned, will be given.

Although all divisions either of general history, or of art history, according to centuries, are to some extent arbitrary, the beginning of the 19th century affords a fairly definite starting-point for an account of modern painting. At this time, the French Revolution and the events which centered around it were controlling factors, not only in general history, but also to some extent in the history of Art. The breaking down of aristocratic and social distinctions, and the gift of legal equality to all citizens, were the inspiring ideas of all that was good in this Revolution, and these ideas continued to make their way over Europe under the ascendency of Bonaparte, whose military despotism continued to represent all the essential ideas of the Revolution and contributed very much to their spread beyond France. The political ascendency of France in Europe was opposed by England, which represented conservative resistance to the excesses of the Revolution and to the personal ambition of Bonaparte, without ultimately antagonizing the social and intellectual changes which were going on in Europe. These had, in fact, as far as liberal government is concerned, been so far especially active in Great Britain. But if the openly manifest political and material forces of Europe are seen in their greatest activity in the rivalry of France and England, Germany played a still more important part in the intellectual movement of the period, and in the later part of the 18th century produced the greatest leaders in literature, in music, and in science. Now the history of art is only a reflex of the society which produces it, and it is no accident that we find in the three countries of Germany, England and France the first important activity of 19th century painting.

The activity and the success of Germany were however greatest in literature and music. In the arts of design her studies were especially those of the antiquarian and historian, and in this field she then outranked every other country, and has since continued to be preëminent. France, in the time of Bonaparte, had need of painters to celebrate his victories, to feed the French love of military glory, and to represent the great historic characters of his time. But of all these countries England was in closest touch with traditions of the older historic painters; for in the 18th century the English School undoubtedly took the lead in European art. In the early 19th century it still held this position.

ENGLISH PAINTING — FIRST QUARTER OF THE 19th CENTURY.

If we wish to present in a few words a clear idea of 19th century painting, we must begin by accenting the superiority of English art during the first thirty years of the century. The names of Constable and Turner certainly outshine those of all Continental artists during that time. In their own department of landscape painting, they may also be regarded as the rivals or equals of their great predecessors of the 17th century. Next to them in importance comes the name of Etty, while Benjamin Robert Haydon deserves mention for his powers as a draughtsman. Sir David Wilkie was another important artist.

John Constable was born at East Bergholt in Suffolk in 1776. His predilections for studying design were not encouraged by his father, who was a yeoman farmer and miller. His first instruction in this field was obtained from a plumber. It is said that his wide knowledge of atmospheric effects was acquired in one of his father's windmills, in which he was employed as a workman. His first encouragement as an artist came from a certain Sir George Beaumont, who owned a very important painting by Claude Lorrain. It is certain that Constable's early work was inspired by Claude, by Ruysdael, and by the earlier English landscape painter, Wilson. Constable began art study in London in 1795, but was obliged to return to work in his father's office two years later. In 1799 he returned to London and to the study of art, and in 1802 he exhibited his first picture. It was, however, nearly forty years after beginning art studies that he sold a picture outside of his circle of friends and immediate acquaintances, and late in life he was still obliged to depend on portrait-painting for a living, although landscape was always his true field. His pronounced success as an artist in the estimation of later criticism dates from his picture of "Dedham Vale," painted in 1811. It was on the continent of Europe that Constable found the greatest appreciation. Eugène Delacroix and the French Romantic School were outspoken in their admiration of him. He was first known in France by a painting, "The Hay-wain," exhibited at the Paris Salon of 1821 by a French purchaser, and he subsequently became still more celebrated by the success of his "White Horse," exhibited at Lille in 1825.

Constable was made a Royal Academician in 1829, but died in 1837 without having achieved either fame or fortune in his own country. Although disparaged by Mr. Ruskin, his standing is now indisputably equal to that of Turner. Two of his greatest pictures were presented to the Louvre in 1873. He is well represented in the National Gallery of London, and in the South Kensington Museum. Two of his greatest works are in the Metropolitan Museum of New York. One of these, "A Lock on the Stour," was exhibited at the Royal Academy in 1824 and was sold on the first day of the exhibition for $775. The other painting is called "The Valley Farm."

J. M. W. Turner.—It has just been said that Constable cannot be considered the inferior of Turner, but there is no doubt that as a matter of popular fame and of every-day popular quotation, the name of Turner is the most famous in the annals of English art. His complete name was Joseph Mallord William, but he signed himself invariably as J. M. W., and is thus generally known. Turner was born in London in 1775. His father was a barber. The boy had no advantages in the way of book education. His English was ungrammatical throughout his life. He never knew a foreign language and had the slightest possible acquaintance with history and literature, as far as the student's point of view is concerned. In person he was unattractive, in manners he was almost boorish, as regards social intercourse he always lived a life of complete isolation. This is the man who left a fortune of $600,000 at his death, for the support of decayed artists, and bequeathed more than one hundred of his own pictures to the British Nation. Most of these pictures were worth large sums on the open market, and many of them he had himself repurchased from the original buyers with a view to this bequest.

Turner acquired fame early in life. He was recognized by the Royal Academy and was made an associate member as early as 1799, and was elected to full membership four years later. We may explain this early success by noting that Turner's early work did not exhibit the imaginative daring of his later life. It was, on the contrary, rather commonplace, and not calculated to rouse that jealousy on the part of inferior men which is generally the real obstacle to the success of a great artist. Having a sure standing, to begin with, he continued throughout his life to hold the highest rank, not only in the estimation of critics like Ruskin, but also in the esteem of his fellow artists and of the picture-buying public. It was certainly the power of genius and of imagination which thus conquered the world, in spite of social and personal disadvantages. But this genius was not simply that of imaginative power; it was also the genius of dogged hard work, of pitiful economy, of slavish labor, of constant self-denial, and of patient observation. Turner's early artistic work was mainly that of a hack illustrator employed to do topographical illustration for magazines, and in this occupation, which led him to visit many parts of England on foot, he acquired his wide experience with visible nature. He subsequently gave much attention to the works of the older landscape masters, but always with the idea of rivalling or excelling them, rather than for the purpose of imitation. In spite of the roughness of his manners and his indifference to appearances, he had a kind heart, in evidence of which many touching incidents are related, and the general nobility of his character is apparent in the peculiar disposition made by his will of his fortune

173 JOHN CONSTABLE. THE CORN FIELD.

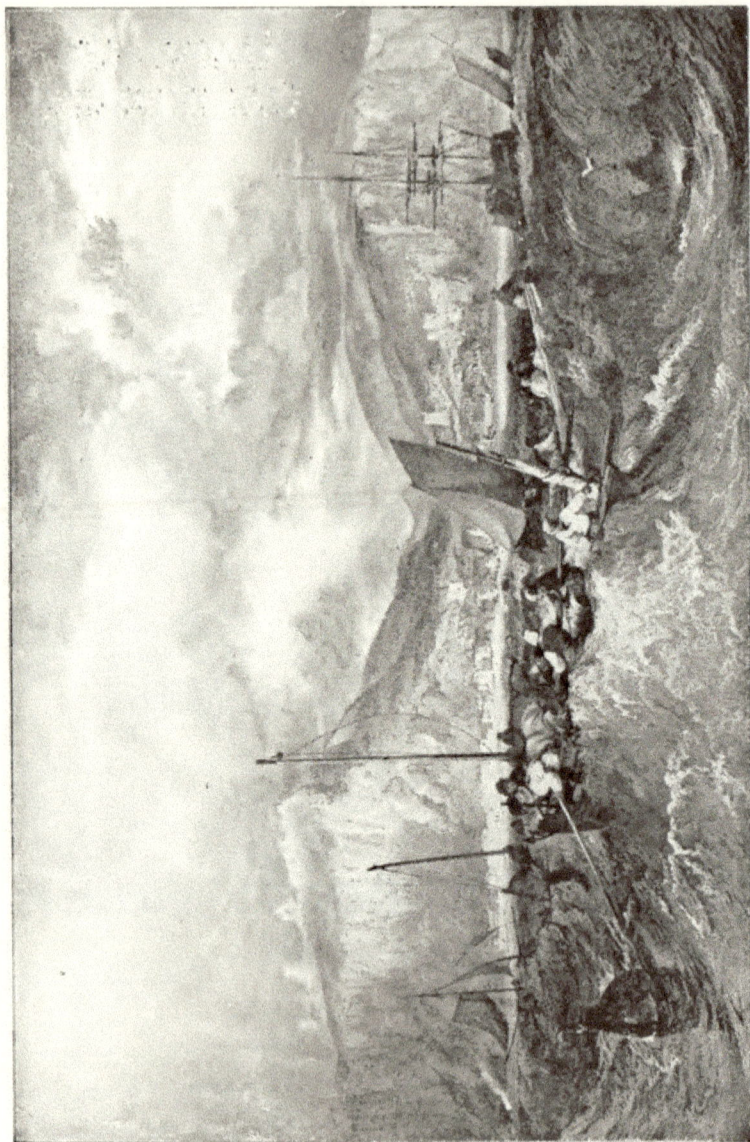

274. J. M. W. TURNER. HASTINGS.

and of the large collection which he had made of his own pictures. He died in 1851. After 1845 his works showed a degeneration in quality due to old age and possibly to his interest in problems of color and atmospheric effect which are more or less beyond the capacities of pictorial art. Owing to the bequest mentioned, the largest collection of Turner's work is that in the National Gallery of London, but there are very fine examples in the Metropolitan Museum and in the Lenox Library of New York.

The Metropolitan Museum purchased in 1896 the magnificent Turner known as the "Whale Ship," or "The Good Ship Erebus." The other great Turner of this Museum is a view of "Saltash," with the river Tamar in the foreground. The "Slave Ship," now owned by the Boston Museum of Fine Arts, is a noted picture, but not one of the best. Ruskin's "Modern Painters" is a work in five volumes largely devoted to the laudation of Turner. This whole work developed from an essay on Turner's greatness. Turner was proficient in water colors, and in etching and engraving, as well as in oil-painting. His "Liber Studiorum" is a series of sketches published between 1807 and 1819, which were professedly issued in rivalry of a similar work of Claude Lorrain, the "Liber Veritatis." It is known that prints from these plates were, at the time of issue, so little valued that some of them were used for lighting fires. They are now worth $1000 apiece.

As regards the points of relation and of contrast in Turner and Constable, it may be said that both were masters of design, and of broad and effective method, and that both were men of great imaginative and intellectual capacity, but Constable was more evenly successful as a colorist, and more strictly attentive to the reproduction of what the eye actually sees. Turner, on the other hand, was rather bent on the use of the matter-of-fact as a starting-point for purely imaginative conceptions. In these imaginative creations he was not uniformly successful from the standpoint of color harmony in a decorative sense; but the masterly quality of his execution as regards design is utterly beyond cavil. So are the true poetic insight and imaginative power of his art. In the numerous cases where his color scheme is irreproachable it is not easy to consider any other landscape or marine painting as superior to Turner's.

William Etty takes the third place in order of distinction among the English painters of the early nineteenth century. Historical compositions and figure pieces rather than landscape were his specialty. As a colorist pure and simple he has had no English superior or rival. His best works are in the National Gallery of Scotland, and it was the Scottish Academy which first discerned his genius. He was born at York in 1787. His father was a miller and baker. He began life as an apprentice to a printer in Hull, in which situation he spent seven years. Although he began work as an art student in London in 1806, he did not achieve any success with his exhibited pictures until 1820, and was not elected a member of the Academy until 1824.

Etty visited Italy on two occasions, and was a faithful student of the old Venetian painters. In his later life he was successful in obtaining appreciation and commissions, and was able, in the year before his death, to make a collection exhibit of his works in London. He died in 1849. The finest Etty in the United States is owned by Mr. Henry T. Chapman of Brooklyn. In London the National Gallery and the South Kensington Museum possess good examples.

Benjamin Robert Haydon was born at Plymouth in 1786. His father was a bookseller, stationer, and publisher. The literary tastes which the son thus imbibed remained with him through life. Haydon's associations with men of letters were subsequently wide-spread and intimate ; for example, with Sir Walter Scott, with Leigh Hunt, and with Wordsworth. The biography published by Haydon's son, which contains his correspondence and table-talk, is the most valuable extant work for a general knowledge of the literary celebrities of that day. Sir Joshua Reynolds had once attended the school in Plymouth at which Haydon was educated, and on the ceiling of the school-room there was a sketch in burnt-cork by Reynolds, to which the boy gave constant attention. He was also drawn to the study of art by the perusal of Reynolds' lectures.

Haydon began studies at the Royal Academy in London in 1804. In 1809 his picture of "Dentatus" was excluded from the main exhibition of the Royal Academy and was hung in a small ante-room. This was the beginning of a quarrel with that body which lasted through his life. About the same time his great interest in the Elgin Marbles, which had recently been brought to London, involved him in controversy with the fashionable critics of the day. This artist was for several years, and until 1815, the sole English appreciator of Phidias. The subsequent purchase of the Elgin Marbles for the British Museum vindicated his judgment, but did not win back to him the friends he had lost by this controversy. His pictures were generally great successes as exhibition pieces, and for several of them he received very high prices, but he was, notwithstanding, always involved in debt and never achieved pecuniary independence. His financial troubles ultimately drove him to suicide, 1846.

Haydon's tragic life and fate were due to a somewhat imperious disposition, and to an impatience of neglect or opposition. He placed a very high estimate on his own abilities, and in this he was undoubtedly right as regards his powers as a draughtsman. Few men since Michael Angelo have possessed equal possibilities as regards mastery of the figure ; but his accessible pictures are in other respects not such as to make his failure in life incomprehensible. His "Entry of Christ into Jerusalem" is now owned by the Cincinnati Museum of Fine Arts. It was for many years in Philadelphia. His "Resurrection of Lazarus" is a large canvas in the National Gallery. His best work is said to be the "Judgment of Solomon" in the Ashburton Collection.

David Wilkie was the son of a Scotch clergyman, and was born at Cults, in Fifeshire, in 1785. At school he used to barter sketches for slate-pencils and mar-

bles, and although his strong bent for design was combatted by his father, it led
to his beginning art study in Edinburgh in 1799.

Wilkie exhibited his "Village Politicians" at the Royal Academy
in London in 1806, and from this time till his death he enjoyed a
career of uninterrupted success. The scope of his art is well described by the titles of his pictures, and we will therefore mention
a series, all of which have become famous through engravings.
Such are the "Card Players," "Rent Day," "Blind Man's Buff,"
"Reading the Will," "The Blind Fiddler," etc. Wilkie's forte, as
here indicated, was the study of every-day humble life, especially
from its humorous or serio-comic side. His pictures are generally
crowded with figures of small dimensions, of which each one is a
study of character. His execution was minute and conscientious,
rather than powerful, but was not ill-adapted to the nature of his
subjects. The matter of his art is well represented by the engravings of it which have been so popular. He was a student and con-
tinuer of the old Dutch and Flemish genre-painters, especially of
Teniers and Ostade, but not a wholly brilliant rival of these painters
in matters of execution.

Wilkie received 1200 guineas, in 1820, from Lord Wellington for his picture
of "The Chelsea Pensioners listening to the News of Waterloo." In later life his
opportunities for foreign travel, and contact with the masterpieces of Spanish and
Italian art, led to a change of style, tending to more ambitious and ideal subjects
and broader methods of execution. The public was not prepared for this change,
and did not approve it, nor does it appear that Wilkie possessed the power of execution and thought which this change should have demanded. There was, however,
no particular resulting detriment to his financial success or general career. In 1830
he succeeded Sir Thomas Lawrence in the position of Painter in Ordinary to the
King. Wilkie died at sea in 1841 during his return from an Oriental trip. He
had been a constant sufferer from ill health since 1824.

FRENCH PAINTING—SECOND QUARTER OF THE 19th CENTURY.

During the first quarter of the 19th century the productivity of the French had
been great, especially in portraits, in battle-scenes, and in historic compositions.
We find the names of David, of Gérard, and of Géricault of main importance during
the period of Bonaparte. Without denying the occasional power and constant conscientious care of the French painters of the first quarter of the century, we must
still place Constable and Turner immeasurably above them; but now the tide turned,
and France became what England had been. The direct influence of Constable, and
in a less direct sense that of Turner, on the rise of the French School "of 1830,"
the "Fontainebleau" or "Barbizon" School, as it is sometimes called, is a most interesting and frequently neglected fact. Constable was better understood at this
time in France than in England. His direct spiritual heir was the French painter
Théodore Rousseau.

Rousseau may be considered, on the whole, as the founder of the most important modern school in French art. This was again in large degree a school of landscape. Its representatives generally made their first appearance in public about 1830, whence the name sometimes applied to them and above quoted. They were, however, not considered as men of mark until a much later date, and an official or academic account of French painting written at the time when their best works were being produced would have entirely ignored their names. Beside Rousseau stands a group of painters among whom we name as especially prominent: Michel, Corot, Dupré, Troyon, Diaz, Decamps, Millet, and Monticelli.

Théodore Rousseau, the son of a tailor, was born at Paris in 1812. He first exhibited at the Salon of 1831. His most important early teachers were the Old Masters of the Louvre. He did not, however, neglect nature for these models, and in this case, as in others, when the influence of the Old Masters on modern art is cited, it will simply appear that the great artists of all times see nature more or less in the same way. Although Rousseau traveled and painted in all parts of France, he had an especial predilection for the Forest of Fontainebleau near Paris, and lived in its neighborhood after 1833. The artists associated with him are thus often known as the Fontainebleau School or the School of Barbizon, the village in which Rousseau lived.

In 1835 the pictures which Rousseau offered for exhibition at the Salon were rejected by the academical authorities in charge, and during the next twelve years he suffered neglect and want, being all this time excluded from the Salon exhibitions. The Revolution of 1848 changed the management of the Salon, and Rousseau became a member of its jury. In the year of his death, 1867, he was president of the jury. His pictures now command enormous prices, and are largely owned in the United States. One of them sold for $21,000 at a New York auction in 1887. Rousseau's strong point was that of all great landscape artists; the ability to seize the broad essential facts without being led astray by a minute rendering of minor details which really escape the eye in open-air vision.

Jean Baptiste Camille Corot is more widely known and more universally popular than Rousseau. He combines the broad treatment of that great landscape artist with a tender and poetic feeling and a certain delicacy of rendering which have made him more comprehensible to the world at large. On the other hand his range of subjects was not wide. Mist effects, or the atmosphere of early morning and of twilight, nearly always engrossed his attention.

He was born in Paris, 1796, and was the son of a clerk. After an elementary education at Rouen he was apprenticed to a draper in Paris and did not begin life

275. THÉODORE ROUSSEAU. LANDSCAPE.
276. J. F. MILLET. THE GLEANERS.

277. J. B. C. COROT. LANDSCAPE.
278. C. TROYON. THE SHEPHERD'S DOG.

as an art student until the age of twenty-six. In 1825 he visited Italy and Rome, where he remained two years. He first exhibited at the Paris Salon in 1827. He reached the age of seventy without attaining wealth. Not till his declining years did he reap his deserved reward in fame and money. He is said to have ultimately earned an annual income of 200,000 francs. The broad style by which Corot is now generally known was not achieved till 1840. He died in 1875. His paintings are largely owned by American collectors.

Jean François Millet was born of a French peasant family in the hamlet of Gruchy near Gréville in 1814. He spent his boyhood working in the fields. His bent for design was assisted only by the study of the engravings in the illustrated family Bible. His education was aided by the village priest, who taught him Latin. The boy's talent for drawing was recognized by his family as a special calling, and he was committed to the instruction of a painter at Cherbourg with their coöperation. His talents here shown procured a small pension from the municipality for his support as a student in Paris; this was not, however, long continued. Millet's talents were recognized by his Paris master, Delaroche, but his wholly unconventional style was against him. He worked in great poverty, painting portraits for two dollars apiece, and selling small copies of two eighteenth-century artists, Watteau and Boucher, whose art was attractive to the public but extremely distasteful to him. After a first success as an exhibitor in 1844, his picture of 1845 was rejected by the Salon. His poverty at this time was such that he was obliged to use the rejected canvas for his next painting, and he actually painted over this rejected painting his "Œdipus Unbound." During one absence in Normandy Millet was obliged to paint sign-boards for a living. It is also related that he fought at the barricades in the Paris revolution of 1848. Having received $100 for his picture of the "Winnower," he moved to Barbizon in 1849, and lived there for twenty-seven years in a three-roomed cottage. Here he was befriended by Rousseau, and was buried beside him in 1875.

Millet's picture of "The Angelus" was sold in Paris in 1889 for $116,000. The ultimate triumph of this painter, much greater since his death than when living, was wholly due to his true soul and simple honesty. He had known the want and the toil of the peasant, and he painted what he knew. The titles of his famous pictures will best exhibit his bent in art — "The Peasant Grafting a Tree," "The Gleaners," "The Sower," "Sheep-shearing," "The Potato-planters," "The Knitting Lesson," "Bringing Home the New-born Calf," etc. The finest Millets are at present generally to be found in the United States, and the American loans at the World's Fair in Chicago comprised several of the most important.

Alexandre Gabriel Decamps (1803–1860) is another artist of the great group in question. He was an Oriental traveller, and devoted much of his art to corresponding subjects. He is said to have been the first to study in Oriental life the true background and accessories of Biblical subjects.

Diaz de la Peña (Narcisse Virgile) (1809–1876) was of Spanish parentage and was born at Bordeaux. He was a pupil of Rousseau. At his best he ranks with the greatest colorists of the 19th century (*as regards color*), having a rival or superior only in Monticelli. Diaz is occasionally frivolous or careless, and at times somewhat mechanical, but he was strong both in landscape and figure composition. In the former class the Forest of Fontainebleau usually furnished his subject, and there is no great variety in his choice of view. On the whole he takes a very high place, but not the first place, in the School of Fontainebleau.

We will not attempt elaborate accounts of Michel, Troyon, Dupré, or **Monticelli**. Of all great artists of the French School the latter is least known, and yet he is one of the greatest, when known at his best. **Dupré** (Jules) and **Troyon** (1810–1865) belong to a class of whom we feel that mercantile success has occasionally led to self-repetition or to work which does not equal their best. At his best it is difficult not to place Troyon as high as any cattle-painter or landscape artist who ever lived. The powers of Dupré in execution and in composition are magnificent when he has chosen to exert them. Michel is less known, but he takes us back to that atmosphere of unselfish art, working for results and not for money, which seems to inspire every canvas of Millet, of Corot, and of Rousseau. Among the more or less mercantile imitators of the School of 1830, Daubigny comes nearest to sincerity. It is doubtful if he has ever reached it.

Beside the Fontainebleau School and its affiliated painters, there are two other French painters who deserve especial mention for the period, closing soon after the first half of the 19th century, Eugène **Delacroix and Couture.** Their distinction from the painters just named lies partly in their choice of subjects, which were mainly historical and ideal compositions. They were like them in opposing the smooth finish and conventional characteristics of the academical artists of that day. Delacroix had a romantic tendency, instanced by his passion for Byron and for the tragic characters of Shakespeare. He was vehement and powerful in his nature and in his art. In the Louvre are his "Dante and Virgil," "Massacre of Scio," etc. Couture's greatest work is his "Romans of the Decadence," in the Luxembourg Museum.

RECENT FRENCH PAINTING.

After the death of the great painters just named, during or after the sixties, we find none of equal importance to take their place. French art now moved in various directions, of which three may be specified here. In one of them we find the name of **Meissonier** (Ernest) as a leading representative. Minutely painted, gayly colored, and generally insignificant subjects were his forte. Considered as costly decorations of luxurious apartments they certainly had their place, but they made no contribution to the intellectual wealth or spiritual force of their time. In cases where Meissonier entered the field of historic composition, as in his "1807," now in the Metropolitan Museum of New York, he departed from his usual choice of subjects without pronounced success.

Meissonier best represents that recent class of French pictures which are carefully executed and well adapted to please fashionable taste, but which are of such frivolous subject-matter that no very serious importance can be given them.

A second direction may be named as that of the correct Academicians, careful in drawing and fairly serious in purpose; but lacking in power, in breadth, and in harmonious color. In this group we may place Bonnat, Cabanel, Carolus-Duran, Bouguereau and others. An artist holding with the Academic School as regards methods of execution, but far outranking them in intellectual power and in the choice of significant and epoch-making subjects, is Gérôme. Puvis de Chavannes has taken high rank as a decorator, but his composition is formal and his color cold.

We cannot overlook the name of **Rosa Bonheur** in view of the fame of her "Horse Fair," now in the Metropolitan Museum of Art. Excellent in drawing and splendid in composition, it lacks only boldness of execution and color. Without detracting from the greatness of Rosa Bonheur, we must award the palm to Troyon among modern cattle-painters.

A third division is that of the **Impressionists** (so called), a much-abused and much-talked-of group of artists, of whom it is impossible to speak collectively. Among the Impressionists may be ranked some of the most talented draughtsmen and most gifted painters of our day. Such would be Courbet, Degas, Manet, and Monet.

As a School it is, however, impossible to pass judgment upon them, and most advisable to comment on the individual artist or the individual picture. No

methods are successful when practised by unskilful hands. All methods are poten-
tially successful which aim at representing serious thought or carefully studied
facts. In our estimate of the Impressionist School we must be careful to distinguish theories of method in technical execution from the success of a given artist
in using these methods, or of a given picture in representing them.

AMERICAN PAINTING.

In the days of the American Revolution and of our early independence, the art
of America was naturally an outgrowth of that of England. The English eighteenth-
century School had been mainly active in portraiture, a field in painting which
has always appealed to the practical taste of the Anglo-Saxon, as it appealed in
sculpture to the practical Roman. Our earliest American painters of greatest
renown are also portrait-painters. Charles Wilson Peale, Rembrandt Peale, and
Gilbert Stuart are leading names, but the greatest name is that of Copley.

The Peales, father and son, hold their rank mainly by virtue of
the historic importance of their sitters. Of the two, the son, Rembrandt, was undoubtedly superior to his father; but Charles Wilson
Peale's portraits of Washington will always keep his name before
the American public, and they are by no means wholly inferior
works. This artist was born in Maryland, but became a Philadel-
phian by residence. He commanded a corps of volunteers in the
Revolutionary War, and was distinguished for skill in various mechanical pursuits and for versatility in various professions. In early
life he studied his art, during four years, in England. He was born
in 1741 and died in 1826.

Rembrandt Peale (1787–1860) also owes his fame especially to
his portrait of Washington, which was purchased in 1832 by the
United States Senate.

The artist was only eighteen years old when Washington sat for the original
sketch, and although the picture was completed after Washington's death, with the
assistance of other portraits and a bust, it is certainly superior, as a work of art, to
the portraits done by the father in Washington's life-time. Several of Rembrandt
Peale's portraits are in the Gallery of the New York Historical Society.

Gilbert Charles Stuart ranks far higher than the Peales. He was
born in Rhode Island in 1756. As a youth, Stuart accompanied a
Scotch artist to Scotland and received lessons from him, but returned
home after his death, and was educated at the Grammar School of
Newport. At the age of eighteen he returned to Edinburgh, and in
1781 began a successful career in London, where he painted the portraits of many famous persons. He was also employed in Dublin and
in Paris, where he painted a portrait of Louis XVI. He returned to

America in 1793, and after residing in New York, Philadelphia, and Washington, moved to Boston in 1806, and died there in 1828. Once more it is the portraits of Washington which have drawn most attention to the artist. Of these, there are said to have been three original paintings and twenty-six copies. The finest is generally conceded to be the one owned by the Boston Athenæum.

Stuart was a man of much wit, and of genial nature, able to draw his patrons into conversation, and to make them lose the self-consciousness which people sitting for their portraits are apt to exhibit. The ability to read character must precede the ability to depict it, and it holds of artists as it does of actors and novelists, that the study of temperament and of human nature is the essential study of art. In the capacity to represent character, which is the true test of the portrait-painter, Stuart takes a high place for his time, and the highest place among American painters next to Copley. As a colorist he was not Copley's inferior.

John Singleton Copley was born in Boston in 1737. He was the leading portrait-painter of New England until 1774. In this year he went to Italy and remained there two years. In 1776 he began living in London, and was joined there by his wife and children, who sailed from Boston on the last New England vessel which bore the British flag. He remained in London until his death in 1815, and was to the last in high favor as a painter of portraits and historical subjects. The Boston Museum of Fine Arts affords the best exhibit to be seen in this country of his works, which are, however, widely scattered among the descendants of the old New England families. His portraits are distinguished for their solidity of execution and strongly-defined character.

Much-quoted names, but of far less importance than Stuart and Copley, are those of Benjamin West, Washington Allston, and **Jonathan Trumbull**. The latter served as an officer in the War of the Revolution, and deserves mention as the leading painter of revolutionary history. His most important works are in the New Haven Yale Art Gallery, and on the walls of the Rotunda of the Washington Capitol. **Washington Allston** (1779–1843) spent much time in England, and achieved distinction there as well as in his own country, but has higher standing as a man of refinement and of letters than as a painter. As a colorist he ranks fairly well. One of his best pictures is the "Paul and Silas in Prison" of the St. Louis Museum. His "Prophet Jeremiah," in the Yale Art Gallery, is an inferior work. An unfinished and elaborate composition is "Belshazzar's Feast," owned by the Boston Athenæum. **Benjamin West** (1738-1820) was a native of Pennsylvania, who studied in England, and rose to be President of its Royal Academy, in which office he succeeded Sir Joshua Reynolds. His work was mediocre, but is historically interesting as that of an early American painter.

The Second Quarter of the nineteenth century would be almost a blank in American art were it not for the great name of **Thomas**

Cole. His five pictures of the "Course of Empire," now in the collection of the Historical Society of New York, are among the greatest works of the century. His "Voyage of Life," in four scenes, is well known by engravings, and shows a tender and poetic spirit.

Cole was born in England in 1801, and was taken to America as a young child. His parents settled in Ohio, and he was originally employed in a wall-paper factory, which was established by his father. He subsequently studied in Philadelphia and New York, and was able to travel abroad extensively. He was ultimately established in New York.

Toward the time of the Civil War American landscape art had begun to develop considerable activity. Its coloring was, however, generally garish, and its execution rather mechanical. Representative names for this period are Albert Bierstadt and F. E. Church. Bierstadt's "Rocky Mountains" and Church's "Heart of the Andes" are typical paintings. Both are enormous canvases illustrating the artistic error of overcrowding large pictures with small details, but valuable as panoramas. Church's "Niagara Falls" was another ambitious picture which acquired great reputation. A more notable artist was William Page, who was born in Albany in 1811, spent many years in Italy, and ultimately settled in New York. He ranks as one of the most serious and able of all American painters. Portraits and ideal subjects were his chosen field.

Rapid strides were taken by American painters during the seventies. Study abroad became general. Exhibitions began to multiply, and buyers to grow more numerous. Among those who appeared at this time as Americans of marked genius we may mention Wm. M. Hunt, George Fuller, Homer Martin, Winslow Homer, Elihu Vedder, and John La Farge. Hunt's influence was especially important as transferring to America the standards which he had drawn in France from the teachings of Millet and Couture. In later life he was head of a School of Art in Boston. George Fuller was one of the most wholly original and intellectual painters that this country has produced. He passed many years of his life as a farm-laborer in Massachusetts, and died before achieving recognition. Homer Martin has been a pioneer among the painters of landscape. Winslow Homer is especially remarkable for his virile and sturdy thought, and his wholly frank and spirited rendering of nature. He is equally strong in figures and in landscape, which is a rare quality among American painters.

In recent years a very important school of American painters has developed from the teachings and influence of Wm. M. Chase, a native of Indiana, whose studio is in New York. Another highly gifted American, James M. Whistler, has spent most of his life in London, and ranks among the first modern artists. The most thoroughly successful and famous of recent American painters is probably J. S. Sargent, whose portraits are world-famous, and who has recently executed a series of very important decorations for the Public Library building in Boston.

To the above names we must add those of Abbott H. Thayer, whose "Virgin Enthroned" was an important exhibit at the Chicago Fair, and George De Forest Brush, whose fine picture of ancient Mexican life, "The Sculptor and the King," was seen at the same exhibit. Wordsworth Thompson and Frederick James are the most successful painters of Colonial scenes. No mention of American painters can afford to omit the names of Albert Ryder, of R. A. Blakelock. and of George Inness. The latter, recently deceased, has a reputation in landscape which stands higher than that of any other American painter. Magnificent specimens of his art may be studied in the Metropolitan Museum of New York. Walter Shirlaw and Edward E. Simmons have been very successful in figure compositions for architectural decoration, as well as in oil painting.

I have endeavored in this brief mention of American painters to include only those of pronounced intellectual quality, men who are thinkers and students as well as painters. There are, however, many such whose names have not been mentioned, and many others whose technical powers entitle them to high rank in their profession.

RECENT ENGLISH ART.

From our short account of American artists we return to England in order to speak of its more recent painters. Since the days of Constable, Turner, and Etty, these men have had no really successful English rivals, but we cannot afford for that reason to ignore the host of meritorious painters that modern England has produced. Some of them, like David Wilkie, had fine satiric powers, and were close students of human nature, following a line comparable to that of Dickens' novels. Others, like Landseer, were successful painters of animals.

Toward the middle of the century (1849) the so-called school of the **Pre-Raphaelites** became prominent. Its leaders were Holman Hunt, John Millais, and Dante Gabriel Rossetti. These were all quite young men when their association was founded. Hunt was nineteen,

Millais was twenty, and Rossetti was twenty-one. The essential aim of
these young painters was to strengthen serious art, and all of them,
especially Millais, became men of prominence. The name which they
chose to attach to themselves has, however, no great significance. It
denoted, among other things, an appreciation for the humility and
purity of early Italian art on the part of these apostles of reform. The
fact that men who were not painters became members of this brother-
hood is an indication that the title had no especial reference to methods
in art. It is, however, true that the want of atmosphere and of chiar-
oscuro which we find in old Pre-Raphaelite painters did to some extent
appear in the works of their spiritual imitators, and in so far their
pictures can hardly be commended for abandoning an improvement of
technical method which has been the common property of civilization
since the 16th century.

Holman Hunt, however, takes high rank as a serious artist. Dante Gabriel Rossetti
never achieved the rank of a wholly successful professional painter, and is best
known as a poet and a man of letters. Some few of his works, widely known by
engravings, show tender and beautiful ideals. The most famous man of the group
is Sir John (Everett) Millais, and it may be added that he is the one who, in later
life, abandoned the technical methods alluded to. These methods may, in fact, be
considered utterly out of date at present, and they never had wide vogue. The
esthetic and literary atmosphere of this school was its really important feature.
Hence we may connect with it some artists who have widely departed from its
presumed technical methods, and who do not strictly belong to it.

Edward Burne-Jones (born 1833) was originally a pupil of
Rossetti. He has become one of the most important representatives
of the imaginative and romantic school in recent English art. He
has also done much in designing for stained glass. Among these
designs are the windows of Christ Church in Oxford. Ford Madox
Brown (born 1821) is distinguished for his series of mural decorations for the history of Manchester in the town-hall of that city.

Sir Frederick Leighton, the recently deceased president of the
Royal Academy, was a most successful artist in imaginative and
classic subjects, a fine draughtsman and an able colorist. A wholly
exceptional position is occupied by George F. Watts, whose greatness
as an allegorist is incontestable. A very complete exhibit of his
works was made at the Metropolitan Museum in New York some
years since.

Another famous painter, long resident in England, is the Belgian
Alma-Tadema. His pictures bring enormous prices. They are most

carefully but rather coldly executed, and are generally devoted to archæologic subjects.

MODERN GERMAN PAINTING.

The history of modern German painting begins with the names of **Carstens** and Cornelius. The former was a Dane and a native of Sleswick (1754-1798). His works are remarkable for their composition and quality of balance in arrangement. The best collection of them is in the Museum of Weimar. The distinction of **Cornelius** (1783-1867) is that of a mural painter. His frescoes in the Campo Santo of Berlin and in Munich are especially noteworthy. The greatest of modern German artists, all things considered, was Wilhelm von **Kaulbach** (1805-1874), whose six great frescoes on the walls of the New Museum in Berlin are his most celebrated work.

In the second quarter of the 19th century the town of Düsseldorf, near Cologne, became the Academic centre of German art. Hence the name of the "Düsseldorf School," which had, however, no really distinctive traits and did not produce any especially noteworthy artists. The leading landscape painters of Germany are the **Achenbachs** — two brothers named Oswald and Andreas. In genre painting **Knaus** and **Meyer** (Von Bremen) are the leading names. In historical compositions, and also as an Academic teacher, Carl von **Piloty** (1826-1886) of Munich held high rank. The greatest modern German colorist was Hans **Makart** of Vienna (1840-1884).

Of late years the Scandinavian painters have developed great power, and among these the name of **Zorn** is most eminent. His pictures at the Chicago Fair attracted much attention.

In Russian art the works of **Verestchagin** are especially remarkable. No other modern painter has so demonstrated the didactic power of art. His pictures of battlefields are the most powerful sermons which have ever been preached on the horrors of wars. A notable Russian picture at the World's Fair in Chicago was the "Cossack's Answer to the Sultan of Turkey" by **Repine**.

To the foregoing brief mentions we must add the names of **Munkacsy** and **Fortuny**. The former, a Hungarian by birth, made his success in Paris. His method is broad, but cannot be called powerful. His large picture of "Christ before Pilate" was widely exhibited in the United States some few years since. A much more distinguished artist was the Spaniard Fortuny (1839-1874).

HISTORY OF MUSIC.

INTRODUCTORY.

Although the arts of design vary fundamentally from that of music in the form of expression, there are still certain points of view from which the history of all these arts may be united in study or considered in association. The art of music is in many ways the most promising art of the present and the future. Its greatest masters have flourished in recent times. Its development is of recent date as regards the perfection of its instruments and the size of its orchestras. Music of the highest classical quality has been written within the limits of the present century. Hence the undeniable relative inferiority of the architecture, the sculpture, or the painting of the 19th century, as compared with the past, is offset and made good by its great success in music. The value of art history is the opportunity it offers for a broad philosophy of history, in which the importance of each epoch is accented and expressed by its ideal art. In a proper presentation of such a philosophy music must be included, if recent modern times and the 19th century are to hold their own in contrast with the past. Gluck may be compared with Phidias, Beethoven may be compared with Michael Angelo, Mozart may be compared with Raphael, and when the great galaxy of musical composers which has flourished in the last two centuries is considered, our period may claim equality with others which have done greater work when the arts of form alone are considered.

The ascendency and superiority of music in modern art correspond to certain obvious facts in modern civilization. Never has there been a time in history when civilization was spread so widely over the earth's surface. Never has there been a time when the size of individual civilized countries was so large. Sculpture and painting appeal to comparatively small audiences. Only in so far as their works are individually accessible can they wield an influence. If copied they lose much of their original power. The classic quality of music, on the other hand, is not damaged by repetition. The same opera, the same symphony, or the same sonata may be repeated a thousand times, or in a hundred places at one time, without loss of spontaneous quality or of original power. The statues of Phidias can now be seen only in London, the Parthenon can be known only in Athens, the Sistine Madonna can be viewed only in Dresden. Photographs and casts are valuable references, but no one considers them equal to the originals. But the works of Beethoven may exert to-day the same influence in Australia or in India that they exert in Germany. Mozart can be studied in New York as easily as in Vienna.

A little thought will show that in so far as art may be considered as an ideal expression of that which is best and greatest in human nature, music has possibilities of influence which can never be claimed for architecture, sculpture, and painting. It is, for instance, the most universally refining of all the arts, because it is an art which most universally appeals to everyday people in advance of special educational training. Special education is certainly needed for the comprehension of many masterpieces, and yet the music of the people and the ballads of the people are everywhere recognized as important factors in culture and of really classic value. Scotch ballads, German songs, Irish melodies, Hungarian dances, and last, but not least, the airs of the negro plantation hands, have their own place and their own importance beside Italian operas and classic symphonies. Still farther, it holds true that the works of the greatest composers have been largely based on themes drawn from these simple sources.

The standards of classic quality in musical art are essentially the same as those which we apply to literature, to painting, or sculpture. There is music which simply pleases the ear without ennobling results, just as there are pictures which have no higher aim than to please the eye, or books which leave us no better than they found us. Then there is music which teaches self-denial and lofty purpose, which stirs the heart, and excites the nobler passions. As connected with poetry and literary dramatic art in the field of opera, music again comes into play as an accessory of vast importance. Music is a rest for the weary brain, and even for the tired body. It softens the heart, stirs the soul, and unlocks pent-up emotions. As the aid and ally of religion it figures in the stirring songs of the Salvation Army, in the hymns of the church, in the Masses of the Catholic ritual. It has led armies to victory, and it has led souls to God. It has been the stay of the patriot and the solace of the wandering beggar. It has thrilled the spectators of the Greek tragedies, and has been united with many of the greatest dramas and greatest poems of modern literature. If we consider such works as the overtures to Goethe's "Egmont" and to Shakespeare's "Coriolanus" by Beethoven, the music of the "Midsummer Night's Dream" by Mendelssohn, the Passion Music by Bach, the biblical oratorios by Handel, the historical operas of Meyerbeer, the preludes and nocturnes of Chopin, the songs of Schubert, and the musical dramas of Wagner,—we shall need no argument to show that the share of music in the history of modern art is the weightiest and the most important.

HISTORICAL SURVEY.

That music played an important part in the life and in the educational systems of the ancients we know well, but we know little more than this. The harp, which is the parent of the modern piano, is figured in an Egyptian tomb at Thebes of the largest dimensions now known to a modern orchestra. The lyre, a smaller kind of harp, is the typical instrument of the Greek god Apollo. Music, both vocal and instrumental, was used throughout the performances of the Greek drama, which prefigured in many ways the modern opera. The trumpet and the flute (double and single) were well known to antiquity. The organ can be dated back at least to Roman antiquity, and the violin had a primitive predecessor among the musical instruments of the early Celts.

It is supposed that the hymns of the Russian church, as handed down from the Byzantine (Greek) Empire, have preserved some surviving traces of old Greek music. That this music was the greatest known to antiquity is generally conceded; also that it passed with other forms of Greek culture to the Romans, and so became the basis of the early Christian science in this art. But as to the exact character of Greek music the most learned theorists are in doubt. That it was simpler than ours is certain. It was, of course, lacking in the complex variety and startling effects which are within the scope of the modern orchestra.

There is a clearer knowledge of the music of the Middle Ages, but as regards its simplicity and comparatively undeveloped forms, the statement made above again holds true. We may most easily date the development of music by the invention or perfection of the modern instruments, and the average dimensions of an orchestra. The violin was perfected in the 17th and 18th centuries by the Amatis and Stradivarius of Cremona; the piano dates from the early 18th century, when it was developed from the spinet and harpsichord, which in their origin go back to forms of the harp. In the late 18th century the symphonies of Haydn were written for an orchestra of about twenty performers. A symphony orchestra now consists of sixty-four musicians. Organs of large dimensions were used in the Middle Ages, but it is not probable that they had any wide range of capacity. The perfected opera dates from the times of Gluck (late 18th century); the perfected symphony and piano sonata date from Beethoven (early 19th century); the perfected oratorio dates from Handel (18th century). All this shows the comparatively recent development of modern music.

Church music, as is natural, was the first to reach perfection. The Masses of Palestrina, which were written in the latter part of the 16th century, are still considered the noblest models of church music. The history of church music, before this time, centres in the Flemish composers during the 14th and 15th centuries, and before these dates is rather vague. Guido of Arezzo, an Italian monk who flourished in the 12th century, is generally quoted as the inventor of the present system of musical notation. For a still earlier time, historians emphasize the importance of the solemn Gregorian chant, which carries us back to the beginnings of Christian history and the connecting links with that now forgotten music of the Romans and the Greeks.

For the period of the Middle Ages we must not forget, however, the minstrels of the Scotch, Welsh, Irish, and English, the troubadours

of the French, and the minnesingers of Germany. The history of
vocal part-music has its most distinct beginnings in the glees and
madrigals of the 16th century in England, which were, however, by
no means the earliest. The beauty of these may still be enjoyed in
the revivals of certain Shakespearian plays. The fugue was a familiar
form of composition to the Flemish musicians whom we have just
cited.

We shall begin our biographical accounts of the composers with
Palestrina — first noting that the invention of movable types for
printing music was made in 1502 in Italy, and that this invention
was of epoch-making importance for the development of the art.

Palestrina is named from his birthplace near Rome, and was born in
1524. He became a singer in the Sistine Chapel at Rome, which
for centuries had the finest choir in Christendom. Previous to this
time, its singers had been very largely drawn from Flanders for reasons
just explained. During the Council of Trent, held for the reform
of the Catholic Church, the question of church music was one of
the points considered, for scandal had been caused by the introduction
of secular music and words in the singing of Mass. It was consequently proposed to abolish all music excepting the plain chant,
but decision was reserved subject to the success of Palestrina in
composing church music which should be deemed worthy of its
sacred mission. Palestrina submitted three Masses to the Commission
appointed to decide the question, and these were unanimously ap-
proved. The most celebrated of all church Masses is still Palestrina's
"Missa Papæ Marcelli," a Mass so named in honor of the Pope Marcellus. The date of these compositions is 1575. The introduction
of congregational singing in Protestant churches is another important
fact for the 16th century, the finest forms being the German "chorals."

In order of time we may next emphasize the production of the
earliest modern opera. This took place at Florence about 1600. The
composer was Jacopo **Peri**, and his work was entitled "Euridice." The
accompaniments were written for four instruments; a primitive kind
of piano known as a clavichord, a guitar, a viol, and a lute. The production of this work was due to a circle of students interested in
old Greek culture, and aiming to revive its musical methods. These
students were among the heirs of that Greek learning which had travelled to Italy, after the Turks had occupied the capital of the Byzantine (Greek) Empire in 1453. It is not clear that the attempted

revival had any direct analogy with the original Greek music, but the general resemblances between modern opera and the old Greek drama, with its musical accompaniment, are none the less certain, and the relations of the two at the very beginning of modern opera are clearly established. This first opera was mainly composed in recitative, but a more elaborately musical style of opera was introduced by Monteverde of Venice, soon after 1600. **Monteverde** is considered the father of modern opera. Only one of his operas, "Orfeo," is now known to print. As a result of his activity there was built in Venice the first public theatre used for opera. This was opened in 1637. Before this the operas had been given only as private entertainments. Many other opera-houses were rapidly opened in Venice, and they spread thence to other Italian cities, as well as to France and Germany. Operatic performances were not introduced into England until the 18th century, and there they long continued to be regarded as a foreign exotic. The first theatre for the performance of opera in Paris was founded in 1671. The cradle of opera in Germany was the city of Hamburg.

The year 1600 is the date of the first oratorio, as well as of the first opera. The word is derived from the Religious Order of the Oratorians, founded at Rome by St. Philip Neri. This Order was so-called because its members were wont to stand outside their church exhorting the by-standers to come and pray (Latin *orare*). The oratorio was originally a religious drama, accompanied by music, and given after the church services on a regular stage. This and other musical attractions were offered in order to draw in an audience to the services, and sustain the interest in them. The oratorio was in reality only another form of the Passion Plays and Miracle Plays by which religious instruction had been given in the Middle Ages.

To the 17th century also belong the names of the famous composers Alessandro **Scarlatti** and **Pergolesi**, active at Naples, which was a very important centre of musical culture at this time. The form of the violin *concerto*, which gives a leading part to the first violin, and uses the other instruments as accompaniment, was also developed in the later 17th century. The use of the term *sonata* also first appears at this time, and its introduction is ascribed to an organist at Venice, Giovanni Gabrieli.

From the foregoing account of musical terms, of the inventions of musical instruments, and of the names of early composers, it appears that Italy was the centre from which the art of music spread in modern times. This fact is in line with the general influence of the Renaissance. During the 17th century the accounts of music in north European countries point generally to Italian influence. The greatest activity of the art during this century, outside of Italy, was in France, and this was the northern country whose general relations with Italy were most intimate. The Italian Cardinal Mazarin, who succeeded Cardinal Richelieu as Prime Minister in the times of Louis XIV., brought a company of Italian singers to Paris and spent vast sums in supporting their entertainments. The entertainment known as the *Ballet* was here developed in great magnificence, but the performers were originally people of distinction and not hired. The *Ballet* was originally a combination of a *Masque*, or performance in which people of quality appeared in allegorical costumes and characters, with dance music and movements. The still celebrated *gavotte*, known as that of Louis XIII., dates from one of these performances, although the music was not composed by that king.

The greatest French composer of the 17th century was an Italian by birth, who was brought from Florence when a boy. His name was Jean Baptiste Lully. He began life in Paris as a scullion, but gained the favor of King Louis XIV. by his performance on the violin. He obtained the right to organize an operatic company, composed many operas and much church music, and until his death was the master of the world of music in Paris.

The triumph of the Puritans in England during the time of the Commonwealth was very detrimental to the progress of music in that country. The church choirs were dispersed and the organs were generally destroyed. After the Restoration the choir of Charles II. produced many fine voices and composers. Among these Henry Purcell ranks as one of high distinction in modern times. He composed, for instance, music for Shakespeare's "Tempest" with the still familiar songs, "Come unto these yellow sands" and "Full fathom five."

In Germany the Thirty Years' War (1618–1648), and the period of distress which followed, were depressing influences for music as well as for other arts. Here was developing, nothwithstanding, the greatness of the following epoch, when the sceptre was to pass from Italy and the whole world was to acknowledge that German music had become the greatest of modern arts. But we again find in Germany a historic continuity as regards development from Italian influence. This appears in the leading position taken by Vienna as a musical centre; for this was the German city to which Italian teachers and performers first naturally gravitated, as being of all German cities the one in closest local relations with Venice and with Italy. Here (in Vienna) flourished a court composer (1698–1740), who is known to have travelled in Italy. Although his musical compositions were numerous, few were published, but his great work on the theory of music called "Gradus ad Parnassum" was the authority of the 18th century, and the basis of the studies of all its great composers.

MUSIC OF THE 18TH CENTURY IN GERMANY.

In the same year, 1685, were born Johann Sebastian Bach and George Frederic Handel. Their careers open, therefore, soon after 1700, and begin the history of 18th century music.

Handel was born at Halle, the son of a barber and surgeon, two professions which were often united in those days. The father destined Handel for the law, and forbade the study of music. The child studied music in secret, and practised on an old clavichord in the garret, where he could be out of hearing. His father had occasion to visit a certain German nobleman, and having declined to take his son with him, the latter, who was then a boy of seven, ran after the carriage on foot for such a distance that his father finally relented. The cause of this persistence, unknown to the father, was the child's desire to play on the Duke's organ. On the next Sunday he obtained access to the instrument, and was caught playing on it. This was the beginning of his career as a musician. Instead of the paternal punishment, about to be visited on him, he received the commendation of the Duke, who declared him to be a genius, and induced his father to place no farther obstacles in the way of his musical studies.

Handel began his career in 1703 as a second violinist in the orchestra of the Hamburg Opera. After composing several operas he visited Italy in 1707, and spent three years in Florence, Rome, and Venice. He was warmly received and highly appreciated in Italy. He next obtained the position of Choral Director to the Elector of Hanover, but with the permission to visit England, which he immediately did in 1710. From this time on most of his life was spent in England. His long absences from his post in Hanover estranged him from the Elector, and when the latter became King of England, as George I., Handel's position at the English court seemed to be endangered. But he was able to make his peace by the composition of some music for a Royal fête and water party. Down to 1720 Handel's work was mainly that of an operatic composer and manager. The many operas thus produced have been supplanted by later works, and are now almost forgotten, but as a composer of oratorios Handel still leads the world, and his productions of this class are as popular to-day as when they first excited the enthusiastic plaudits of an English public. Among these oratorios may be mentioned "The Messiah," "Israel in Egypt," "Saul" (which contains the famous "Dead March"), and "Samson." Handel died in 1759.

,t was a remarkable fatality which led Handel to England as a musician holding office under the House of Hanover, which itself subsequently succeeded to the English throne. The favor and support of the English court were his through life. Handel thus became in music the connecting link between Germany and England, and has exercised a vast influence on the later history of English music. His personal character was choleric but lovable, and many curious stories are told of his petulance, and also of his amiability.

Johann Sebastian Bach died nine years before Handel (1750). He was born at Eisenach, in Thuringia, and belonged to a family whose members had been musicians for several preceding generations. His favorite instrument was the organ. He occupied positions succes-

sively at Weimar, at Coethen, and at Leipzig. Being, in his capacity
of organist, a director of church choirs, he wrote much church music.
His "Passion Music" belongs to a type which was in general use in
Germany for the services of Holy Week. It still ranks as the grandest
of all religious music. The later pianoforte *sonata* has developed from
the *suites*, or compositions, with a series of movements, which he
wrote for various instruments, but especially for the harpsichord (the
predecessor of the piano). These *suites* were originally combinations
of dance tunes of different measures. The sons of Johann Sebastian
were all eminent musicians, and one of them, Carl Philip Emanuel,
ranks as the predecessor, in pianoforte compositions, of Haydn and
Mozart.

In order of time we must, however, emphasize the importance
of **Gluck**, the first and among the greatest of all operatic composers
whose works still hold the modern stage. Christopher Willibald
Gluck was born in Bohemia in 1714. As an Austrian subject he
made his way to the Austrian capital, Vienna, and thence to Milan,
where he completed his musical education. The operas which he
composed here secured him an invitation to London. He next
visited Paris, and then returned to Vienna. In 1762 he brought
out his immortal opera of "Orfeo" (Orpheus). This was followed in
1772 by "Iphigenia in Aulis," which was first produced in Paris,
through the favor of the Queen of France, the Austrian Marie An-
toinette. Gluck died in Vienna in 1787, having spent most of his
life after 1772 in Paris. His "Iphigenia in Tauris" is another opera
which still holds the modern stage.

The astounding wealth of melody in the "Orpheus" is such that, to one who
hears it for the first time, it almost seems as though all later music had been drawn
from it. The overture to "Iphigenia in Aulis" is still considered one of the best
of operatic overtures. To fully appreciate the greatness of Gluck we must, however,
have some knowledge of the general conditions of operatic composition in his own
day. We have seen that Italy was the birthplace of the opera, but during the 18th
century the Italian operatic style had fallen more and more into artificial and conventional trammels. The development and display of the voice of the singer had
become the test of success in writing opera. The operatic singers had become the
despots and lords of the composers, dictating their style of music, and frequently
refusing to sing any song which did not suit them. The habit of composing music
to display the gifts of individual singers was, of course, fatal to true music; for no
art can maintain its greatness when *technique* and mechanical execution are considered more important than meaning and inspiration.

The story told of Handel is doubtless true, that he once seized and was about
to throw out of the window an Italian prima-donna who had refused to sing one of

his songs because she conceived that it did not display her voice to advantage. This story illustrates the tyranny to which all composers had been subjected. It was the greatness of Gluck to abandon absolutely all the tricks and decorations of vocal gymnastics which had thus become the ruling fashion. In other words, he wrote music for music's sake, and not for the sake of personal display. But there was still another conventional weakness in the ruling style of Italian opera. Its choice and development of plot and story were hampered by a rigid system of musical conventions as to the number and style of arias, duos, and trios to be sung. This system had also developed from the habit of making concessions to the singers, and of avoiding that jealousy of one or the other of them which might result from an unequal distribution of the opportunity to make a display before the audience. As a consequence once more of this conventional system of arranging operas, the story or libretto had grown to be a matter of complete indifference. Gluck set his face against this system by insisting on the value of the libretto, and the necessity of having an intrinsic worth in the *subject-matter* of the opera. But to all this common sense of theory and justice of reason, we must add that he was a composer of melody whose only rivals have been Mozart and Schubert.

We may venture to break with the strict sequence of time, according to which Haydn's name should next appear, in order to place in immediate connection with Gluck his great successor and rival in operatic composition, **Mozart** (Johann Chrysostom Wolfgang Amadeus). His father was a professional musician in the employ of the Prince-Archbishop of Salzburg, where the composer was born in 1756. The precocious ability of young Mozart is still the wonder of the world. He was a performer on the harpsichord at the age of three, and a composer at five years of age. At the age of seven he was taken by his father on a starring tour through Europe as a performer on the harpsichord and violin. His first published work, four sonatas for violin and harpsichord, appeared in Paris at this age. This tour had lasted five years when Mozart wrote his first opera, at the age of twelve. The tour was subsequently continued in Italy, the same phenomenal success being met with everywhere. In spite of this success, the finances of the Mozart family ultimately became straitened. A new Prince-Archbishop of Salzburg succeeded in 1772. He treated the young composer, who held the place of music-master in his service, with great unkindness and neglect. A new position was therefore sought, but could not immediately be obtained. Having moved to Vienna, Mozart made a precarious living by teaching music, and was best known there as a pianist. His early operas were highly successful, artistically speaking, but did not relieve him from want. He married in 1782 — happily as regards association, but unhappily as regards matters of domestic economy, and died in 1791, aged thirty-six. His three immortal operas are "Don Giovanni" (or "Don Juan"), the "Marriage of Figaro," and the "Magic Flute." These still hold the stage as unexcelled masterpieces.

Three or four other operas have great excellence but are now rarely performed. Several of Mozart's symphonies have high reputation, especially the "Jupiter" symphony; but the supreme master of the symphony was Ludwig von Beethoven, who was twenty-one years old when Mozart died. We must, however, before speaking of the greatest of orchestral symphony composers, go back to Haydn, the father of the symphony, who in time preceded both Mozart and Beethoven, but outlived the former eighteen years, although born twenty-four years before him.

Franz Joseph Haydn (1732–1809) was born at Rohrau, on the borders of Austria and Hungary. His father was a wheelwright. As a boy Haydn was a chorister in Vienna, and he subsequently entered the service of a famous Italian singing-master (Porpora) as accompanist. He first made a reputation as a composer of string quartettes for first and second violin, viola and cello, and so obtained the direction of a small orchestra in the service of an Austrian Count. From this employment he passed to the service of Prince Paul Anton Esterhazy, whose death, however, soon followed. Under the Prince's successor, Prince Nicolaus, he became sole director of his orchestra, spending his time partly in Vienna and partly at the summer residence of the Prince. Thirty years of Haydn's life were passed in the service of the Esterhazys, and this entire period was one of uninterrupted activity in musical composition. He subsequently made two visits to London. During these visits, and for English production, he wrote the twelve symphonies which are considered by some his most important works—the *Salomon* set, so called from the name of the violinist and manager who induced him to come to London. "The Creation," an oratorio composed for production in England, is still second in popularity only to Handel's "Messiah." The French bombardment and occupation of Vienna in 1809 are thought to have hastened his death, which occurred at that time.

The character of Haydn's music corresponds to the peaceful and serene tenor of his life. Without great climaxes or strong dramatic power, it is a wholly simple and wholly classic flow of melodious measures. His art prepared the way for the still more beautiful works of Mozart and the still sublimer style of Beethoven.

GERMAN MUSIC IN THE 19TH CENTURY.

Ludwig von Beethoven was born at Bonn in 1770. His father was a singer in the choir of the Archbishop of Cologne, whose residence was at Bonn. The boy's education in music was pushed by the father, who hoped to profit by his precocious talents. At the age of twelve, Beethoven was harpsichord player in the orchestra of the Opera. At the age of seventeen he was enabled to visit Vienna and to make the acquaintance of Mozart. In 1792 he made another visit to Vienna in order to study under Haydn. His connection with this master was not of long duration, but after this time Vienna was his place of residence. His first compositions show very close relation to those of Haydn and Mozart, but they subsequently develop an originality of massive and overwhelming power. Among his early works are the first and second symphonies, the sonata "Pathetique" and the "Moonlight" sonata. The third symphony (dating 1804), called the "Eroica" (the Hero symphony), was written to celebrate the greatness of Bonaparte, for whom Beethoven had a passionate admiration; but the coronation of Bonaparte as Emperor shattered his idol, for Beethoven was a republican, and the dedication to Bonaparte was abandoned. There are nine of the symphonies in all. These are generally known by their numbers, which specify the order of production. All of them are sublime masterpieces. The ninth symphony has as a finale a choral setting of Schiller's "Hymn to Joy."

Beethoven's life was embittered by deafness, which grew on him rapidly after 1801. The calamity was not only a bitter trial to him as a musician, but he felt his resulting isolation in society deeply, and has recorded his suffering in words that show a breaking heart. In matters of worldly welfare he was not subjected to the tortures of pecuniary want, but his life was one of continued domestic discomfort, and also of domestic loneliness. Changes of lodgings and servants were a constant source of petty annoyance, and another cause of unhappiness was the ungrateful behavior of a scapegrace nephew to whom the composer devoted his thoughts and all his savings. When these life trials are made known to us, the whole significance of Beethoven's music begins to dawn upon us — it is the music of self-conquest, of sublime resignation, of the triumph of the spirit over matter. It could have been written only by a man of very great intellect and of a very pure soul, but it is also the music of strength and power and vigor. There is a creative Titanic quality in Beethoven which can be compared only with that of Shakespeare. Beethoven's death took place in 1827. In his last hours his thoughts were still devoted to his unworthy nephew, and to him were left all his savings. This musician's greatness was that of an instrumental composer for the piano and the string quartette, as well as for the orchestra. His sole opera, "Fidelio," has never been popular. This is due partly to the lack of dramatic interest in the libretto; the music is of great beauty, but belongs rather to the sphere of symphony than that of opera.

The history of instrumental music in Germany after the death of Beethoven centres especially in Mendelssohn, Schubert, and Schumann.

Felix Mendelssohn Bartholdy was a Hebrew, born in Hamburg in 1809. His family was well-to-do, and of wide literary culture. His early life was spent mainly in Berlin. Here he developed precocious talents as a musician and composer which were stimulated and encouraged in every possible way. At the age of twenty he visited London and then travelled in Italy. He subsequently settled as Musical Director in Düsseldorf, but in 1835 became Conductor of the famous Gewandhaus concerts in Leipzig. In 1841 Frederick William IV., the Prussian king, invited Mendelssohn to Berlin with appointment of Musical Director in a new Academy of Art. The position proved uncongenial, and the result was a partial return to the work in Leipzig without abandoning that in Berlin. The founding of the famous Leipzig Conservatory was due to Mendelssohn, who persuaded the king of Saxony to apply a legacy which had been left the town of Leipzig to this purpose. The death of the composer occurred in 1847, and seems to have been hastened by his grief at the sudden decease of his gifted and favorite sister.

Mendelssohn made, in all, ten visits to England, where he was much appreciated, and many of his works were composed during or for these English visits. Since his death his reputation in England has continued to hold its own. His music is generally admitted to be that of a most refined and cultivated nature, with wide knowledge of harmony and of technical problems. It is as a composer for the piano that he ranks best ; for instance, in the famous "Songs without Words." His symphonies are classic compositions, without rising to the heights of his great forerunners. His most ambitious works, the music to "Midsummer Night's Dream," and the oratorios "St. Paul" and "Elijah," still enjoy great popularity, especially in England and the United States. Mendelssohn's music is generally that of a highly refined, but not of a powerful personality. It has, however, undoubted original value, and it is *music*.

The "Scotch" symphony is the most popular. The "Fingal's Cave" overture and the overture to "Ruy Blas" are great works.

The instrumental compositions of **Robert Schumann** (1810–1856) are of a somewhat dreamy and introspective character, not very definite in form, or strong in their organism. They may be regarded as the reveries of a man of genius, and so regarded they must take high rank.

Schumann was born in Saxony in 1810. He studied law in Leipzig and Heidelberg, but drifted gradually into musical composition, after so injuring one of his

fingers that he could not aspire to success on the piano in the way of public performance, which had been his ambition. He also founded a journal in Leipzig for musical
criticism, and contributed to it many notable articles. He was for a short time a
Professor in the new Leipzig Conservatory founded by Mendelssohn (1843), but was
too shy for success in this capacity. Overwork also produced nervous exhaustion.
Hence a removal to Dresden for rest and seclusion. He remained here till 1850, and
then took a position as musical conductor in Düsseldorf. He failed in this capacity,
and his mind gave way. His madness took the shape of a delusion that he heard
constantly a particular musical note, and that the spirits of Mendelssohn and Schubert were about him. He died in an asylum in 1856. Schumann attempted all fields
of musical composition, and succeeded in all excepting opera. His piano compositions,
symphonies, string quartets, quintets, and especially his songs, are his best works.

Next to and after Beethoven the greatest musical geniuses of Germany in the 19th
century have been Carl Maria von Weber and Franz Schubert. In order of time
Meyerbeer follows, and to his appearance succeeds that of Richard Wagner.

Carl Maria von Weber was born in 1786. His father had been a soldier and
courtier in the train of the Elector of the Palatinate, at whose court he was a famous
musical amateur. Late in life the father undertook to recruit his fortunes by man-
aging a travelling operatic company. The son thus grew up in contact with the machinery and life of the stage. He wrote an opera at the age of fourteen, and became
a pianist of renown. After many changes of position and residence Weber was made
Director of the Opera in Prague (1813), and he subsequently occupied a similar position in Dresden.

Weber's world-renowned opera, "Der Freischütz," was first produced in Berlin in 1821. It had an instantaneous and wide-spread
success, and has ever since ranked as the greatest of romantic operas.
This was followed by the production of "Euryanthe" at Vienna;
the libretto was less successful, but the music not less beautiful.
"Oberon" was produced in London in 1826, under the personal direction of the composer, who was, at the time, in the last stages of
consumption, and died immediately afterward. He had been crippled
at birth by hip disease, and was an invalid through life. Weber's
nature was as refined, as imaginative, and as lovable as his music.
His "Invitation to the Waltz" is a well-known piano composition,
brilliant and sparkling, but also tender and pathetic. The wide range
and subtlety of Weber's perceptions in art suggest a comparison with
the qualities of Leonardo da Vinci, and all these great qualities cul-
minated in the romance of "Der Freischütz."

Giacomo Meyerbeer (1794–1864), the greatest of all composers
of opera on historic subjects, was five years the junior of Weber,
whose romantic tendencies he continued, and whose acquaintance he
had enjoyed. It is somewhat suggestive of this composer's character that his real name was Jacob Meyer Beer, but Giacomo Meyerbeer was a more romantic and a more euphonious name, which he

consequently adopted. There is no doubt that there is an element of show, perhaps even of tinsel, occasionally to be found in Meyerbeer's work. He loved effect, and popularity, and success, crashing sonorous climaxes and dramatic situations, fine ballets, and gorgeous scenery. All these things he lived to attain; but he also had an imaginative insight into the forces and vast mazes of history. In the music of "Robert le Diable" we have all that poetry and music can do for the Normans in Sicily. "L'Africaine" represents the whole period of the Maritime discoveries. "Le Prophète" gives us the picture of the Reformation period and the time of the Peasant Wars in Germany. "Les Huguenots" pictures France in the 17th century. Meyerbeer possessed power, and firm grasp, and comprehensive insight as a musician; but he preferred to master the world rather than to be its slave. Whatever the tastes of a Parisian public demanded for popular success Meyerbeer gave that public in the matter of details. He wrote for the stage of the Grand Opera at Paris, and wielded all the vast machinery of that stage at will.

Meyerbeer was born in Berlin in 1794 (or 1791?). He was the son of a rich Jewish banker, and had throughout life full command of money. He was a hard student, and became a great pianist. His musical education was first carried on in Berlin, and was completed in Darmstadt under the master who instructed Weber. He then appeared in Vienna as an operatic composer and public performer on the piano. His first success in writing operas was made in Italy, where he won great fame; but the works there produced are now forgotten in the fame subsequently achieved in Paris, where he lived from 1826 till his death in 1864. This Parisian success dates from the appearance of "Robert le Diable" in 1831. He also wrote lighter operas for the Opéra Comique of Paris—among others "Dinorah" and "L'Étoile du Nord."

The life of Franz Schubert (1797–1828) carries us once more to Vienna, where his father was a schoolmaster. He had a fine voice, and sang as a boy in the Imperial choir. He had no regular musical education, but began to compose at an early age. His great embarrassment for music paper was supplied by another schoolboy, when his own pocket-money was exhausted. After his employment in the choir ended with the change of voice, he became an assistant in his father's school. His later life was one of scanty means and small encouragement. He died at the age of thirty-one.

Schubert's first song was published when he was twenty-four. This was the now famous "Erlkönig," composed at the age of eighteen, which was brought out by the assistance of friends, after refusal by a publisher. Some other songs were also published by subscription with fair success, and it began to appear that there was a market for them. From this time he spent his life in working for his publisher as a song-writer, for such small remuneration that the highest income he ever reached was $500 a year. Only after his death did the world realize his true greatness. His now famous symphonies, string quartets, etc., had, at the time of his death, never been given either in public or in private. Schubert is now known as the greatest song-writer who ever lived. He wrote over 600 songs, and many of them, like the "Serenade," "Haidenroeslein," the "Muellerlieder," "Winterreise," and the "Swan Songs," are still universal favorites.

Without dwelling on the names of other great Germans like Spohr (opera of "Jessonda") Nicolai, ("The Merry Wives of Windsor"), Flotow ("Martha"), Franz Lachner (fine orchestral works), Raff (symphony "Im Walde," etc.), Robert Franz (the successor of Schubert and Schumann in the realm of song), and Johannes Brahms, who is considered by many to be the greatest living composer, we come now to the epoch-making name of Richard Wagner.

Richard Wagner was born at Leipzig in 1813, and was the son of a clerk in a police court. His father died in the year of his birth, and his mother soon remarried an artist and actor named Geyer. A removal to Dresden resulted. Young Wagner's early tastes were literary. He studied the piano, but never succeeded in mastering this instrument. At the age of fourteen he wrote a tragedy for which he conceived a musical accompaniment to be necessary; hence he began to study composition. His studies in music were continued at Leipzig, and were devoted especially to Beethoven. At the age of twenty he became chorus-master in the theatre at Würzburg, on a very small salary. After various wanderings and struggles (Magdeburg, Königsberg, Riga, London), Wagner made his way to Paris and lived there from 1839 to 1842 without securing any sort of recognition or foot-hold.

Wagner's first success was his opera of "Rienzi," which was produced at Dresden in 1842. He left Paris to superintend the performance of this opera. It was written in Meyerbeer's style, and does not represent the later tendencies of the composer. These began to appear in the "Flying Dutchman," a marvellous piece of imaginative music, which was brought out at Dresden in 1843. "Tannhäuser" followed in 1845. In 1849 Wagner was involved in the revolutionary troubles which then afflicted Dresden, and was obliged to take refuge in Paris and ultimately in Zurich, where he lived for several years. It now happened that Wagner was passing through Weimar on an occasion when Liszt, who was conductor of the Court theatre, was producing "Tannhäuser." This led to the revival of an acquaintance first begun in Paris, and to a close friendship between the two. Thus was brought about, under Liszt's encouragement, the completion and production of "Lohengrin" (1850). Work on the "Ring of the Nibelungen" was now undertaken in Zurich.

The scope of this work, which consists of four separate operas intended for performance on consecutive days, seemed destined to prove fatal to a public production. But the publication of the poem of the libretto attracted the attention of the King of Bavaria, who invited Wagner to Munich, gave him a pension and a residence, and engaged him to complete the "Ring of the Nibelungen." The king's enthusiasm created an opposition to the composer, which obliged him to leave Munich, but the pension was increased, and the royal favor was continued. A special theatre was completed at Baireuth in 1876 for the performance of this work, consisting of four operas — "Das Rheingold," "Die Walküre," "Siegfried," and "Götterdämmerung." Meantime "Tristan and Isolde" and the "Meistersinger" had been produced. The last of Wagner's operas was "Parsifal," which was brought out in 1882. The composer died in 1883 at Venice, and was buried at Baireuth.

The standing and quality of Wagner's art are still a subject of contention. His theory of opera was to make the subject-matter, as developed by the libretto, the main feature. All music was destined to support and express the meaning of the text. The theory was impregnable, and makes it difficult to understand the number of Wagner concerts in which the music is given without the text — for which inconsistency the author of the music is, of course, in no wise responsible. In spite of brilliant exceptions, Wagner's music is generally wanting in conventional melody, but it always faithfully interprets his idea. His power, versatility, and mastery of instrumentation are beyond cavil. What is needed for comprehension of this master's work is strict attention to his literary idea and literary method. There is no other case known to the history of opera in which the composer has been himself able to create his subject-matter and cast it into literary and poetic form. Wagner's admiration for the great masters who preceded him was passionate and sincere, especially for Gluck, Mozart, and Beethoven. In so far as some of his supporters have tended to ignore these masters, *their* influence is not to be commended.

The name of Liszt has been mentioned as that of Wagner's great friend and supporter. **Franz Liszt** (1811-1886) was a Hungarian by birth, who studied in Paris, and became one of the greatest pianoforte players of our time. In an age when the piano is so popular, and when critics and appreciators are so numerous, it is not difficult to understand the adulation and worship which were lavished on one of the most successful masters of the instrument. After an extraordinary success in Paris, Liszt became conductor of the Court Theatre in Weimar. He resigned this position in 1859, and subsequently distributed his time between Weimar, Pesth, and Rome. In later life he became a priest, but without abandoning his musical career, and is known as the *Abbé* Liszt. His compositions, especially those for the piano, are noted for their daring harmonization, and their difficult "bravura" embellishments which tax to the utmost the technique of the pianist, but which are in great favor with virtuosos who use them in order to give a brilliant conclusion to their programmes. His personal character was of marked nobility.

MODERN ITALIAN OPERA.

We have given due weight to the precedence and greatness of Germany in modern music. In songs and in orchestral compositions there is scarcely a show of successful rivalry by other nations, but in the field of opera both France and Italy have done great work. Little of it will, however, bear comparison with the opera of Germany. The artificiality into which Italian opera had fallen in the 18th century, and its causes, have been explained in our account of Gluck. From this condition of decadence it again rose to greatness in the 19th century with the names of Cherubini, Rossini, Donizetti, Bellini, and Verdi. Paisiello (1741–1815) and Cimarosa (1754?–1801) were, however, notable 18th-century composers. Boccherini (1740–1805) takes high rank as a composer of instrumental chamber music. He was a resident of Madrid.

Cherubini (1760–1842) was a native of Florence, but finally resided at Paris. His great surviving opera is "Les deux Journées" (otherwise named in Germany the "Water-Carrier"—"Der Wasserträger"), a rarely simple and classic work. He stands (with Boccherini) nearest of all Italians to the classic style of German music.

Gioachino Rossini (1792–1868) was born at Pesaro, and studied music in Bologna. The "Barber of Seville" is his world-renowned work, full of movement, vitality, and good music. "Semiramide" was produced in 1823. The first act is one of colossal power; the second act is weaker. After this production Rossini visited England with brilliant success, and then settled in Paris, where he became Director of the Italian Opera. Here he wrote "William Tell" (1829), of which the famous overture is the best feature.

Rossini's character was pleasure-loving and jovial; he was not fond of work, and after writing this opera preferred to rest on his laurels for the remainder of his life. In church music he, however, subsequently, wrote his famous "Stabat Mater."

Gaetano Donizetti (1798–1848) was born at Bergamo. The familiar titles of "Lucrezia Borgia," "Lucia di Lammermoor," "La Favorita," "La Figlia del Reggimento," "Linda da Chamounix," and "Don Pasquale" all belong to his creations.

Donizetti's music is light, but catching and vigorous. The frequency of repetition which these operas have enjoyed is due to the fact that they are not especially serious, either as regards music or libretto, or as regards connection between the two. In so far as some fashionable people have felt bound to attend the opera, without very much caring to do so, Donizetti has not been too taxing to their patience. For people who go to the opera because they are ashamed to stay away, Donizetti is a good programme. Schumann characterizes his "Lucia" as "Puppenmusik" (puppet-show music).

Vincenze **Bellini** (1802–1835) was a native of Sicily. He wrote "Norma," "I Puritani," and "La Sonnambula," all of them sonorous **and** meritorious works. Bellini shows gravity and capacity for climax **in** his methods of composition, together with the melodious quality **which** is the charm of all the Italian operas.

Giuseppe Verdi was born in 1814. He is the composer of the familiar works, "Ernani," "Il Trovatore," "Rigoletto," "La Traviata," and lately the more serious operas "Aïda," "Otello," and "Falstaff."

The most recent success of the Italian opera is the "Cavalleria Rusticana" of Mascagni, which has found wide appreciation in America.

MODERN MUSIC IN FRANCE AND ENGLAND.

François Frédéric Chopin (1809–1849) was born in Poland, but being the son of a French father and having spent his art life in France, his name may be entered here. From the age of nineteen this famous pianist was generally a resident of Paris. His delicate health and tender nature unfitted him for public appearance, but in private circles he became the idol of all who knew him. As a composer for the piano, Chopin wrote down what he was himself—heart-weary, pleading, romantic, tender, and delicate compositions. He cannot be called capricious, but his compositions are full of moods and changes of mood. Chopin has, in a word, written down the music of life's emotion, as felt by a highly nervous and delicate organism. He is considered by many as the greatest master of pianoforte composition, and his works appear in the programmes of every "virtuoso."

The leader in modern French opera is **Auber** (1782–1871), a disciple of Cherubini, and author of the "Mute of Portici" or "Masaniello" (the name generally adopted in England). Beside this great and serious work, he is known for his "Fra Diavolo" and other light operas.

Charles Francis Gounod was born in 1818. His "Faust" was produced in 1859. It is one of the most deservedly popular of recent operas.

Bizet (1838–1875) born at Paris, is famous for his "Carmen," which was brought out in 1875. **Massenet, Thomas** and **Saint-Saens** are recent composers of distinction. One of the greatest French composers was **Hector Berlioz** (1803–1869). In the recent light operas and comic operas of France there is much that is tuneful and charming. Planquette's "Chimes of Normandy" may be quoted as an illustration. Adam's "Postillon de Longjumeau," of earlier date, is almost a classic.

In the field of light opera Sir Arthur **Sullivan** has made a name with "Pinafore," "The Pirates of Penzance," "Patience," "Iolanthe," "The Gondoliers," "The Mikado," etc. The high literary quality of the librettos of these operas, as furnished by Mr. John Gilbert, has not always been appreciated, and it can be fairly said that the music of Sullivan is worthy of these clever librettos. **Balfe's** "Bohemian Girl" (1843) and **Wallace's** "Maritana" (1845) are earlier operas of very light quality, which have had a certain kind of popularity. Sir William Sterndale **Bennett** (1816–1875) was the greatest of modern English composers. He was proffered in 1853 the appointment of Conductor of the Gewandhaus Concerts at Leipzig. Orchestral composition was **his** specialty.

INDEX AND CLASSIFICATION OF MATTER.

Where more than one page reference is given, the first reference is that for pronunciations and definitions, when supplied by the text. Reference numbers for illustrated subjects refer to the page, not to the number of the illustration.